Poetry of Discovery

Poetry of Discovery

The Spanish Generation of 1956-1971

ANDREW P. DEBICKI

THE UNIVERSITY PRESS OF KENTUCKY

Scholarly publisher for the Commonwealth,
serving Berea College, Centre College of Kentucky,
Eastern Kentucky University, The Filson Club,
Georgetown College, Kentucky Historical Society,
Kentucky State University, Morehead State University,
Murray State University, Northern Kentucky University,
Transylvania University, University of Kentucky,
University of Louisville, and Western Kentucky University.

Editorial and Sales Offices: Lexington, Kentucky 40506-0024

Library of Congress Cataloging in Publication Data

Debicki, Andrew Peter.
  Poetry of discovery.

  Bibliography: p.
  Includes index.
    1. Spanish poetry—20th century—History and
criticism. I. Title.
PQ6085.D4   1982   861'.64'09   82-40171
ISBN 0-8131-1461-6   AACR2

Contents

Preface

This book grew out of perceptions developed over a period of several years during which I read and taught Spanish poetry of the 1950s and 1960s. In so doing, I realized the importance of this poetry and some of the ways in which it represented a departure from the styles and canons of earlier post-Civil War verse. Above all, I came to see that these more recent poets were using everyday language and narrative techniques in highly inventive ways. Though some of their works superficially resembled the "realistic" verse of their predecessors, they exhibited originality and a novel artistic control, and conveyed a wealth of meanings and perspectives. Meanwhile, little critical work was being done on this poetry and many writers tended to place it in the context of earlier work and to ignore its special features.

In dealing with these writers, it soon became clear that traditional thematic and analytic approaches to poetry were of limited value. The themes they dealt with, for one, tended to be themes common to poetry of many periods and rarely gave a clear indication of the novelty or significance of their works. (Their tendency to philosophic as opposed to social or historical topics did signal a shift from the immediately preceding period, but did not reveal the value of their production.) Commonly used methods of analysis and close reading likewise proved of limited value. In sharp contrast to the poetry of the 1920s, for example, that of the 1950s and 1960s did not exhibit complex patterns of imagery or elaborate formal structures, and rarely revealed its uniqueness when examined by conventional stylistic and "New Critical" techniques.

In attempting to find more effective methods of inquiry, I discovered that I could often make useful statements about ways in which these works established certain points of view for their speakers, adopted certain perspectives, and also elicited certain responses in their readers. They did so less through traditional poetic devices than through tone, intertextual references, and patterns of development that build up and modify reader expectations. In pursuing these discoveries, I was able to gain insights from recent theory on reader response as well as from some criticism of fiction, as will become clear throughout this book.

One of my greatest difficulties arose in trying to find objective grounding to reader-response studies. In several chapters, especially those devoted to Francisco Brines, Claudio Rodríguez, and José Angel Valente, I was able to support my insights by critical approaches derived from semiotic and formalist works; in others (those on Carlos Sahagún and Eladio Cabañero) I used imagery patterns to pin down my conclusions; in yet others (Gloria Fuertes, Angel González) I employed intertextual schemes. In all cases, I tried to confirm my insights on reader reactions by careful examination of textual patterns.

Even so, the nature of much of this poetry as well as the problems raised by reader-response criticism (chiefly the difficulty of defining accurately the "implied reader" and describing one set meaning for a given text) brought into question a premise of my previous criticism, that of the integrity and permanence of an individual poem. I began to place less emphasis on finding the most accurate interpretation for every work and more emphasis on considering how these works raised fundamental questions about reading and about intertextual relationships. As I did so, I was helped by "deconstructive" criticism, especially regarding the "traces" present in a literary sign, the reversibility of figures, and the ways in which texts evolve in successive readings. In the final analysis, my work is still centered on interpretation, if only because the poetry I study has not been often interpreted systematically and because my main goal is to help others understand it better. Nonetheless, I have on the one hand avoided the assumption that my analyses should be absolute and exclusive, and on the other used these analyses to explore some underlying questions concerning the reading process and the diverse factors which influence it.

I started work on this book several years ago, and the chapters on Rodríguez and Brines constitute substantially expanded and changed versions of studies previously published in Spanish. Parts of the chapter on Fuertes and most of the chapter on González have appeared as articles; the rest of this book has not been published before. But all of it was conceived as a single project, a sustained inquiry into the poetry of what I see as a single generation and into a set of critical approaches which to my mind illuminate this poetry and are in turn illuminated by it. At the same time, I have not tried to make this book a history of a period of Spanish poetry. In chapter 1, I have examined the general developments of post-Civil War Spanish poetry insofar as they constitute a background for the understanding of the major poets of the generation of the 1950s and 1960s; all other chapters attempt to elucidate the works of those poets, the approaches they elicit, and the resulting view of an extremely valuable corpus of poetry.

I have adopted one stylistic convention in order to avoid the awkwardness of double pronouns ("he/she") when referring to the reader. I am arbitrarily assuming a male reader for poems written by male authors, and a female reader for poems written by female authors, and leaving it to my reader to make the necessary adjustments. Minimal background information on each author and his/her poetry is provided in an unnumbered note placed at the beginning of the note section for the relevant chapter.

This book could not have been written without the aid of the John Simon Guggenheim Foundation, which made possible a year's leave devoted to developing and writing it. It was also facilitated by the National Humanities Center, which invited me to work in its ideal setting and created circumstances suited to reading, learning, and writing, as well as by the financial support given to me by the University of Kansas and its General Research Fund. I am most grateful to the Guggenheim Foundation, to William Bennett and the whole staff at the National Humanities Center, and to Frances Horowitz, Ronald Calgaard, and Robert Cobb of the University of Kansas.

I also owe a great debt to many friends and colleagues: to Robert Magliola, Emory Elliott, John Brushwood, and Robert Spires for their critical insights and their reading of parts of the manuscript; and to my friends Nancy Denney, Nancy and David Dinneen, Susan Kemper, and Judith Liskin-Gasparro. My students and the participants in my NEH summer seminars, especially Douglas Benson, Carole Bradford, Santiago Daydí, Nancy Mandlove, Martha LaFollette Miller, and Margaret Persin, taught me a great deal of what I needed to know to write this book. Susan Brown's and Margaret Mohatt's research help and the typing of Jan Paxton, Gretchen Nolle, Vicki Melton, and Joy Zinn were indispensable to its completion. My daughters Margaret and Mary Beth proved patient and supportive at key moments. I thank them all.

Poetry of Discovery

1 The Generation of 1956–1971

Beginning in the late 1950s and extending through the 1960s, there appeared in Spain several young poets whose work reveals a high degree of originality, coupled with significant value. Because they were writing in a seemingly direct language and dealing with themes that had also been dealt with by earlier writers, these poets were at first considered mere continuers of the general tendencies of post-Civil War verse and were not accorded the importance they deserved. But as their work has grown and unfolded, as their ideas on poetry have been expressed and linked to their work, and as critics have begun to highlight their originality, their significance has become more and more apparent.[1] Not only does their poetry possess value comparable to that of the major writers of the early twentieth century, but it also forces us to reconsider earlier views on the characteristics and development of contemporary poetry in Spain, and on the critical methods and approaches which are most fruitful in dealing with it.

To undertake a general appraisal of this poetry, one must first recall the characteristics of the works that preceded it. Standard interpretations of Spanish post-Civil War poetry begin by noting the formalism and lack of transcendence of most works of the early 1940s.[2] Grouped around the magazine *Garcilaso* (1943-1946), the salient poets of this era —José García Nieto, Rafael Morales, Rafael Montesinos—produced serene and skillful verse, most often written in traditional forms (sonnets abounded). Although the "garcilasistas" mentioned the importance of feelings in poetry, the feelings that predominated in their works were an admiration of nature, nostalgic love, and well-contained religious fervor. Although one can find superficial parallels between the perfectionism of this poetry and the stylistic excellence of the works of the great poets of the Generation of 1927, the contrasts between its timidity and the originality of that earlier poetry are quite apparent.

A more significant development in post-War Spanish poetry was marked by the magazine *Espadaña* (León, 1944-1951). Although it published works by many diverse writers, this magazine, unlike the much

more eclectic journal *Proel*, was dominated by poets concerned with
social issues and with the problems of daily life in Franco's Spain.
Victoriano Crémer and Eugenio de Nora were the most important of the
poets writing in *Espadaña;* the former also articulated very clearly its
antiformalist stance.[3] Somewhat later, in the early 1950s, Blas de Otero
and Gabriel Celaya published books dealing with social issues and
written in everyday language and a seemingly direct expression—and
gained a wide reading public. The social and apparently "realistic"
current of the late 1940s and early 1950s is very clear when one examines the two main anthologies of the period, the *Antología consultada de
la joven poesía española* (whose selection was based on a questionnaire
sent to writers) and Rafael Millán's *Veinte poetas españoles.* The presence
of social themes, the concern with daily life, the use of colloquial language and of everyday settings are apparent in the works of almost all
the poets included. On the negative side, both anthologies reveal suspi-
cious uniformity, a certain dullness, and many works that quickly
became dated. The best of the "social" poets handle language in a very
creative fashion, but others seem to be expressing social messages in
verse.

Not all poetry of the time fits into a social current. Less obvious,
perhaps, but equally significant is the appearance of works which deal
with the human situation from a more individual and emotional perspective. Much of Crémer's poetry and some of Otero's deals with the
anguish of an individual living in a hostile and at times meaningless
environment. The first-rate religious poetry of Carlos Bousoño is filled
with anguish, doubt, and a search for some reality beyond illusions. The
early (and excellent) work of José Hierro already reveals a concern for
the impact of time on human life, and for the search for understanding
in the face of surrounding enigmas. One can see this existential and
perhaps neoromantic current of post-War poetry as another side of the
impulse to "rehumanize" verse and bring it into consonance with the
preoccupations of the times. It leads to some superb poetry, more lasting
perhaps than the social works of the time; but it also brings forth a lot
of confessional verse, full of exaggerated anguish and rhetorical lament.

The social and existential currents that I have been noting gained
much of their impulse from books published at this time by poets of the
Generation of 1927.[4] The appearance of Dámaso Alonso's *Hijos de la ira*
in 1944 marked a key turning point for Spanish letters. Its presentation
of human anguish in a colloquial tone and its highly artistic use of
everyday terms, of the grotesque, and of dramatic monologue directed
younger poets to a new form of expression; they also opened the possibilities for a poetic treatment of hitherto "banned" topics. Although it

cannot be classified as overtly "social," this book certainly inaugurated the treatment in verse of the ills of Spain of the 1940s. Less individually significant perhaps, yet nonetheless important, was the appearance in 1944 of Vicente Aleixandre's *Sombra del paraíso.* Neither social nor "existential," this book nevertheless placed stress on the emotive and subconscious aspects of human existence, and fit into the tendency to "rehumanize" poetry. Its use of visionary imagery and blank verse suggested ways in which the new tendencies could find successful artistic embodiment, though it did not influence later poetry directly. And although Gerardo Diego's religious poetry had even less direct impact on the works of younger poets, it certainly fit in with the spirit of the period. (Much more important, in a sense, were the generosity and the personal help offered to these younger poets by Diego, Aleixandre, and Alonso, all of whom, in various ways, contributed significantly to their development.)

One should also note the work written at this time by poets who had already made themselves known in the 1930s and who are often classified as the "Generation of 1936" (questionable as such a classification may be). Luis Rosales and Leopoldo Panero published significant books in this period: *La casa encendida* by the former illustrated the tendency to emotional meaning as well as collective concerns, while *Escrito a cada instante* by the latter exemplified the use of private allusions and remembrances in poems which nevertheless point to larger subjective meanings.[5] Rosales and Panero, together with Luis Felipe Vivanco, Germán Bleiberg, and José María Valverde, continued after the Civil War to write poetry based on subjective and philosophic concerns (we think of the importance of love poetry, of religious poetry, of metaphysical inquiries) which dovetailed with the climate of the late 1940s. In general, it is important to remember Carlos Bousoño's observation that after the Civil War the issue of generations and of the age of the poets played a much less important role than it had previously.[6] At a certain moment, under the impact of given circumstances and a given intellectual climate, poets of different ages and groups revealed many similarities.

In a speech delivered in 1955 and published as a monograph, Aleixandre summarized admirably the main features of Spanish poetry of the late 1940s and early 1950s: "Yo diriá que el tema esencial de la poesía de nuestros días es . . . el cántico de hombre en cuanto *situado,* es decir en cuanto *localizado;* localizado en un tiempo, en un tiempo que pasa y es irreversible, y localizado en un espacio, en una sociedad determínada, con unos determinados problemas que le son propios.'"[7] Aleixandre notes that this definition helps explain the presence of specific themes, such as the social, the religious, and the national, and fits in with the tendency to simple language, to narrative devices, and to specific recollections and personal remembrances.[8] It is clear that this first epoch of post-Civil War poetry marks a significant new direction—though as I will later suggest, it is a new direction that poses at least as many problems as it opens paths for future poetic expression.

Before looking ahead, however, it is useful to take into account the cultural atmosphere in which this poetry of the first post-War period took place and the way in which its creators viewed and used the literature that had come before them. Félix Grande and other critics have noted the significant effect that the poetry of César Vallejo and Pablo Neruda had on the younger poets of the period. Not only did it offer them examples of social poetry, but it gave them models of poets deeply committed to specific human problems and tragedies, individual as well as collective.[9] Miguel Hernández, widely read by these poets, clearly furnished a model for the expression of emotional meanings through language, and offered a link, as Grande has noted, to a whole tradition of poetry going back to Quevedo and the *Romancero*. Just about every poet and critic of this period paid homage to Antonio Machado: he became almost the symbol of the poet preoccupied with fundamental "human" issues, both individual and national, as well as a representative of the writer who attempts to write in plain language and direct fashion. Of the poets of the Generation of 1927, the one most praised and read in this period was Luis Cernuda, both for his social consciousness and for his expression of subjective meanings. There was, on the other hand, an initial lessening of interest in Juan Ramón Jiménez as well as Jorge Guillén and even Federico García Lorca, and a tendency to stereotype their work and that of other poets as excessively "pure" and "inhuman."

These literary tastes already point to some of the blind spots and limitations of the poetic climate of the first post-War period. Even the earlier writers praised in this period were read in a one-sided fashion: Vallejo's verbal virtuosity and tremendous creativity were not stressed, nor was Hernández's use of language, nor Machado's innovativeness in making seemingly anecdotal subjects acquire universal dimensions. The tendency to oppose the dangers of empty formalism by overstressing the content and message of poetry led the writers of this period to exaggerate the separation between form and meaning, and to ignore the fact that the latter exists only through the former. Although this occurred for understandable reasons, the overall vision of literature and literary history became extremely one-sided in a way that was perilous for the impulses to creativity and innovation through poetic language.[10]

This is not to say, however, that none of the poets who emerged in the first period after the Spanish Civil War—the late 1940s and early 1950s—produced significant verse. Blas de Otero and Angela Figuera wrote consistently first-rate works, as valuable today as they were when they first appeared; whether addressing social questions or expressing anguish at man's situation, their poems embody their meanings in carefully crafted language and imagery. The poetry of Gabriel Celaya, though very uneven, includes works of force and originality. José Hierro uses evocations of the past to capture poetically the sense of loss caused by time; Carlos Bousoño's early work, neglected by critics, conveys through perfect forms the poet's concern with death and nothingness, and his search (religious as well as worldly) for life's meanings. But the poetry produced, published, and anthologized in this period also included a mass of undistinguished works which declaim social messages or stridently cry out their authors' anguish.

The limitation of this period is also apparent in the lack of attention given in the 1940s and 1950s to a very interesting poet and a poetic movement that did not fit the "realistic" canons. The poet was Carlos Edmundo de Ory, who founded the magazine *La Cerbatana* in 1945 and developed the theories of the vanguardist movement *Postismo*. Ory's manifesto of *Postismo* places emphasis on the role of the imagination in poetry, as well as on the creative power of the poetic word: it asserts correspondences between its vision and those of surrealism and expressionism. Ory's own poetry is difficult, rich and varied in form, filled with verbal and imaginative play; as Pere Gimferrer has noted, it is centered on the themes of eroticism and poetic creation. (The erotic impulse and verbal creation are linked.)[11] *Postismo* and Ory have remained largely ignored until the present (only thanks to Félix Grande's efforts is there an edition of the poet's work), and it is difficult to find specific correspondences between Ory's verse and the works of other poets. Yet his stress on the imaginative, his vision of poetry as highly creative and transcendent, and his rebellion against realistic didacticism contrasted with the general poetic atmosphere of the time and presaged, at least indirectly, significant developments of the 1960s. (Angel Crespo and Gloria Fuertes had links with *Postismo*.) One other group of poets noted for their careful use of language, those centered around the review *Cántico* of Córdoba in the late 1940s and early 1950s, was also largely ignored. Thanks to a recent and excellent study and anthology by Guillermo Carnero, we can see that these poets (Pablo García Baena and Ricardo Molina were the outstanding ones) wrote beautifully crafted works which, as Carnero notes, provide a bridge between Spanish poetry of the 1920s and that of the 1960s.[12]

All in all, it is clear that the "realistic" and existential trends of the 1940s and 1950s led to a neglect of the visionary dimensions and possibilities of poetry, and to a climate of opinion which devalued these dimensions and saw the poet's task as one of moving away from the supposed aestheticism of the Generation of 1927. It became the role of the poets who came to the fore in the late 1950s, and are the subject of my study, to redirect attention to more creative tasks. And they were to do so not by going back in time but by building more significant visions and more significantly creative poems on the basis of—and with the materials used by—post-War poetry.

The emergence of these more recent post-War poets was not marked by a single event, magazine, publication, or pronouncement. Most of them published significant books of poetry between 1953 and 1960 and were given importance by critics and reviewers at that time; several of them were given an impetus by the *Adonais* review and series. Yet it was not until well after 1960 that much attention was paid to the differences between their works and attitudes and those of earlier post-War writers. Somewhat like the Generation of 1927, these poets began by quietly cultivating their craft, and only later were recognized for their innovativeness. Two anthologies pinned down their importance: Francisco Ribes's *Poesía última* (1963) and José Batlló's *Antología de la nueva poesía española* (1968). The significance of these anthologies was increased by their inclusion of statements on poetics by the individual poets—statements which made clear the differences between their attitudes and those of the dominant writers who had come before them.

The vision of poetry espoused by these poets is extremely important for the understanding of their role and their works. Most noteworthy is the opposition that several of them express to the previously dominant stress on theme, message, and "communication." José Angel Valente, for example, puts renewed importance on style: "Me parece especialmente saludable pensar en el estilo. Porque no es el formalismo en sentido estricto el único rigor que el estilo puede padecer. Por vías distintas, el antiformalismo ha venido a parar en un formalismo de la peor especie: el de los temas o el de las tendencias." Claudio Rodríguez stresses the importance of the poetic word: "Las palabras funcionan en el poema, no sólo con su natural capacidad de decir o significar, sino, además, en un grado fundamental, en el sentido de su actividad en el conjunto de los versos. Por eso son insustituibles." Carlos Sahagún likewise underlines the value of style: "Un poema sólo es válido cuando el sentimiento que le ha dado origen, además de ser auténtico, va unido a una expresión única e insustituible."[13] Through these and other similar statements, the poets modify the utilitarian notions of poetry prevalent before them, and give back to poetic language some of the importance that it held for the Generation of 1927.

More novel yet and more important is the stress placed on poetry as an act of discovery and knowledge rather than mere communication. In a well-known essay to which many of these poets will later allude, Enrique Badosa unfolds a detailed attack on "communication" in poetry, and stresses that the work's meanings only emerge in the process of its composition: "En la poesía el poeta se conoce más a sí mismo y a las cosas, gracias a su poema, e—igual que el lector—tiene ocasión de hallarse en una nueva experiencia con que engrandecer sus perspectivas y logros espirituales."[14] Sahagún echoes the same idea: "En el fondo, al poeta no le importa la comunicación. . . . Lo verdaderamente importante, para él, es esa afirmación de sí mismo, esa indagación en lo oscuro mediante la cual, una vez terminado el poema, conocerá la realidad desde otras perspectivas." Claudio Rodríguez speaks of a "participación que el poeta establece entre las cosas y su experiencia poética de ellas, a través del lenguaje. Esta participación es un modo peculiar de conocer." And Valente devotes a whole essay to the question of the knowledge obtained in the process of composing a poem, concluding: "La poesía aparece así, de modo primario, como revelación de un aspecto de la realidad para el cual no hay más vía de acceso que el conocimiento poético."[15]

In a certain sense these statements go even beyond the creative role attributed to poetry by symbolist and postsymbolist writers. In stressing that the poet only perceives the meanings of his work in the process of writing it, they constitute a strong statement of poetry's uniqueness and irreductibility to other ways of knowing and saying. They represent a more extreme assertion of poetry's independence than those formulated by the writers of the 1920s.

Badosa does, in fact, assert the independence of the poem, even from its creator: "cuando hablo del conocimiento poético lo hago sin tener para nada en cuenta al poeta . . . sino la aprehensión y el conocimiento que surgen a partir del poema cuando ya ni el poeta es dueño de modificarlos." Such a vision leads him to attribute transcendent value to the poem: "Por otra parte, la poesía fija los puntos cardinales de la realidad que descubre y a cuya vivencia nos lleva. La poesía, en fin, es un modo de vivir las cosas."[16] The poets of this group have expressed different versions of this attitude, fitted to their particular interests. Thus Angel González finds poetry's transcendence linked to its ethical value; Rodríguez believes that "La finalidad de la poesía . . . consiste en revelar al hombre aquello por lo cual es humano"; and Valente keeps stressing the ways in which poetry is a unique way of finding and inventing reality.[17] All of this constitutes a firm denial of any purely instrumental view of poetic expression. It is also a response to what Pere Gimferrer has classified as the inertia and fossilization of the poetry and poetics of the 1940s, in which the supposedly "revolutionary" goals of the poets led them to a linguistically conservative, uncreative, and intranscendent vision and expression.[18]

The stress on the uniqueness and independence of poetry does lead these writers to some skeptical attitudes: if the poem's meanings are inexplicable and its language untranslateable, then the bonds it can establish between author and reader may be elusive and incomplete. In *Insistencias en Luzbel,* Francisco Brines includes a poem titled "Al lector," in which he points out the limitations of the poem, whose "manchas negras del papel" do not really capture the speaker's meaning; in "La mentira," José Angel Valente envisions words as empty balloons, uselessly attempting to embody their creator's meanings.[19] Such skepticism distinguishes the poets of this group from those of the Generation of 1927. Where the latter looked upon the good poem as a successful objectification of meanings, the former see it as a vehicle for a creative but necessarily incomplete journey of discovery, a journey in which both speaker and reader participate and in which the language of the text does not always provide definitive answers.

This vision of poetry as a unique act of creation via language affects the views held by these writers concerning social verse. Angel González, generally considered the most "social" of them all, has indicated that the term itself is not very meaningful: "Decir 'poesía social' no es decir nada, es caer en una simplificación que puede falsearlo todo. Pero, por debajo de tanta confusión, hay una alusión directa a realidades más profundas, poéticas y extrapoéticas, con las que, sinceramente, no me desagrada sentirme relacionado."[20] González here reveals the consciousness, common to these poets, that it is not the mere presence of the social subject that defines the work, but the particular meanings expressed and the way in which they are expressed. Carlos Barral, like González, has noted the vagueness and uselessness of the term "social poetry"; Claudio Rodríguez has indicated that it is not the materials referred to but the reach of the poem ("capacidad del alcance") which defines its subject.[21] When we examine seemingly "social" poems written by these poets, we will find a variety of ways in which they make their subjects acquire richness and dimensions that are not present in any simplistic message.[22]

These poets do assert, on the other hand, the need for poetry to deal with the basic themes of life. José Olivio Jiménez has noted the predominance in their work of the themes of time, of the mystery of existence, of the relationship between the specifics of life and its larger issues.[23] In their statements on poetics, they make it clear that they are conscious of poetry's role in dealing with such subjects. Thus Rodríguez speaks of poetry as an adventure, a discovery of essences, and gives it a moral dimension; Valente, as we have seen, makes poetry a way of knowing; and Sahagún speaks of the poem as "indagación en lo oscuro mediante la cual, una vez terminado el poema, el poeta conocerá la realidad desde otras perspectivas."[24] This stress on the larger issues to be embodied in poetry derives, of course, from the view of its transcendent value which I have already noted; it links these poets not only with José Hierro and Carlos Buosoño but also with the Generation of 1927.[25]

All these views of the necessity of finding an original expression, of the work as an act of discovery, and of its transcendence lead these writers to strive for new methods of using language in a creative fashion. In later chapters we will see different ways in which they impart to a seemingly everyday vocabulary and a seemingly anecdotal reality, novel meanings and dimensions. Eladio Cabañero has already indicated the need to look for new ways in which this poetry relates form and content: "Lo primero que se advierte es el redondeamiento de una nueva forma-fondo. El poema . . . es ya una unidad dinámica sin preciosismos ni versos sueltos o estáticos, posee una estructura argumental . . . ; se logra una superior sencillez expresiva en el tratamiento del verso libre."[26] Without abandoning the use of common language and colloquial reference, without simply going back to the vocabulary and the forms of pre-War traditions, these poets find innovative verbal strategies which make extremely significant meanings and experiences out of their apparently ordinary materials. And these strategies inevitably call for new approaches and perspectives on the part of the critic elucidating their work.

In attempting to illuminate this poetry, I have tried to adjust my approach to the characteristics of each poet's work, though always with an eye to the relationship which it establishes with the reader. In the cases of Francisco Brines and Claudio Rodríguez, this relationship can be examined through objective features of the poems: Brines's way of transforming natural scenes specifically determines the reactions of his implied reader, and Rodríguez's use of identifiable "codes" of language clarifies the experience elicited by his works. In these cases a close reading of the poems, enriched by insights gained from formalist criticism, is quite effective, although it becomes even more so when the critic gives special attention to the bond between the work and its reader. A standard analytic approach is also useful in dealing with Jaime Gil de Biedma and Eladio Cabañero, since language, imagery, and stylistic devices are their main ways of conveying meanings. In the cases of Angel González, Gloria Fuertes, and José Angel Valente, however, the relationships between text and reader, and the consequent range of meanings of the former, are harder to pin down. In studying their works, I have placed emphasis on ways in which the text is played off against various contexts, and in which the process of reading and re-reading has to unfold. Here insights from recent "reader criticism" have proven quite useful.[27] In dealing with Carlos Sahagún, I needed to combine an examination of his metaphorical language with an awareness of the contexts and systems from which this language emerges.

Two issues with which I deal several times are those of intertextuality and self-referentiality. On several occasions I will be noting ways in which a poem relates to previous texts and traditions. More often yet, a text alludes to its own process of composition or involves the reader in an interplay with itself or with some of its premises. This is, of course, one way in which these poets can infuse deeper dimensions into a seemingly ordinary reality. It is also an exemplification of their belief that writing is an act of discovery. If the process of writing a text is a way of finding fresh meanings, then the poet is necessarily conscious of the process itself and expects to gain insight by reflecting on it. The reader, in turn, also acquires a more creative role. He is not merely being handed a set meaning which the poet has placed in a text, but is examining something which constituted a gradual act of discovery for its maker. He can presumably follow the same process that the poet underwent in writing. Quite clearly the vision of poetry as a gradual act of knowledge both stresses and complicates the whole question of the relationships between reader and poet and between reader and text. It makes it even more necessary to combine an analytic sense of the text with a concern for the interactions and suggestions produced by it and by its contexts.

In addition, the view of a poem as a gradual act of discovery rather than a static repository of meanings calls into question its immutability (which analytic critics have generally taken for granted). If a poem's and a poet's meanings grow and evolve in the process of its compositions, could they not also evolve through successive readings in time? In this sense, the poetics of these writers coincides with the challenge posed to a logocentric view of writing by recent "deconstructive" critics, and forces us to deal with the issue of a work's evolution through successive readings. As I noted in the preface, this issue led me to less absolute goals in my analyses, to a greater concern with ways in which texts form parts of larger systems, and to some attempts to explore several questions underlying the reading process.

We can observe in the poetry of these writers a decided stress on personal subjects and specific events: love relationships set in particular times and places, recollections of episodes from a speaker's past, detailed happenings and discoveries. In a sense, these subjects collaborate with the ordinary vocabulary and the references to everyday matters to create an illusion of "realistic" verse. But as Carlos Buosoño has pointed out, the writers of the second post-Civil War generation accent the individual rather than the collective, and distinguish themselves from their predecessors precisely by this emphasis on personal rather than communal experience.[28] In addition, the reality and the events portrayed are so presented and "coded" that they point to larger issues. Very often they constitute a way of dealing with metaphysical subjects (time, death, the value of life, human integrity) without falling into excess abstraction or sentimental declarations. Throughout this book, we will see many specific scenes and remembrances used to evoke larger visions or to cast ironic perspectives on social issues or literary commonplaces.

The greater stress on the personal as opposed to the communal which Bousoño finds in this generation brings with it also a tendency to relate individual concerns to larger patterns of life, and not just to the issues of one society or one political moment. It also brings with it a tendency to self-reflection and self-commentary, which clearly leads to the abundance of intertextual relationships in this poetry, and to the impression that the poets are creating and discovering their view of reality as they are composing their poems, and are inviting us to do likewise as we read those poems. The specificity and the "personalism" of this poetry, in this sense, differs radically from the confessionalism of other periods (nineteenth-Century romanticism, for example): it leads not to the mere expression of irrelevant private concerns but rather to the creative representation and recreation of individual visions which acquire wider resonance and applicability.

This use of the personal and the specific, as well as the tendency to self-referentiality and to intertextual relations, helps the poetry of these writers avoid didacticism on the one hand and lachrymosely confessional verse on the other. They allow it to overcome the major pitfalls of earlier post-Civil War verse, while making use of similar materials —ordinary language, detailed remembrances, common events. This poetry demands that we pay close attention to the interplay between various levels and conventions, as I have noted, and not focus exclusively on the immediate reality portrayed or even on the text in itself.

At first glance the language used by the poets I am studying does not seem to differ much from that of their immediate predecessors: it is mostly everyday modern Spanish, devoid of any "poetic diction" and often quite colloquial in nature. But unlike many of the earlier social poets, these newer writers never let their expression become hackneyed. Everyday expressions, on the contrary, often become the basis for compellingly original verbal creations. Very much in keeping with their views on creativity, these poets make artistic use of their apparently common language. Some of them do so mainly by vocabulary selection and by using codes and symbolic patterns; others employ humor, juxtapositions, and intertextuality to give new dimensions to ordinary words and events. All in all, they discover the artistic possibilities of everyday speech and move Spanish poetry away from clichés, from sentimental overstatement, and from empty rhetoric. The originality of their poetry resides not so much in the subjects they treat or the novelty of their language, as in their precise and creative way of handling common human themes on one hand, and ordinary language on the other.

When assessing the work of this group of poets, it is important to set it in the context of other works written in the same period by older writers, and to try to determine the extent to which we can speak about a separate group or generation as opposed to a period in Spanish poetry. It is clear that many of the attitudes and traits I have been describing are also applicable to other authors, notably José Hierro and Carlos Bousoño, both of whom figured prominently in earlier post-War poetry.[29] From its very beginning, Hierro's poetry deals with metaphysical issues on the basis of specific remembrances. Particular scenes are recalled and transformed poetically, leading us to an apprehension of such themes as the sense of loss caused by time. This is perhaps most evident in his *Libro de las alucinaciones,* published in 1964 and therefore contemporary with many works of the poets I am studying. As José Olivio Jiménez has noted, the book is based on the poet's battle to affirm reality, fighting against meaninglessness and time.[30] Whether it be in a more descriptive fashion (in the "reportajes") or in a more evocative and symbolic one (in the "alucinaciones"), Hierro's works constitute a search for meaning through poetic language. They resemble those written by younger poets in their ways of transforming everyday scenes and in their creative and careful use of language. Bousoño's poetry shows a constant concern with the fleetingness and inapprehensibility of human life, and a constant search for a poetic expression which can seize life's fragile reality. *Oda en la ceniza,* first published in 1967, is centered on the poet's struggle to assert himself against nothingness through his creative use of language. Although perhaps less evidently than Hierro's work, this book fits many of the tendencies I have noted in the poetry of the group I am studying. One can even find likenesses between their

work and Vicente Aleixandre's *En un vasto dominio,* in which this great
writer of the Generation of 1927 searches for a poetic expression to seize
the basic meanings of human existence. (José Olivio Jiménez, it might
be noted, deals with Hierro, Bousoño, and Aleixandre in his study of
the poetry of the 1960s.[31])

These correspondences remind us not to place excessive emphasis
on generational distinctions, and to recall Bousoño's 1964 opinion that
after the Civil War in Spain generational distinctions tended to vanish;
as literature focused more on surrounding reality and on timely issues,
claimed Bousoño, writers of different ages produced more similar works
within a given period, and the concept of period became much more
important than the concept of generation.[32] I would maintain that the
generational distinction is nevertheless important to understand the
poetry I am studying here, even if it does not hold as fully as it might
have in the 1920s. Bousoño himself went back to it in his 1974 introduction to Brines's poetry, writing about two different poetic generations
after the Civil War. (He used this idea to indicate the stress on individual experiences by the second generation.[33])

The concept of generation also allows us to make distinctions concerning intertextuality and the role of the writer and the reader. Much
as the poetry of Hierro and Bousoño may resemble that of González or
Valente in its creative use of personal evocations, in its transformation
of the everyday, or in its formal excellence, it does not reveal either the
self-referentiality or the frequency of intertextual play that we will find
in the latter. Bousoño's statements about poetry, in sharp contrast to
those of Valente, accept a logocentric view of the text: the excellence
of his criticism resides in its ability to define the objective features of
the work studied. Valente, as we have seen, sees the poem as an evolving act of discovery,[34] an attitude also expressed by Sahagún and Rodríguez, as I have noted. And it is precisely this new accent on the poem
in an evolving process and on its self-referential and intertextual features that invites the critic to study it differently. Analyses of such a
poem have to take into account not only the text's objective features but
also the way in which it unfolds, the way in which it motivates gradual
discoveries, and the diverse relationships that it establishes between
implied author, speaker, and reader. This alone justifies the study of the
works of this generation apart from others written at the same time.

This generation's stress on the personal and the subjective, which
Bousoño has highlighted, may call for futher discussion. In general
terms, we can find personal, subjective evocations in the poetry of
Bousoño and Hierro as well as in that of González and Sahagún. But the
works of the latter (and also those of Cabañero and Gil de Biedma) are

more filled with specific remembrances of childhood and youth. Quite
often such remembrances are linked to the period of the Civil War and
to that immediately following. These poets, all but one of them born
between 1929 and 1938, constitute precisely that generation which grew
up during the war but reached adulthood after it. The traumas of the
war and of the ten years following it were engraved upon them with the
intensity of formative experiences, and formed a reservoir on which the
poets drew in their later writings. They also found themselves caught
between the restrictions of a very traditional upbringing and growing
impulses to break with that upbringing. They grew up with censorship
and read clandestinely the works of Neruda and Vallejo; yet they could
also see the corruption and the forthcoming breakdown of the system
of repression. These factors clearly distinguished them from older poets
who had reached (or were reaching) maturity when the war broke out,
and from younger ones born after the war. They may account, to some
degree, for the use of personal evocations as means to a process of poetic
discovery, and also perhaps for the tendency to view society from an
ironic, critical, and yet detached perspective. As José Batlló has indicated, these poets can be distinguished from earlier ones in their effort
to overcome the division into two neatly separated camps which had
dominated Spanish thought.[35] Transcending simplistic distinctions between Right and Left and the polemics that these engender, they
adopted more complex critical postures which we will see reflected in
their verse.

   If we are to consider the Spanish poets who come to the fore in the
late 1950s as a generation, we must briefly appraise the methodology of
generational studies and the degree of their usefulness. Quite clearly the
study of writers who were born in the same period and exposed to the
same circumstances is valuable in several ways: it allows one to take into
account the effects of their background, it facilitates the discussion of
relationships between the writers' outlooks and their works, and it helps
distinguish traits common to the group from individual characteristics
of given authors. Used with care, it can offer a system of classification
less arbitrary than one based on decades or centuries. Efforts to define
an exact system of generations have at times clouded these pragmatic
advantages and have led to very detailed and perhaps useless discus-
sions of which traits define a generation. Julius Petersen, for example,
set out eight conditions which determine and define a generation: inher-
itance, date of birth, education of the members, the ways in which they
form a community, common experiences, leadership, a generational
language, and stagnation of the previous generation.[36] Other scholars
have questioned the importance of some of these factors and criticized

Petersen for mixing biological and social criteria.[37] It seems preferable to me to leave aside the question of an exact definition and to accept the concept of a generation as a pragmatic way of grouping and examining a set of writers who clearly have much in common, whose backgrounds and work differ in significant ways from those of their contemporaries who are older or younger, and who can be best understood when studied in relation to one another.[38]

The group I am studying does meet many of Petersen's criteria. As I noted, these poets were born just previous to the Civil War and share it as a basic childhood experience; they also grew up and reached maturity during the Franco regime and its institutions. Although their early schooling differed considerably, all but one of them went to Madrid in their formative years, most of them studied there, and all but one formed part, at least temporarily, of the Spanish literary world. (Most of these writers, in contrast to many younger ones, are still based in Madrid rather than in Barcelona.) Although they do not form a single cohesive group, all of them have had extensive contacts with at least some of the others and have been very much aware of each other's work. It is impossible to define any one of them as a "leader" of the group. We cannot say that a previous generation had stagnated when they came to the fore, nor can we define a specific generational language for this group. But they clearly brought forth a new posture toward literature and a new poetics, and these, as well as their poetry, irrupted upon the Spanish literary scene when realistic social verse was losing its impact and when the most significant older poets (Aleixandre, Guillén, Alonso, Hierro, Bousoño) were moving in new directions.

The amount of time to attribute to the predominance of a given generation and the frequency with which generations succeed each other are issues that have long perplexed critics using this term. Julián Marías, developing a system envisioned by José Ortega y Gasset, attributes fifteen years to each generation and suggests that its era of predominance occurs while its members are from around forty-five to around sixty years old.[39] This particular scheme does not seem applicable to poets, who quite often publish their influential works much earlier in life. Having generations succeed each other every fifteen years also makes for many divisions. (José Arrom's scheme, which attributes thirty years to each generation and allows for subdivisions, is neater.[40]) Again, efforts to codify the concept of generations into an inflexible system can lead to arbitrariness and needless quibbling. It seems better to look at works and events as they really emerged and to define generations and their periods of predominance pragmatically. Thus one can avoid excess fragmentation on the one hand (major changes in intellec-

tual climate do not occur every five years, nor do people group themselves only with others of exactly the same age) and, on the other,
periods so long that they must encompass too many literary currents.
Periods of approximately fifteen years each seem to allow for the time
of predominance of a given group or orientation, and can often be linked
into sets of two somewhat related units.

What we have already seen suggests that a new generation of poets
did indeed emerge in Spain around 1956-1960. Although the dominant
notes of Spanish poetry until the mid-1950s still seemed to be social
consciousness on the one hand and existentialist anguish on the other,
critics were already decrying their limitations and pointing to the need
for new directions. By 1958 Enrique Badosa's essay attacking "communication" in poetry and asserting the need for creativity was published
and read, becoming a touchstone to which the new poets would often
refer.[41] Important books of poetry by the new writers appeared in or
just before this period: Claudio Rodríguez's *Don de la ebriedad* (1953),
Eladio Cabañero's *Desde el sol y la anchura* (1956) and *Una señal de amor*
(1958), Jaime Gil de Biedma's *Compañeros de viaje* (1959), Francisco Brines's *Las brasas* (1960), Angel González's *Aspero mundo* (1956), José
Angel Valente's *A modo de esperanza* (1955) and *Poemas a Lázaro* (1960),
and Carlos Sahagún's *Profecía del agua* (1958). Several of these books
won important poetry prizes.[42] All of their authors were between eigh-
teen and thirty-one years old in 1956. The youngest, Sahagún, began
publishing early in life, while the oldest, González, did so rather late;
the older poets seemed to delay their work and the younger to anticipate
it, bringing all of them together even more than their ages alone would
do. The net effect was the appearance of a cluster of new poets and a
considerably different poetic orientation within a short span of time.

If the late 1950s marked the appearance of this generation, the
decade of the 1960s was clearly its apogee. Most of the key books of
poetry by its members were published during this decade, with a special
concentration in 1965-1966 (Rodríguez's *Alianza y condena,* González's
Palabra sobre palabra, Brines's *Palabras a la oscuridad,* Valente's *La memoria
y los signos,* Gil de Biedma's *Moralidades*). Ribes's and Batlló's anthologies appeared in 1963 and 1968, respectively; they not only made the
poetry of this generation more readily available but also revealed to the
general reader the poetics and the attitudes of its members. Also during
this decade the "Colección Collioure" in Barcelona published works by
several of these poets in rather large editions, which reached more
readers than most poetry series. The poets of this generation continued
winning prizes throughout the decade, their books were more widely
reviewed, and critical studies on them began to appear.

By the early and mid-1970s the generation was clearly established as the dominant group of poets in Spain. Almost every member of the group published a collection of his or her poetry to date, many of them in the "Selecciones de Poesía Española" series of Plaza and Janés. Major critical appraisals appeared which not only defined the work of individual writers but assessed the generation as a whole (these would include José Olivio Jiménez's *Diez años de poesía española* and Bousoño's long introductory essay to Brines's poetry, both referred to above).[43] The series "El Bardo" became in effect a generational organ, publishing Batlló's anthology and many individual works of these poets. At the same time, a new and rather different group of poets made its appearance, announced in the anthology *Nueve novísmos poetas españolas,* edited by José María Castellet.[44] These poets—the most important were Manuel Vázquez Montalbán, Pere Gimferrer, Ana María Moix, Guillermo Carnero, and Leopoldo María Panero—revealed a new set of tendencies. Although some of them were included in Batlló's anthology and are but a few years younger than the poets studied here, their writing reveals different characteristics: a more aestheticist and decorative note; playful references to popular culture, film, and music, mixed with literary allusions; a breaking away from philosophic concerns in favor of aesthetic and sensorial ones; a renewed interest in surrealist features and the frequent use of *collages;* and a search for new heroes including authors as diverse as Octavio Paz and Carlos Edmundo de Ory.[45] In a sense one can see these younger writers carrying to an extreme the creative premises and the view of poetry as elaboration of new insights espoused by the previous group; in another sense one can see them leaving behind the philosophic and moral orientation of that group (as well as its tendency to recall and reelaborate the past and personal evocations), and moving to more playful and imaginative posture with respect to their art. In any event, these new poets represented a distinct change; they need to be studied as either a new "promoción" (in Arrom's generational scheme) or a new generation (in that of Marías). If the key years of the Rodríguez-Brines generation seem to have been 1956-1971, the key years of the Gimferrer-Carnero group would be from 1971 to the present.

Without attempting to make claims for the absolute value of the scheme, I find the ordering of Spanish post-Civil War poetry in fifteen-year periods extremely useful in highlighting important characteristics. In this scheme, the 1940s and early 1950s mark the path from *garcilacismo* to social poetry; 1956-1971, the dominance of the Rodríguez-Brines generation; and 1971 to the present, the appearance of a new poetry and a new sensibility which may take more time to define itself

fully. As I have already indicated, such a scheme must be used with
great care, keeping in mind the way in which poets of different generations often reveal common characteristics, and also the fact that many
poets write major works before or after the dominant period of their
generation.

One author studied in this book requires special discussion within
this generational scheme. Gloria Fuertes, who will be considered as part
of the 1956-1971 generation, was born in 1918, nearly a decade before
its next oldest member. Yet almost all of her works were written and
published between 1954 and 1970. (Only one small book, which became
almost inaccessible, came out before.) More importantly, her poetry
exemplifies the intertextuality and the way of conveying meaning of the
other writers of the generation, and her sensibility and creativity tie her
more closely to younger writers and readers than to members of her own
chronological generation. She illustrates, in fact, the limitations of any
mechanical scheme of generations, and proves that an author can fit an
orientation predominant in another generational group.

The Generation of 1956-1971 includes several important poets
whose work I do not study here. Carlos Barral, best known as publisher
and essayist, has written carefully crafted verse in which wider meanings emerge from descriptions. José María Caballero Bonald is the author of many excellent poems, leading from detailed evocations of past
events to significant perceptions and philosophic insights. Joaquín
Marco and José Agustín Goytisolo also have written valuable poetry, as
has Enrique Badosa, the author of the essay "Hablemos primero de
Júpiter." None of them, however, has produced as sustained and significant a body of poetry as the authors I am studying. José María Valverde
has published a significant amount of excellent verse, and chronologi-
cally belongs to this generation; his poems, however, are much closer
in style and orientation to those of earlier writers. Lorenzo Gomis,
another very good poet, also reveals a different orientation. I have
decided to forgo including studies on all these writers in order to give
greater cohesion to my book. As noted in chapter 10, I have studied two
poets (Angel Crespo and Manuel Mantero) who have been neglected by
the critics of this generation, but who have produced excellent poetry,
well fitted to the characteristics of this period.

All in all, the poets of the Generation of 1956-1971 do stand as a
group. Their work introduces new ways of using everyday language
creatively, and of drawing on anecdotal events and personal evocations
to forge new visions and to perform new discoveries through poetry. It
leads us to develop and revise our notions on the relationships between
a work and other preceding texts, and to consider novel ways in which

our act of reading (and rereading) a poem must be performed so as to discover its full significance, and perhaps even to expand further that significance. And it sets the ground for later poetic works written by younger writers. Most importantly, perhaps, it extends our horizons, our vision of both the lives we lead and the language we read and experience. In the following chapters, we will see how all this is accomplished.

2 FRANCISCO BRINES
Text and Reader

The work of Francisco Brines exemplifies some of the main features of Spanish poetry in the 1960s. Meditative and philosophical, often centered on the themes of time and death and on the reactions that these evoke, Brines's poetry is also marked by the very careful and artistic use of seemingly ordinary language. Critics have observed the symbolic nature of his work and its way of giving impact to seemingly common vignettes and expressions by juxtapositions, superpositions, and linguistic devices.[1]

Yet the studies so far published on Brines have not managed to explain his work adequately, to pin down fully the ways in which its language functions to create original meanings. This occurs, in my opinion, because a large part of the meaning of his poems is not determined by the words and verbal structures themselves, and hence cannot be explained by a stylistic analysis alone, nor by a combination of stylistic and thematic study. This meaning emerges, rather, from the interplay that takes place between the objective text and the reactions of the reader—an interplay that develops gradually in the act of reading the poem. By studying this process we will be able to see how the poem's techniques (many of them already studied in isolation by José Olivio Jiménez and Carlos Bousoño) contribute to the gradually unfolding reading of the text, and to the experience that it conveys.

In order to study this interplay between the text and the reactions of the reader, we have to try to assess the latter as objectively as we can, overcoming as much as possible the variations between individual readers and the differences in subjective judgments. The concept of an "implied reader" as defined by Wolfgang Iser can be helpful.[2] Iser suggests that the nature and structure of a text anticipate the standpoint from which any reader will look at its "world." That standpoint is not a specific part of the text, such as an image or a word; it is nonetheless a necessary and developing vantage point, which any reader must take if he is to follow the clues given him. Each individual reader will of course also have private reactions, and these will differ from person to person; but he will share the general standpoint set up by the text, and to this extent be its "implied reader." It will be this standpoint and this necessary role as implied reader, rather than his idiosyncratic responses, which will combine with the objective features of a given section to produce the interplay that we will be studying.

One of the processes indicated by Iser occurs when the reader, guided by the way in which the text develops, is led to modify the reaction that he would otherwise have to a word, image, or section of a poem.[3] The objective features of that given section or element are played off against attitudes and expectations that have been built up before. This produces an interplay which makes the reader deviate from the attitude he might have otherwise taken and develop a new vision and experience. This process is in my opinion central to many poems of Brines, and necessary for an understanding of their meanings. Despite some variations in interpretation that individual readers may develop, the way in which the poem unfolds dictates a certain pattern of response, and this pattern is essential to the poem's final effect.

In *Las brasas,* Brines's first book of poetry, the main theme is the passing of time; most of its poems reveal a serene and resigned contemplation of time's destructive effects although there are different shadings and variations of this outlook. This theme is expressed in a seemingly ordinary language in poems which refer to anecdotal scenes.[4] Brines often presents a speaker whose situation reveals some aspect of temporality, or describes a scene or event which reflects an attitude in the face of time's passing. He often uses "disemic" symbols, which allow him to impart wider meaning to seemingly realistic poems.[5] Other characteristics of the book also contribute to the impression of a language lacking in artifice, and yet endow it with a great expressive precision, as we shall see later on. In almost every case, the devices of a text interplay with the reader's expectations to produce an unusual and significant experience. The way in which this occurs can be seen in the following work, which forms part of a section titled "Poemas de la vida vieja":

> Está en la penumbra el cuarto, lo ha invadido
> la inclinación del sol, las luces rojas
> que en el cristal cambian el huerto, y alguien
> que es un bulto de sombra está sentado.

Sobre la mesa los cartones muestran
retratos de ciudad, mojados bosques
de helechos, infinitas playas, rotas
columnas: cuantas cosas, como un puerto,
le estremecieron de muchacho. Antes
se tendía en la alfombra largo tiempo,
y conquistaba la aventura. Nada
queda de aquel fervor, y en el presente
no vive la esperanza. Va pasando
con lentitud las hojas. Este rito
de desmontar el tiempo cada día
le da sabia mirada, la costumbre
de señalar personas conocidas
para que le acompañen. Y retornan
aquellas viejas vidas, los amigos
más jóvenes y amados, cierta muerta
mujer, y los parientes. No repite
los hechos como fueron, de otro modo
los piensa, más felices, y el paisaje
se puebla de una historia casi nueva
(y es doloroso ver que, aun con engaño,
hay un mismo final de desaliento).
Recuerda una ciudad, de altas paredes,
donde millones de hombres viven juntos,
desconocidos, solitarios; sabe
que una mirada allí es como un beso.
Mas él ama una isla, la repasa
cada noche al dormir, y en ella sueña
mucho, sus fatigados miembros ceden
fuerte dolor cuando apaga los ojos. [pp. 111-12]*

The poem focuses on a very common scene: a man sitting in his room recalling his past. But its first section creates an unusual impression on the reader. In the first lines the man is not individualized, but rather described as though he were an object ("es un bulto de sombra"); the things around him, on the other hand, become animated and almost personified (the sun invades, the lights "change the garden," the boxes "show" pictures). By thus reversing the normal roles of the man and the inanimate objects, the poem achieves several effects. Above all, it converts an ordinary scene into something rather unusual, producing a "defamiliarized" effect that makes us aware that the scene before us is not just being portrayed objectively, but is being modified literarily.[6] In

*For information on the editions quoted in the text, see the Selected Bibliography and the first (unnumbered) note to each chapter (below).

this fashion Brines, while using common words and descriptions, manages nevertheless to gain the reader's attention (overcoming the normally routine reaction the reader might have to a common scene) and to make him feel that what is being portrayed is an original vision and not an objective representation. Besides, the reversal of roles evokes a specific attitude toward the situation of the man here described. We come to feel that in some fashion his life has become static and stagnant, and that he has ceased to participate in the continuous vitality of nature which surrounds him. This prepares us for the middle part of the poem, which portrays the man as a witness of his past, and for the ending, which points to his death. In this sense, the inversion of roles is a key device which interplays with later sections of the work, governs the implied reader's reaction to them, and to a large extent determines the reading of the whole.

The view presented at the outset continues to some extent as the poem develops. The portrayal of the man as static and of things as dynamic extends to the scene in which the man examines his past. The poem stresses the importance of the photographs and of what they reveal (lines 5-9), and the way in which they create vivid memories of the past ("y retornan, / aquellas viejas vidas"). The protagonist, on the other hand, plays a passive role, both in the present (in which he recalls his past) and in the past (in which he had boyhood dreams [lines 9-11]). All this contributes to our view of the protagonist, and perhaps of man in general, as witness rather than actor in the process of life.

Beginning with line 21, the poem stresses how the protagonist not only recalls his past but actually remakes it in his mind. The more he becomes absorbed in the process of remembering, recreating his memories, and constructing dreams, the more passive he becomes in relation to his present and to the reality surrounding him. At the end of the section he gives way to tiredness and sleep. Were we to read this part of the poem by itself, we might simply say that the protagonist has become tired of recalling his past. But the previous sections of the poem dictate a less literal reading. The initial reversal of the roles of man and nature, in defamiliarizing the scene, has already forced us to move away from a literal reading of the poem and of the speaker's situation and has made us notice the contrast between the static quality of the man and the dynamic properties of nature and of the memories evoked. This invites us, now, to ascribe wider meaning to the man's tiredness at the end. We relate it to the sense of stagnation portrayed at the beginning, and come to feel that while nature and life in general continue on, the individual who looks at his existence in more specific terms notices his temporality and the limits of his life. This may provide him with wisdom, but at the price of depriving him of any active role in the course of things. (The image of taking time apart [line 15] underlines the process and is one of the few specific references to this wider pattern of meaning.)

If we read the poem in this fashion, we can even link the speaker's recollections with the act of poetic creation. We notice that he does not repeat events the way they were but thinks of them in another fashion ("de otro modo / los piensa"). His process of remembering and remaking constitutes an effort to overcome, by means of a creative act, the wearing down to which he is subject. The end of this effort suggests the tragic limitation of poetry as well as of life itself.

Reviewing our reading of the poem, we can see that it has made use of the reversal of the roles of protagonist and nature to create an initial defamiliarizing effect, and thus to convert a seeming anecdote into a vision of human temporality. Once this vision is set up, it governs our reading of the rest of the poem. In this sense, the poem is clearly disemic: the specific reality that it describes carries wider meaning, although this meaning is not essential to understand the literal level of the text.[7] But in contrast to the more typical disemic poems of other authors, which contain specific words and elements to which we can attribute symbolic value, this one depends to a large extent on the reader's reactions and attitudes. Almost the only objective device that defines its focus is the initial reversal, with its defamiliarizing effect and its way of leading us to the view of man as affected by time. Once it has established this view, the poem relies on us to continue reading with the same defamiliarized perspective and the same interpretation of the speaker as the image of a man stopped and limited by time. This lets the reader see in wider terms the idealization of the past that the speaker undertakes, and the allusions to the city and the island. And it makes very clear why this work, seemingly focused on anecdotal details, is in the last analysis philosophic and symbolic rather than descriptive or realistic.

Given the perspective established by the poem, we have to read its ending as symbolic:

> Un día partirá del viejo pueblo
> y en un extraño buque, sin pesar,
> navegará. Sin emoción la casa
> se abandona, ya los rincones húmedos
> con la flor del verdín, mustias las vides;
> los libros, amarillos. Nunca nadie
> sabrá cuando murió, la cerradura
> se irá cubriendo de un lejano polvo. [p. 112]

The allusions to the strange ship and to weightlessness suggest a death trip, an impression which is confirmed in the next-to-last line of the poem. In a certain sense, the protagonist's death is no more than the culmination of the passivity that we have witnessed from the beginning: his leaving the old town merely continues and completes the process of estrangement produced by time, which had already separated him from the old lives that he could only recall in his memory. In view of the earlier sections of the poem, therefore, the ending merely clarifies the theme of the work, stressing the way in which temporality limits and defines man. (Even his memories and their recreation only lead the protagonist toward death; implicitly, at least, poetic creation does likewise.) The surrounding world goes on, but without the human being who lived in it.

We can now see that the whole poem has made us feel the emptiness of human life, an emptiness caused by its temporality. The poem's key procedure has been a disemic symbolism, which has given deeper value to an apparently realistic description. But that procedure has depended on the reader's collaboration, and cannot be explained just by analyzing words or images. The initial reversal of roles and the resultant defamiliarization have established an attitude from which the reader has transformed and interpreted succeeding sections, applying the vision of man's temporality to anecdotal details which, in themselves and in isolation, would not have embodied it.

A similar effect is achieved in another poem of *Las brasas,* which comes from the third section of the book:

> Esta grandiosa luz, que hay en el cuarto,
> desplegada regresa de los montes
> altos del Guadarrama. Gran tarea
> es dar la flor a verdecidos troncos
> o ser el aire suave que los mueve.
> Mas yo qué solo estoy, Madrid se va
> saliéndose a mi calle por ver pinos.
> Miro la habitación, en el espejo
> desvanecida mi figura seria,
> ya sin dolor el alma. La fatiga
> rinde el cuerpo del hombre, le da un punto
> de paz, lo aleja de la vida libre.
> Los bultos que dejó, sus cartas, tocan
> mis dedos en silencio, como al campo
> la tarde de febrero que se ensancha.

Me miro en el espejo, y estoy fijo
como un árbol oscuro que han podado.
Mi extraña seriedad es porque pienso
que aquello fue por un azar (las hojas
así caen del arbol, por el roce
de una rama vecina, por el aire),
y todo ha de empezar de nuevo. Ay,
que el furioso dolor nace de encuentros
indiferentes, se conocen pronto
cuerpos a veces débiles, las fuerzas
sin voluntad se rinden al espíritu
y enamorados quedan. Los guijarros
son más fuertes que el hombre, la alegría
muy robusta no crece si es que nace.
En contra de esta lanza que se clava
no hay escudo de bronce, ni edad vieja
que libre de esa lucha; tal tesoro
no custodia un gigante ni hace suyo
quien tiene el corazón más puro y fuerte.
Era bello decir, tú como un monte,
y tú como un león, y delicado
como la paz de una doncella. Tristes
quedan los ojos en el hombre siempre,
es un dolor ver que los frutos caen
o que el tordo se cansa de volar.
Mas es mayor el mal si la arrogancia
de respirar en la mañana sufre
sin aliento esforzado, y el fervor
de la vida se encorva como un viejo. [pp. 139-40]

The roles of speaker and nature are again reversed; while the latter
is vivified, the former presents himself as static and alone. In the first
stanza a contrast is set up between the vitality of the light (which
moves, returns, fulfills a task, makes tree trunks flower) and the passivity of the speaker, who sees himself as an inanimate figure in a
mirror, who remains static and solitary, and whose letters are only
shapes ("bultos") that he left behind. Just as in the poem analyzed
before, this reversal produces a defamiliarizing effect, and makes the
reader feel the unusual quality of this seemingly common scene. It also
conveys a similar view of man, again described as stagnant in contrast
to a much more vital nature. In this poem even the presentation of a
protagonist who speaks in the first person, which normally would make
him more active, creates the opposite effect: by seeing himself as a
reflection in a mirror, by switching to the third person in lines 11-13,

and by setting his passivity off against the activity of the surrounding world, this protagonist seems to be consciously effacing himself, turning himself into a thing.

Our reading of the first parts of the poem determines our reaction to the later ones. When the speaker stresses his temporality (beginning in line 30) and links his inertia and his pessimism with the limitations of time, we relate his view to the scheme of reversals seen before. If we had read this section by itself, we might have said that the speaker tries to link with nature, since he identifies himself with natural processes (falling leaves and fruit). Our reading of the previous parts of the poem, however, makes us stress the differences between man and nature. We therefore observe how the protagonist's consciousness of old age sets him apart from nature, in which everything will begin again: for him, temporality is a much more absolute process. This makes us feel very dramatically the protagonist's plight, and gives greater importance to the aging and destruction portrayed in the poem's ending:

> Tras del rojo horizonte la ceniza
> de la tarde ha caído, y en el cuarto
> queda marchito un hombre. Lucen fuera
> las primeras estrellas, es la noche
> quien entra en el espejo su gran sombra
> borrándome, las ramas de la calle
> vacilan moribundas bajo el frío.
> Siento dura la espalda y hace daño
> dar movimiento al cuerpo, mis mejillas
> arden como la leña y están secas. [p. 140]

Although the protagonist himself links his temporality with that of natural elements (the evening, firewood), we come to feel that his evanescence is much more fundamental. While the changes in nature represent succeeding moments in a continuous cycle, and while the "death" of light is only an illusion, the dissolution of man is an absolute tragedy.

Again we have seen how the defamiliarizing effect of the first stanza has governed our reading of the whole poem and has determined its meaning. By separating man from nature, and by stressing the vitality of the latter and the immobility of the former, the work has made us feel something that the protagonist himself barely seems to suspect: the fact that his temporality is much more final and tragic than that of the surrounding world. This gives the poem some of the qualities of a dramatic monologue, the reader of which sees more clearly than its speaker the situation in which the latter finds himself.[8]

The process of defamiliarization and the reversal of man and nature work somewhat differently in the two poems analyzed so far. In the first one they are used mainly to highlight the symbolic level; in the second (where the symbolic level is clear) they serve to separate us from the protagonist and to underline his tragedy. But in both cases they are a way of fixing the perspective of the poem and determining the attitude of the implied reader at the outset; in both they serve to guide the reading throughout, and to produce a vision different from, and richer than, that produced by the words and images if seen in isolation. Both poems use apparently common scenes in a unique fashion, building up expectations within the reader so as to create significant patterns of response, experience, and meaning.

Palabras a la oscuridad, Brines's next major book, portrays the conflict between the vitality of nature and human life on the one hand, and the destructiveness of time on the other.[9] In very general terms one can say, with José Olivio Jiménez, that a positive attitude and an exaltation of life in the face of temporality are more evident in this book than in the previous one. Greater stress is also placed on the speaker or *persona;* far from making the work confessional or private, this speaker dramatizes general attitudes in the face of time.[10] In this sense, he fulfills a role similar to that of the descriptions and scenes of *Las brasas.* In several poems the speaker contemplates objective reality and addresses a second person in order to obtain a deeper insight and a deeper understanding; his contemplation and his monologue are ways of examining the surrounding world poetically and of discovering its significance.

The ways in which these poems elicit the implied reader's reactions are related to the book's characteristics. Instead of focusing on an external reality, reversing its appearance, and defamiliarizing it, Brines now uses the speaker and his attitude to lead the reader to the poem's meanings. (He still defamiliarizes the poem's subject matter.) Again and again the outlook or attitude of the speaker is unusual or fluctuating, and alters the reader's reaction so as to give him a new vision of the subject. If in *Las brasas* the defamiliarization of apparently common episodes led to more original meanings, in *Palabras a la oscuridad* the transformation of the speaker's observations and reactions is the main device for leading us to significant visions.

The importance of this process and its effect on the reader will be clearer if we keep in mind that the speaker of a poem is a device constructed and manipulated by an implied author detached from him;

the attitude of the author and the experience of the reader may differ significantly from those of the speaker.[11] The author may in fact use these differences in order to construct his meanings. The speaker may be characterized so as to set his judgments apart and against ours; when this occurs, our experience (and the work's meaning) depends on the interplay between the speaker's attitudes at given points in the poem and our evolving judgment of him and of the situation—a judgment based on our overall view and on the context in which he and the work operate. "Tránsito de la alegría" offers a good example of such an interplay:

>Sube, cae tu voz,
>se mueve el sol, nos besa.
>Y en la vida del aire
>se renuevan las hojas,
>cantan pequeños picos
>desde las ramas altas.
>El la luz, es la vida
>que se va, la triunfal
>muerte, tú, yo, y el pájaro
>que canta, que cantamos.
>
>Sentado aquí, contigo,
>después que la felicidad
>deviene súbita
>para que la tristeza
>la desborde después,
>¿qué le falta a mi pecho
>para ser ya ceniza?
>
>Ah, sí, sólo la fuerza
>que, aquí abajo, concilia
>la carne con la sombra,
>el sueño con la nada,
>puede en su voluntad
>hacerme eterno y árido.
>
>Después que la felicidad
>deviene súbita
>para que la tristeza
>la desborde después,
>queda inservible el mundo;
>y aun la tristeza misma,
>nacida de misterio,
>se ha de tornar, inútil
>a su cueva.

> Serena,
> irá ocupando el sitio,
> sin demasiada prisa,
> la alegría que vuelve. [pp. 239-40]

The situation seems very ordinary, and in fact constitutes a literary
commonplace: the speaker, sitting beside his loved one in a natural
landscape, meditates on the happiness of the moment as well as the
effects of time. The reader's reaction, however, is not so conventional.
The beginning of the first stanza suggests a fusion between the lovers
and nature, a fusion underlined by the sun's kisses, the song of the
birds, and the rebirth of the leaves. (The fusion seems even more
stressed by a reversal of roles: the sun kisses while the beloved's voice
rises and falls.) Any reader familiar with the tradition of bucolic love
poetry recognizes immediately the *topos* of the lovers happily ensconced
in nature, and comes to line 7 ready to accept the optimistic vision of
a beautiful and harmonious world of love. (We observe that line 7
invites us, on first reading, to see it as a complete sentence, stating
clearly the value of life.)

But at this point the poem takes an abrupt and unexpected turn: on
reading line 8 and seeing how it continues and changes the thought of
the previous one, we are forced to change our interpretation and to
realize that what is portrayed is a negative view of time's passing. The
speaker (and the poem) seem to have put us to sleep with their supposed
and conventional idealism, only to play a trick upon us. Another trick
awaits us in the next line. By ending line 8 with the adjective "triunfal,"
the poem tempts us into thinking that it might refer to life and reestablish some of the initial optimism. But the adjective ends up modifying
"death," and repeating the shift to a negative view! The run-on lines of
7 and 8, and 8 and 9 destroy dramatically the positive vision with which
the poem tempted us at the beginning, and leave us contemplating the
bird and the lovers as images of temporality and tragedy rather than of
happiness. The effect of this stanza depends to a great extent on its
progressive development: it is the illusion of a positive view, abruptly
undercut by the changes that I have indicated, that makes us feel the
destructive impact of time and death. The shift we have witnessed
serves to give impact and originality to a theme and a view which
otherwise could have seemed quite commonplace.

Our reading of the following stanzas is based on the experience
produced by the first one. If it were seen independently, the speaker's
declaration in stanza two would be just an example of a conventional
pessimism, and its last lines would seem a romantic exaggeration. But

the dramatic destruction of a positive view that we have witnessed in stanza 1 makes the speaker's pessimism more understandable. We go along with it and with the growing resignation of stanza 3, in which he manages to reconcile his illusion (the dream) with his perception of temporality (shadow and nothingness), ending up with an enigmatic vision of himself as "eternal and arid."

But the poem has not yet come to its end: one more surprise awaits us. When we start reading the fourth stanza, and especially when we realize that its first four lines repeat, exactly, four lines of the second stanza, we assume that the speaker is repeating his loss of illusion and his pessimism and adding a yet more negative touch in line 28. Precisely at this point the poem again changes direction: the speaker comes to see sadness itself as part of the world he is leaving behind, again reverses his outlook, and asserts the happiness which was so dramatically destroyed in the first stanza.

The reader is disoriented, seeking desperately some objective explanation for this renewed optimism. On not finding any in the last lines he is forced to reexamine the whole work, the general attitude of the speaker, and the total experience conveyed by the poem. The two shifts in attitude, both so dramatically presented, seem contradictory. But if we look at them together they make us see the speaker as a person in constant struggle, never really resolved; they also make us realize that we have been forced to participate in this struggle, as we have seen our expectations destroyed each time. Having followed the speaker step by step through the poem, we can now stand back, take a wider view of his experience (and our own), and come to a new understanding of the poem's meaning. We now realize that its true theme is, precisely, the struggle between an assertion of life on the one hand and a recognition of its limitations on the other.[12]

One could object that my analysis of the poem was based on words and technical devices more than on the reader's reactions as such: the changes in attitude are clearly signalled by objective features of the text. But the final value of these changes cannot be understood until one examines how they interfere with the normal expectations of the reader, how they determine his reactions and produce an interaction between reader and speaker, and how they make the reader into both participant and witness of a paradoxical vision of life and temporality. The context of the poem—our previous knowledge of certain traditions, the way in which we normally react to a first-person speaker, the normal attitudes we take to certain views—are also a integral part of our experience. In the final analysis we can say that in "Tránsito de la alegría" Brines has again manipulated and defamiliarized his subject and his material to create a unique experience, just as he did in the poems from *Las brasas*. But now he has made use of a more elaborate play of perspectives in the speaker as well as an intertextual pattern, and has produced a richer vision of the theme of temporality.

Several other poems in *Palabras a la oscuridad* achieve a similar effect. In "Aceptación," for example, the speaker splits his perspective and addresses himself in order to recall his past and to come to realize the fleetingness of life. At the moment at which he is most conscious of this fleetingness, however, he paradoxically affirms his acceptance of life:

> El tiempo va pasando, no retorna
> nada de lo vivido:
> el dolor, la alegría, se confunden
> con la débil memoria,
> después en el olvido son cegados.
> Y al dolor agradeces
> que se desborde de tu frágil pecho
> la firme aceptación de la existencia. [p. 238]

In somewhat similar fashion, Brines ends the poem "Oscureciendo el bosque" by following a pessimistic vision with a declaration of faith in life:

> Cercado de tinieblas, yo he tocado mi cuerpo
> y era apenas rescoldo de calor,
> también casi ceniza.
> Y he sentido después que mi figura se borraba.
>
> Mirad con cuánto gozo os digo
> que es hermoso vivir. [p. 216]

This tension between a realization of the limitations which time and death impose on human life, and the impulse to affirm human vitality, forms the cornerstone of *Palabras a la oscuridad*. The book's success, however, depends on the ways in which the tension is conveyed by the play of perspectives and by the resulting interactions between the speaker and the implied reader.

Aún no is focused even more exclusively on time and death; its dominant vision, however, is much more pessimistic than that of *Palabras*. The destructive effects of time are constantly stressed, and their portrayal provides some of the most intense moments of the book. The negative vision of the book is often embodied in the outlook of a first-person speaker. But the book reveals a great variety of tones, perspectives, and situations; in several poems the speaker steps back into a remote past and invokes literary and artistic works of antiquity.

Carlos Bousoño, in his excellent prologue to Brines's collected works, has described the unusual language of this book, noting that elements of reality appear in roles that are totally unexpected but that always serve to express the poet's intuitions.[13] Bousoño refers to "Signos vanos," showing how objects and allusions that do not make logical sense correspond to the atmosphere communicated by the poem. He does not analyze the poem in detail, however, and leaves unexplained how these elements manage to convey the atmosphere and the experience to the reader.

The explanation, in my opinion, lies in a more extreme version of the process of defamiliarization that we have been studying. In Brines's previous books, the reader's reactions to the text were guided by defamiliarizations or changes in perspective which led him to original experiences created around apparently ordinary scenes (in *Las brasas*) and apparently insignificant narrations or presentations (in *Palabras*). The external reality portrayed seemed at first glance to correspond to our ordinary one; in the final analysis, however, common elements were being manipulated to create new visions. In "Signos vanos" the only change is the disappearance of an apparently ordinary reality. The elements which are presented to us do not relate logically to each other, and function from the outset as correlatives of the speaker's attitude. That attitude, and not any scene or episode, becomes the explicit basis of the poem. We can see it in several excerpts:

> ¿Por qué llego furtivo
> si en la casa me esperan sólo sábanas fúnebres,
> y el único habitante, de celosa vigilia,
> tiene el oído seco,
> y es yacente marchito entre las sombras,
> y su nombre no es vicio ni virtud,
> sino silencio?
> En esta escasa noche que aún desvela,
> el gemido amoroso del cansancio y el sueño
> debe tardar aún, la fosca tregua
> ha de llegar con la herida del día;
> ahora sepulto muerte al recordar
>
>   la música del negro, su rosa paladar, y la penumbra
> lasciva de los humos, la escalera reciente
> de arracimadas manos, vasos desiertos, derramadas
> miradas y licores, la remisa invasión.
> . . . .

> . . . Esta lenta vejez
> no la remedia nada; el sueño, con su máscara,
> va impidiendo mi muerte, pero no este derrumbe
> sucesivo y constante de la carne,
> mi floja compañera, que arroparé en las sábanas.
> Es acto decidido, necesario.
>
>   Y a este día
> de confusa costumbre
> lo canso un poco más, y en el papel
> he trazado palabras, signos vanos
> del tiempo, porque pido bondad,
> y me rodean cosas que no me dan bondad, aunque acompañen,
> y esta casa está sola. [pp. 309-10]

The house and the speaker's arrival at it carry an obvious symbolic meaning, and evoke man's path through life. The details presented are fitted to this theme and point to a perception of mortality and a loss of the experiences of life. The speaker is able, for a time, to "bury death" by remembering happenings or actions that occurred in life, but he finally has to accept his temporality and dress himself in sheets that have already been described as funereal. The dominant technique of this poem seems to be the presentation of symbolic actions and scenes (in Bousoño's terminology, they seem monosemic rather than disemic) which embody and reflect the attitude of the speaker as well as the vision offered by the poem. We might say that the poet has defamiliarized not only some selected elements but also the whole scene of which his work consists. In this fashion he leads the reader directly to his theme.

We also observe an allusion to the very process of writing poetry at the end of this poem. Just as he did in some works of *Las brasas* and *Palabras a la oscuridad,* Brines here links the limitations of poetry to those of human life in general. This not only reinforces the theme of temporality but also adds a metapoetic dimension to his work and underlines dramatically the limitations of the very act of communication that is taking place before our eyes.

In other poems of *Aún no,* Brines combines seemingly anecdotal elements and events with obviously symbolic ones. "Mendigo de realidad," for example, focuses on a detailed action, the beloved's withdrawal of her hand from the speaker; this action, however, motivates a whole vision of loss and failure. At the end of the poem, the speaker embodies his attitude in the image of howling:

> Con un hambre cruel de realidad
> aúllo sordamente con los perros,
> miro apagar el alba las estrellas,
> Y he sentido mi mano desechada
> como si ajena fuese. [p. 306]

What appears to be a single description is in fact a combination of several different levels: whereas the withdrawal of the beloved's hand refers back to the poem's literal level, the images of hunger and howling are concretizations of the speaker's philosophic outlook and subjective attitude, and the dimming of dawn light by the stars seems to represent the negative state of the world. By combining all these levels in a single picture, the poem makes it impossible to separate neatly the anecdotal from the symbolic; ultimately this leads the reader to leave behind any concerns with literal reality as such, and to focus on the way in which the whole scene captures the subjective theme of the work. We might say that all elements of the poem have been defamiliarized and restructured to fit that theme.

Several poems in this book seem to be descriptions of trivial events or characters: we are given conversations between two women adulterers, an address to a bad poet, thoughts on a conversation. But even in these the speaker's attitude is often shockingly unusual and serves to underline his general pessimism in the face of life and time. He describes, for example, the banality to which well-known poetry will be reduced in time in "Poeta póstumo" (p. 399). In other poems, references to epitaphs of antiquity likewise capture the impermanence of life and art, which unites the poets of the past and of the present in a trip to oblivion: "Quien lea, debe saber que el tuyo / también es mi epitafio. Valgan tópicas frases / por tópicas cenizas." ("Epitafio romano," p. 319). Much of this poem's effect is intertextual and depends on our awareness that the meaning of this "epitaph" contradicts the conventional intent of an epitaph, that of making us remember.

As Brines's negative vision becomes intensified in *Aún no,* the descriptions, images, and events portrayed are transformed in more obvious ways than in the earlier books; instead of a gradual process of defamiliarization that leads us through a text, we are given recreated images and vignettes which picture a doomed world. The interplay between reader and work becomes somewhat different. It does not simply occur within each individual poem as the development of that poem modifies the reader's expectations. It develops, instead, throughout the book as a whole. The reader, as he witnesses the already defamiliarized reality of the text, and senses the effects of the transformations, finds himself leaving behind his ordinary vision and experiencing the created world of the book.

This process is even more apparent in *Insistencias en Luzbel,* Brines's latest book of poetry.[14] External reality now appears totally transformed to fit the subjective vision of the poet, and serves as the correlative of a negative yet rebellious outlook on life and art. The story of Lucifer is the basis for a whole new myth of existence: In the first part of the book ("Insistencias en Luzbel") Lucifer's rebellion is a sign of modern man's existential battle against a meaningless and time-limited existence. The second part ("Insistencias en el engaño") is more heterogeneous, reflecting various aspects of man's efforts to affirm himself within an absurd world by means of love, sex, and poetry.

In many poems, external reality is transformed from the very beginning into a correlative for the speaker's feelings. In "El extraño habitual" (*Insistencias,* pp. 44-45), which recalls "Signos vanos" of *Aún no,* an empty house is transformed into an image of loss, emptiness, and death. At times the speaker combines evocations of past and present to construct a subjective vision of loss (see "Sucesión de mí mismo," pp. 74-75). All these individual transformations, however, function as parts of a recreated reality encompassing the whole book. The reader sees individual poems against the backdrop of a system in which traditional meanings have been reversed, in which God is "el engaño," the Angel "la nada," and Lucifer "el olvido" (p. 13). These reversals are extended in poem after poem: in "Invitación a un blanco mantel," for example, an attempt to define oneself in the condition of nothingness leads to a situation in which the only possible creation is self-destruction (p. 15). By making this context for itself, the book essentially defamiliarizes all reality as we know it and creates a situation in which every recognizable item or situation presented can no longer be assumed to have its normal connotations. Any insights or meanings must be formed anew.

A good example of the way in which this affects our reading of individual works is provided by "Canción de los cuerpos":

> La cama está dispuesta,
> blancas las sábanas,
> y un cuerpo se me ofrece
> para el amor.
> . . . .
> Que no hay felicidad
> tan repetida y plena
> como pasar la noche,

> romper la madrugada,
> con un ardiente cuerpo.
> Con un oscuro cuerpo,
> de quien nada conozco
> sino su juventud. [p. 64]

Read by itself, the poem seems to offer a basically negative view of the event. Despite the speaker's affirmation and the apparently positive nature of the love described, the details given limit the episode. The beloved lacks individuality (she is simply "un oscuro cuerpo"), the speaker emphasizes the impermanence of the experience, greater stress is placed on the beloved's youth than on anything else. We are tempted to deem the love trivial and insignificant.

Yet in the context of the whole book such an evaluation would be simplistic. The work's constant reversal of traditional views, for one, makes us loath to render quick judgments. The use of love and erotic force as antidotes to meaninglessness throughout the book would also make us view this episode more positively than we would otherwise. And the stress on the beloved's youth, in this context, is a positive rather than a negative factor: it highlights the speaker's use of love in his battle against time and oblivion.

All this does not completely destroy the impression of a limited erotic love, but it does modify it. We are left, in the final analysis, with a paradoxical vision of a love that is limited yet significant as an assertion of existence and as a rebellion against oblivion. The defamiliarization produced by the book as a whole has created a context which greatly contributes to the richness and meaning of the poem.

This situation is even more apparent in the case of several poems dealing with the theme of poetic creation—a subject of great importance in the book. In "Al lector," for example, the author/speaker desperately tries to express and continue himself in the lines that he has written and that we are reading:

> En las manos el libro.
> Son palabras que rasgan el papel
> desde el dolor o la inquietud que soy,
> ahora que todavía aliento bajo tu misma noche,
> desde el dolor o la inquietud que fui,
> a ti que alientas debajo de la noche
> y ya no estoy.
> Crees que me percibes en estas manchas negras del papel,
> en este territorio, ya no mío, de la desolación. [p. 37]

The poem's impact is greatly increased when we see the speaker's act of writing as part of his rebellion against temporality and death: whether sucessful or not, his effort to continue himself in his poem embodies his struggle against nothingness. And the theme of the struggle, in turn, acquires greater force when presented in this form. The device of having the poet speak about his writing in the very text that we are reading provides a dramatic method of highlighting it and involving us in its process.

The metapoetic allusions that appear in other parts of the book likewise serve to highlight the same struggle: several pictures of the speaker creating poetry make us feel both the dilemma created by temporality and the battle waged against it. "Días finales," one of the last works in the book, ends as follows:

> Alguna noche intenta algún poema
> personal, aunque vago, como escrito
> por él, cuando era joven, presintiendo
> los días venturosos de vejez.
> Y es el último engaño de la vida. [p. 81]

The increasing stress on the theme of poetry in Brines's work, and the metapoetic nature of some of his recent texts, seem part of a general process of development. They constitute a way of moving beyond a "realistic" presentation of his materials, of intensifying the play of perspectives, and of including the reader within a complex poetic inquiry into the theme of temporality. By commenting on the process of creation while undertaking it, the speaker invites us on the one hand to take part in it, and on the other to contemplate it as part of his general struggle against the order of things.

We have seen throughout Brines's poetry a variety of ways in which the reader's reactions have been developed and modified. By defamiliarizing individual elements, by setting up attitudes and then modifying them, by creating intertextual relationships, and by forging whole new visions of life, Brines has created contexts which govern and modify the specific images and words of his poems. Each one of his books offers excellent examples of how the meaning of a given text depends not only on its devices but also on the reader's reactions—reactions produced and guided by the contexts of the words (and of the reader's own background). Seen as a whole, his poetry shows an increasing complexity in the ways of relating text and context and of fitting individual poems into larger and fuller visions and experiences.

The importance of contexts which guide the reactions of the implied reader in Brines's poetry is related to the language used by the poet, to the themes of his work, and to his attitude to poetry. Like other members of his generation, Brines avoids a consciously artful style and uses common events and experiences in his work. By modifying his materials through the contexts in which they are set and through the manipulation of reader reactions, he can impart significance to seemingly ordinary scenes and happenings. He can also make these elements lead us to the philosophic themes which infuse his work. And the complex interplay often produced in his poems serves to embody these themes (especially temporality) with all the nuances of complex experiences. The processes we have been studying therefore let Francisco Brines achieve what he himself envisioned as a goal of poetry—the embodiment, preservation, and communication to others of an experience threatened by time:

> La poesía consigue este milagro de prolongar en el
> tiempo una emoción de vida, perecedera por temporal;
> así le da ocasión al poeta de ejercitar ese fortísimo
> instinto de conservación . . . y ese otro de comunicación
> y reconocimiento en los demás.[15]

3 CLAUDIO RODRÍGUEZ
Language Codes
and Their Effects

As has often been noted, Claudio Rodríguez's poetry illustrates attitudes and tendencies that came to the fore in Spain in the 1960s. Its seemingly everyday language and its allusions to common events link this poetry to earlier tendencies of post-Civil War verse. Yet a close look at individual texts makes clear that Rodríguez employs that language in a highly unusual and creative way, imparting significance to common words and expressions and making ordinary events suggest very fundamental meanings. His work avoids easy social and conceptual messages, and deals in complex fashion with such subjects as the conflict between negative and positive forces in the world, the search for a joyous vitality in life, and the quest for knowledge through poetry. Again and again, a specific experience evokes a much more general vision, pointing beyond the problems of one individual or even one particular society.

Critics have explained these characteristics of Rodríguez's work by noting that the poet adds a metaphoric and allegorical dimension to common events and thus expands their meaning. By applying to this work the concepts of "metaphorical realism" and "disemic allegory," Carlos Bousoño and William Mudrovic explain quite effectively how poems impart universal meaning to apparently limted subjects.[1]

These explanations of Rodríguez's work do have one limitation: they make us see the concrete level of the poems as somehow separate from their wider significance. Bousoño tries to overcome this separation by stressing the disemic nature of Rodríguez's allegory; he observes that the representational plane does not become submerged in the more universal one, but coexists with it and conveys its own meanings to the reader. In Bousoño's words: "His intention is not to annihilate the object. The object is seen and understood as itself . . . although it is presented, at the same time, as carrying a more universal meaning."[2] Even so, this way of interpreting Rodríguez's poems leaves unexplained a key characteristic of the poet's work. When one reads this work, one does not focus separately on the representational plane and the universal one. Quite on the contrary, one senses the unity (often a paradoxical one, combining conflicting perspectives) of the experience being offered; one *simultaneously* apprehends the diverse realities and perspectives which are part of that experience. These encompass not only immediate perceptions and universal themes, but also cultural patterns, literary allusions, diverse ways of seeing one event. On sensing all this, the reader feels that the experience produced is an irreducible mystery which combines multiple elements not according to some logical scheme but in response to some integrative impulse that transcends any such scheme. To explain how Rodríguez's poetry manages to convey this sense of paradoxical unity, one needs to look more closely at the levels of language operating in his poems. These reveal patterns which can be defined with some objectivity, and which suggest ways in which the poems convey their meanings to the "implied reader"—the reader led by the text to a specific vantage point whose perspective is governed by the characteristics of that text.[3]

Roland Barthes uses the term and concept of "codes" to suggest ways in which a literary text contains several different levels of meaning which coexist in it and which come together to form the experience conveyed to the reader. Barthes has stressed that the interpretation of a text is not a process of uncovering a variety of separate meanings hidden in it but rather that of trying to appreciate the total significance produced by its different levels, evocations, and values.[4] When a critic examines a code he is identifying a related group of words and devices which act as signifiers. In this fashion he can define and highlight one of the text's values and go on to relate it to others, gradually building up a coherent vision of the work's total range. This way of dealing with the text has a great advantage when studying the poetry of Rodríguez: it allows the critic to examine and relate various levels of a work without creating excessively neat oppositions between a representational plane and a symbolic or allegorical one.

Barthes discusses five codes in his study of Balzac's *Sarrasine:* the proairetic (which identifies the meanings that determine the work's action), the hermeneutic (which focuses on the formal devices which define and resolve the work's enigma), the *seme* code, the symbolic one, and the cultural one. His list, however, should not be taken as an inflexible system but rather as a way of approaching a work that can be modified and adjusted to the requirements of the work. I will use a somewhat different list of codes in examining Rodríguez's poems, selecting levels which seem to play major roles in their structure and meaning. My main purpose is to discover the ways in which the multiple values of a work are generated and related to each other so as to produce its total experience. Despite some variation from poem to poem and from book to book, certain language patterns and codes can be identified in many of Rodríguez's works.

"A mi ropa tendida," from the book *Conjuros,* exemplifies the way in which several codes produce different levels of meaning. Two of these levels, one representational and the other symbolic and allegorical, are immediately evident on reading the poem: one can apprehend the washing of clothes described in it as on the one hand a specific event and on the other a way of pointing to the more abstract theme of a search for purification. The presence of both levels becomes evident in the very title: while the main title highlights the specific event, the subtitle, "El alma," underlines the symbolic level.[5] From that point on, the poem keeps on shuffling and developing both levels simultaneously. Its total effect depends on both, on the two language codes—one representational and the other symbolic—which are used to embody and reveal these levels, and also on two other codes, a humorous one and a cultural one, which modify the total effect produced on the implied reader.[6]

A Mi Ropa Tendida

(El alma)

Me la están refregando, alguien la aclara.
¡Yo que desde aquel día
la eché a lo sucio para siempre, para
ya no lavarla más, y me servía!
¡Si hasta me está más justa! No la he puesto
pero ahí la véis todos, ahí, tendida,
ropa tendida al sol. ¿Quién es? ¿Qué es esto?
¿Qué lejía inmortal, y qué perdida
jabonadura vuelve, qué blancura?
Como al atardecer el cerro es nuestra ropa
desde la infancia, más y más oscura
y ve la mía ahora. ¡Ved mi ropa,
mi aposento de par en par! ¡Adentro
con todo el aire y todo el cielo encima!
¡Vista la tierra tierra! ¡Más adentro!
¡No tendedla en el patio: ahí, en la cima,
ropa pisada por el sol y el gallo,
por el rey siempre! [p. 101]

Mudrovic has observed that the poem makes us relate two levels, stressing on the one hand a literal cleansing and on the other a process of purification.[7] If we adopt the concept of codes, we can see more clearly how these levels are developed and juxtaposed. The allusions to the process of washing and the words "refregar," "lejía," "jabonadura," and "patio" form a code calling attention to the representational level, while "el alma," "inmortal," "aclara," and the archetypal resonances implicit in washing produce a symbolic code and level. The words "aclara" and "blancura" form a kind of bridge, since they allude to both levels, as does the phrase "lejía inmortal." This way of looking at the poem and its two levels makes very clear the precision with which the latter are produced, shuffled, and intertwined; it lets us see that the work's impact depends on the contrast between levels and on the tension produced on the implied reader, who is forced by the text to switch from one code and one level to the other. The expression "lejía inmortal" ("immortal bleach"!), for example, combines one representational and one symbolic word and produces an extreme juxtaposition. Seen in this light, the experience created by the poem turns out to be quite different from what it would have seemed if we had given it a conventional allegorical reading. The text does not really impart deeper meaning to a common scene; rather it juggles two language patterns or codes, forming two simultaneous levels and two perspectives which do not fit very well with each other. By alternating these patterns, levels, and perspectives, the poem inevitably produces a disorienting tension within the implied reader.

All this becomes even more evident as we observe the workings of the representational and symbolic levels in the rest of the poem:

> He dicho así a media alba
> porque de nuevo la hallo,
> de nuevo al aire libre sana y salva.
> Fue en el río, seguro, en aquel río
> donde se lava todo, bajo el puente.
> Huele a la misma agua, a cuerpo mío.
> ¡Y ya sin mancha! ¡Si hay algún valiente,
> que se la ponga! Sé que le ahogaría.
> Bien sé que al pie del corazón no es blanca
> pero no importa: un día . . .
> ¡Qué un día: hoy, mañana que es la fiesta!
> Mañana todo el pueblo por las calles
> y la conocerán, y dirán: "Esta
> es su camisa, equella, la que era
> sólo un remiendo y ya no le servía.
> ¿Qué es este amor? ¿Quién es su lavandera?" [pp. 101-02]

Now both levels and both codes emerge from the same words and objects. The river in which the clothes were washed forms part of the representational level but is at the same time "the river in which everything is washed," hence an image for purification. "Sin mancha" also points to both levels. The speaker's challenge for someone to put on the shirt seems part of the poem's anecdote but makes sense only if we attribute symbolic value to the shirt and see it as signifying essential purity. The joy of the people at the end also seems anecdotal but is explainable only in terms of the symbolic level. This combination confuses and shocks the reader. Having been able to identify separately the two levels before and to see how the representational led to the symbolic, this reader is now unable to distinguish which one is being developed when. A literal reality is clearly present before him, but it seems incomprehensible and absurd without some more abstract explanation (the speaker's challenge and the people's joy would be ridiculous if they were dealing only with a real shirt). By abandoning its initial procedure of juxtaposing two levels by two separate codes, and by combining them, the poem offers an even stranger and more disorienting vision which makes the reader feel that he has been removed from a world governed by logic and by the normal rules of reality.

This tension caused by the combination of codes and levels therefore makes something which we would ordinarily judge understandable seem very strange: the act of washing clothes on the one hand, and the theme of purification on the other, have been wrenched out of their normal context. This has caused something like the defamiliarization of ordinary reality in literature studied by Viktor Shklovsky.[8] By making the common seem strange, the poem makes us aware that we are looking at a literary work, a reconstruction of a reality and a theme rather than reality itself. Despite its "realistic" appearance, "A mi ropa tendida" turns out to be a highly stylized text.

The defamiliarizing and disorienting effect produced by the juxtaposition and combination of codes in this poem is further intensified by the use of humor. Rodríguez employs several humorous and parodic expressions which come to form a level and perhaps a code of their own, and which accentuate the reader's confusion.[9] Having underlined the symbolic meaning of the clean clothes by situating them on top of a hill in line 16, the poem suddenly describes them as stepped on by the sun and by a rooster. To be stepped on by a rooster would not contribute to the literal or the figurative cleanliness of the clothes, and the image can only startle us, and may suggest a self-parody. The vignette at the end of the poem definitely seems parodic: the people's joy in the face of the shirt's cleanliness is understandable in symbolic terms, but is presented so dramatically that it seems ridiculous in representational terms. And the final juxtaposition of a question about a washerwoman and an inquiry about the nature of "this love" is not only startling but makes us see the literal question as a sort of parody of the universal one. All of this contributes to the poem's general effect: it makes us feel not only that a specific reality symbolizes a universal view of purification but also—and more importantly—that both a literal and a symbolic view constantly modify and alter each other. As they do so, the parodies and the resultant juxtapositions produce unexpected reactions within the implied reader, making highly questionable any impulse on his part to reduce everything in the text to one easy pattern of meaning. In the final analysis, they make him feel the enigmatic and illusory nature of all meanings that can be attributed to things and ideas. (Although I have dealt with the parodic and humorous level separately, it is intermixed with the representational and symbolic ones, and helps combine both of them into a single puzzling experience.)

One other code bears examination, the cultural one; it also contributes to the unity and originality of the experience produced. By using as its anecdotal base the action of washing clothes, and by alluding directly to bleach, soap, scrubbing, a washerwoman, and the placing of clothes in the sun to dry, the poem calls our attention to a daily activity most easily related to the life of a lower or lower-middle class in Spain. This anchors it in the everyday and makes it impossible for us to see the poem's meaning in purely metaphysical terms. The use of colloquial expressions and exclamations, and the repetition of words which focus on the literal scene ("tendida, ropa tendida") also contribute to this code of daily lower-class life. The whole code, in addition to helping the poem avoid artificiality and excess "elevation," adds to the sense of enigma that I have been noting. The ordinary details and the lower-class activities seem so remote from the larger theme of purification that their simultaneous presence and their mixture accent the feeling of estrangement and confusion.

All the codes that I have noted, and the levels of meaning produced by them, allow us to see the poem in a new light and to understand the way in which it produces disorientation. This effect underlies the specific meaning the poem offers, the way in which it presents its theme of purification. It makes us feel that although the reality portrayed symbolizes a more essential vision of purification, it does so in a very tensive, ambiguous, and enigmatic way. The many nuances of the poem do not merge into a single and simple message; its "world" is a mixture of diverse realities, tones, and perspectives, and its unity lies in the counterposition of all these elements, much as the unity of any human experience arises out of a puzzling mixture of different things.

The defamiliarization produced by the intertwining of different codes and planes stresses this variety of perspectives; it also seems to have a metapoetic function. Given the disorientation produced by the poem and the impossibility of resolving all of its perspectives into one single attitude, we are made more aware that what we have in front of us is not a single message but a text made up of words and images which combine and mix creatively a variety of planes and outlooks—and which produce, in the final analysis, an experience of mystery, a view of things in which everything both is and is not like something else. The counterpositions and the confusions they generate may in fact invite the reader to extend this experience further, to continue the examination of ways in which the specific literal realities present here do and do not evoke wider patterns—the ways in which this washing of clothes both is and is not a vision of purification.[10] Whether we let the poem keep unfolding in this fashion, or whether we pull it together by calling it a paradoxical if fundamentally unified vision of the theme of cleansing, it demonstrates how Rodríguez uses apparently everyday language to create a compelling literary work and to embody a unique experience.

My analysis of this poem helps place it in the mainstream of Claudio Rodríguez's earlier verse. As José Olivio Jiménez has shown, that verse is centered on the theme of the fundamental meanings and mysteries that underlie daily existence. Rodríguez's first book, *Don de la ebriedad,* is a single, sustained work in which the *persona* contemplates and comments on natural scenes and derives from them a sense of the order and integrity of life. *Conjuros,* his second book, is more varied in subject and technique, but it reveals the same striving to uncover the transcendence of life in a seemingly ordinary outer world. Yet this outer world is never simplified, deprived of its concrete reality, made into a simple pretext for abstractions: it is out of its concreteness and its ambiguities that any deeper vision springs. That vision involves a sense of mystery, an awareness of the inexplicability and irreducibility of the meanings of things; it has to be uncovered by a poet living in and verbally exploring reality, not by an abstract thinker.[11] In speaking about poetry, Rodríguez once described it as follows: "Quizá la poesía no consiste en definiciones sino en aventuras. En la aventura de la experiencia expresada. Lo que no quiere decir irracionalidad, sino investigación, invención, en el sentido etimológico de esta palabra de descubrimiento, sorpresa."[12] The interplay of codes and levels that we have seen in "A mi ropa tendida" produces exactly this sense of mystery, pointing to the larger positive meaning of life without simplifying it into an abstraction.

We can find a similar process and a similar effect in other poems of *Conjuros*. In "El baile de Águedas," for example, a village dance is linked to a sense of participation in life, while the speaker's not fitting into the dance evokes his initial lack of participation:

> Veo que no queréis bailar conmigo
> y hacéis muy bien. Si hasta ahora
> no hice más que pisaros, si hasta ahora
> no moví al aire vuestro estos pies cojos.
> Tú siempre tan bailón, corazón mío.
> ¡Métete en fiesta; pronto,
> antes de que te quedes sin pareja!
> ¡Hoy no hay escuela! Al río,
> a lavarse primero,
> que hay que estar limpios cuando llegue la hora!
> Ya están ahí, ya vienen
> por el raíl con sol de la esperanza
> hombres de todo el mundo. Ya se ponen
> a dar fe de su empleo de alegría.
> ¿Quién no esperó la fiesta?
> ¿Quién los días del año
> no los pasó guardando bien la ropa
> para el día de hoy? Y ya ha llegado.
> Cuánto manteo, cuánta media blanca,
> cuánto refajo de lanilla, cuánto
> corto calzón. ¡Bien a lo vivo, como
> esa moza se pone su pañuelo,
> poned el alma así, bien a lo vivo!
> Echo de menos ahora
> aquellos tiempos en los que a sus fiestas
> se unía el hombre como el suero al queso. [p. 140]

The representational level stands out from the very beginning of the poem: specific allusions to the dance, to the speaker's inept stepping, to a school vacation, to the details of the dancers' dress, all produce the sense of a very immediate village reality. The reader of course anticipates that some further meaning will be ascribed to this reality, and he may have some archetypal notion of the dance as participation in life. But the symbolic level does not really appear until line 11, although it is hinted at in line 5 (the heart's desire to dance suggests a more essential striving). When in lines 11-13 the dance becomes an activity for hopeful men from everywhere, when the urge to participate is extended to one's

soul (line 23), and when past feasts are seen as times of idyllic participation (lines 25-26), we are obliged to see the event as symbolic of participation and compenetration in life.

Just as was the case in "A mi ropa tendida," a tension is engendered
between the representational and the symbolic levels. The initial emphasis on the former and the profusion of details condition us to see the
scene realistically; the appearance of a symbolic meaning therefore produces a certain sense of disproportion. The disproportion is increased by
some of the specific images to which symbolic meaning is explicitly
ascribed: arranging one's soul is like fixing a scarf, and men's union is
like the joining of curds and whey. The sense of a clash between the
everyday and the transcendent may be increased even more when we
go back and ascribe symbolic values to the process of getting washed
for the dance (lines 10-11) and saving one's clothes for it (lines 17-19).
Initially these fit very well in the literal picture being drawn; once the
symbolic level of the poem becomes apparent, we are led to work them
into it, and they fit quite easily: cleansing oneself and saving special
clothes are good embodiments for the preparations needed for a transcendent experience. Yet the difference between the literal actions and
their symbolic value is so great that the reader cannot completely inte-
grate both levels.

As Bousoño has indicated, this makes the poem disemic: its concrete
and its universal levels remain simultaneously in our minds.[13] But it also
has a further effect: the clash and the disproportion between planes
make us aware that particulars and universals do not fit together sim-
plistically and that the wider significance of our lives is a mysterious and
complicated subject—one that the poet can uncover and portray
but never quite explain. And one that the reader, in turn, can sense
only as an enigma created in the poem and recreated in the process of
reading.

As "El baile de Águedas" develops, the two codes and levels are
present in the same lines and images, very much as in "A mi ropa
tendida." An invitation to dance contains both a literal reference to
one's posture and a symbolic one to order and participation; another
dancer is addressed both as a specific character in the story and as a
representative of man seeking union:

> Óyeme tú, que ahora
> pasas al lado mío y un momento,
> sin darte cuenta, miras a lo alto
> y a tu corazón baja
> el baile eterno de Águedas del mundo,

. . . .
tú, que pisas la tierra
y aprietas tu pareja, y bailas, bailas. [p. 141]

The specific details of dancing by and of holding one's partner fix this
man in the story, while the words "eterno" and "Águedas del mundo,"
as well as the reference to looking up, underline his symbolic search.
The condensation of both levels joins them into a single experience, yet
also accents the feeling of disorientation and strangeness.

There does not seem to be a pattern of humor in this poem. There
is, however, a very clear "cultural code" that functions much as did the
one in "A mi ropa tendida." The detailed references to village life and
customs create a whole network, a seemingly anecdotal picture which
recalls "costumbrista" writing. That Rodríguez uses this picture as a
basis for an elevated philosophic vision increases the feeling of strangeness, while suggesting that it is in the most ordinary reality that the poet
must discover (or create) his meanings.

We can find a number of other poems in *Conjuros* that function in
much the same way as the one I have been examining. In "Alto jornal"
(p. 116) a workman's salary is presented both representationally and as
a sign for life's meaning. In "Incidente en los Jerónimos" (pp. 129-32)
the speaker is a crow whose specific activities evoke meaningful and
meaningless patterns in life and in the search for union and significance.
The tensions between levels reach an extreme state in this poem, and
are fully exploited by the poet. The interplay of codes and levels, in
sum, is a central feature of the book, and a key to its unusual way of
engendering experience.

Alianza y condena, published in 1965, marks a deepening of the
themes and the vision of Rodríguez's earlier books. As José Olivio
Jiménez has indicated, the poet's attitude to nature and reality now
stands more clearly as a sign for a larger commitment to life's forces, and
the book acquires some of the characteristics of a search for truth.
Commenting on the book, Rodríguez himself stated that its subject was
"la vida, en sus múltiples manifestaciones."[14] Despite variations in their
meaning, the term "alianza" is generally linked with the search for
union with life and with other men, while "condena" suggests the
negative forces of our existence; the two, however, are in a constant
dialectical relationship with each other.[15] All in all, the book marks one
of the high points of the poetry of this era, and is a superb example of
poetry oriented to "discovery" ("conocimiento," a key term of this
period) in its deepest sense: not simple messages but a deeper understanding of life's patterns and paradoxes.[16]

We can find in this book patterns of codes and levels which recall those of *Conjuros*. Generally, however, the process is more complex and harder to define. Bousoño has described very perceptively one of the difficulties of the book, which comes from its way of presenting us with a seemingly strange reality, one that only makes sense when we discover an essential meaning which it represents.[17] Fitting this into the perspectives of codes, we might say that the representational code of a poem is now less independently explainable, and that its relationships to symbolic codes are more pervasive and more complicated. Furthermore, many poems contain more than one symbolic code each, and the interplay between various codes becomes more complicated. At the same time, humor seems to play a much lesser role, and the cultural patterns are less specific—the events portrayed are not so tied to particular local or social situations.

The poem "Girasol" offers an excellent example of the way in which Rodríguez combines two different symbolic codes to embody a double view of life, one which connects positive harmony and a negative, tragic sense (echoing the duality present in *Alianza y condena)*:

> Esta cara bonita,
> este regazo que fue flor y queda
> tan pronto encinta, y yo lo quiero, y ahora
> me lo arrimo, y me entra
> su luminosa rotación sencilla,
> su danza, que es cosecha,
> por el alma esta tarde
> de setiembre, de buena
> ventura porque ahora tú, valiente
> girasol, de tan ciega
> mirada, tú me hacías mucha falta
> con tu postura de perdón, tras esa
> campaña soleada
> de altanería, a tierra
> la cabeza, vencida
> por tanto grano, tan loca empresa. [p. 180]

If we focus on the symbolic meaning of the sunflower, we will relate on the one hand to harvesting and fulfillment, and on the other to sacrifice; the personification of the flower as a pregnant woman underlines the first of these meanings, and its portrayal as a defeated soldier at the end of the poem stresses the second. Once we see this, we may be tempted to combine both patterns into a single view, and to see the sunflower as representing a life of sacrifice, a giving of oneself in order to further the continuation of the natural world. This way of reading the poem, however, simplifies and impoverishes it, eliminating tensions which are present within it and which contradict the seeming simplicity of the "message." By examining the levels and the language codes present in the work, we can see these tensions more clearly. The two personifications I have described, for example, produce two different codes and levels which lead us in different directions, and do not coalesce easily into a single view.

The image of the flower as pregnant woman is developed through a series of words which evoke not only fertility ("cosecha") but also natural order ("luminosa rotación sencilla," "danza," "tarde de setiembre"). The speaker identifies himself with this order ("yo lo quiero," "me lo arrimo, y me entra"). This series of words therefore forms a code which evokes the sense of order and the speaker's participation in it. That participation is emphasized by the poem's syntax: the whole poem is composed of a single sentence. In the first part, the flow of that sentence is interrupted several times by phrases which inject the speaker's feelings into the description of the flower. In lines 4-7 the speaker's statement is in turn interrupted by the description of the flower's movement; Rodríguez changes what would have been the normal word order, "its luminous rotation enters my soul," into a phrase which alternates and confuses elements and perspectives. He thus mixes and combines the image and the speaker's reaction to it, stressing the latter's participation in the vision of the sunflower as symbolically evoking order.

The personification of the sunflower as a defeated soldier is also linked to a code which evokes a symbolic pattern. The expressions "valiente," "de tan ciega mirada," and "la cabeza, vencida" not only make apparent the personification but also suggest that the soldier / flower's sacrifice is extreme, almost senseless. We can observe that now the speaker does not link himself with the flower as he did in the first part of the poem; instead he speaks to it as to another person. Where before he identified himself with the flower / woman and the order it represented, he now stands back and admires from the outside the sacrifice of the flower / soldier.

This poem clearly contains two separate symbolic codes, each of them underlined by a different attitude on the part of the speaker. It is true that both codes can be integrated into a single vision, in which the flower is fulfillment as well as sacrifice. But the differences between the two codes, between the language used in the first part and that used in the second, and between the attitudes of the speaker in each, produce inevitable tensions for the implied reader. The first part evokes a much

more integrated and positive view, accenting the continuous harmony
of nature; the second leads us to stand back more and feel the tragedy
that is a counterweight to that harmony. The overall experience of the
poem depends on the counterposition of both attitudes, and cannot be
reduced to a simplistic message concerning the order of nature. By
defining in specific terms the codes that are constructed around the two
personifications, one can see much more clearly this counterposition and
the resulting experience. In "Girasol," in contrast with "A mi ropa
tendida," there is no pattern of humor; nor can we find here a specific
cultural code. The poem depends mostly on the symbolic codes for its
meaning.

"Lluvia y gracia" also suggests a double view of life, using the image
of rain to point to suffering on the one hand and purification on the
other. Unlike "Girasol," the poem begins with a detailed picture of a
man running in the rain:

> Desde el autobús, lleno
> de labriegos, de curas y de gallos,
> al llegar a Palencia,
> veo a ese hombre.
> Comienza a llover fuerte, casi arrecia
> y no le va a dar tiempo
> a refugiarse en la ciudad. Y corre
> como quien asesina. Y no comprende
> el castigo del agua, su sencilla
> servidumbre; tan sólo estar a salvo
> es lo que quiere. Por eso no sabe
> que le crece como un renuevo fértil
> en su respiración acelerada,
> que es cebo vivo, amor ya sin remedio,
> cantera rica. Y, ante la sorpresa
> de tal fecundidad,
> se atropella y recela;
> siente, muy en lo oscuro, que está limpio
> para siempre, pero él no lo resiste; [p. 179]

The very specific description in lines 1-4 anchors the poem in an immediate reality, making us see the man's running as part of a literal scene.
If these lines were omitted, the symbolic level would dominate and we
would lose the feeling that the wider meaning lies in and emerges from
concrete reality. Then the poem builds its symbolic view of the rain as
both punishment and regeneration: "castigo" and the image of the man

as escaping assassin point to the former, while the reference to his exhilaration and the words "renuevo fértil," "amor," "cantera rica" and "limpio / para siempre" highlight the latter. Rodríguez has used a very common scene to dramatize the view of life that underlies his book.

At times the symbolic codes and levels do not form such neat patterns. In "Espuma," for example, the foam caused by waves breaking becomes linked with various aspects of life:

> Miro la espuma, su delicadeza
> que es tan distinta a la de la ceniza.
> Como quien mira una sonrisa, aquella
> por la que da su vida y le es fatiga
> y amparo, miro ahora la modesta
> espuma. Es el momento bronco y bello
> del uso, el roce, el acto de la entrega
> creándola. El dolor encarcelado
> del mar, se salva en fibra tan ligera;
> bajo la quilla, frente al dique, donde
> existe amor surcado, como en tierra
> la flor, nace la espuma. Y es en ella
> donde rompe la muerte, en su madeja
> donde el mar cobra ser, como en la cima
> de su pasión el hombre es hombre, fuera
> de otros negocios: en su leche viva. [p. 175]

The foam is clearly seen as a life-giving element: it is tied to love in lines 8, 11, and especially 14-16, with their specific references to the sexual act and to semen. Lines 7 and 8 stress the process of giving as a source of creation, while 8 and 9 indicate regeneration through suffering. The reference to creation may also suggest artistic activity. Yet all of these images and references form one general symbolic pattern, pointing to the theme of regeneration; they lead us to the poem's ending, in which the protagonist paradoxically both drowns and feels renewed in the foam, embodying an acceptance of life's pattern. In this poem, as in so many others of *Alianza y condena,* the poet's vision of life emerges from the multiple symbolic "coding" of a scene.[18]

The quest for a deeper vision of life through poetry which became so noticeable in *Alianza y condena* also underlies Rodríguez's most recent book, *El vuelo de la celebración* (1976). Critics have noted the speaker's search for transcendent reality in this book, and the use of love as an image for life in all its joys and sorrows.[19] We often find a combination of representational and symbolic codes and levels that recalls those of

Alianza: frequently a poem contains more than one symbolic pattern. On the other hand, several poems of *El vuelo* contain humorous levels that recall those of *Conjuros,* and use them to defamiliarize their subject matter and offer an even more complex and enigmatic vision. "Ballet del papel" offers a good example of the use of codes and levels in this book:

> ... Y va el papel volando
> con vuelo bajo a veces, otras con aleteo
> sagaz, a media ala,
> con la celeridad tan musical,
> de rapiña,
> del halcón, ahora aquí, por esta calle,
> cuando la tarde cae y se avecina
> el viento de oeste,
> aun muy sereno, y con él el enjambre
> y la cadencia de la miel, tan fiel,
> la entraña de la danza:
> las suaves cabriolas de una hoja de periódico,
> las piruetas de un papel de estraza,
> las siluetas de las servilletas de papel de seda,
> y el cartón con pies bobos.
> Todos los envoltorios
> con cuerpo ágil, tan libre y tan usado,
> bailando todavía este momento,
> con la soltura de su soledad,
> antes de arrodillarse en el asfalto. [*El vuelo,* p. 23]

The poem creates a very evident juxtaposition between its representational and symbolic codes and levels. The detailed description of the flight of sheets of paper at the beginning, the specific examples of different paper products (a piece of newspaper, a napkin, cardboard), and the references to pavement and to a given moment of the day, all help to produce a strong sense of immediacy. On the other hand, the musical allusions ("celeridad tan musical," "la entraña de la danza," the very title, the references to dance in the last lines quoted above) make the flight of the paper into a sign for a higher kind of life, an artistic vitality that can be experienced even in the course of an ordinary day and event. The higher value of the paper's flight and its symbolic function are stressed even more at the end of the poem, when the image of kneeling adds a religious dimension to the act. The poem's representational and symbolic levels are intertwined at several points: the phrase "aleteo sagaz," for example, both produces a specific visual impression and suggests a wider meaning by endowing the paper with a conscious purpose. This procedure recalls the "immortal bleach" in "A mi ropa tendida."

This juxtaposition of codes and levels produces a defamiliarizing effect, making us wonder about the relationship between the reality described in the poem and its symbolic significance. We come to feel, on the one hand, that the scene does represent a higher vitality, and yet also to realize, on the other, that the relationship between the two levels is rather strange and points to an enigmatic world presented by the poem.

But "Ballet de papel" also involves another tension in meanings, this one present within the symbolic pattern itself. The flight of the paper suggests two very different kinds of processes. It evidently stands for an artistic activity which captures the vitality and order of existence; all the musical images accent this meaning, making the paper's flight a beautiful and lasting act. But it simultaneously suggests something more negative: the image of the falcon, the phrase "de rapiña," and the allusions to the paper's falling and to its kneeling at the end add up to another code, one which makes the paper's flight an action leading to loss and destruction. Very much like the poems from *Alianza y condena* that I have examined, "Ballet del papel" lets its symbolic codes point in more than one direction, and thus embodies a paradoxical vision—one in which life's patterns are both creative and destructive.

The different tensions present in this poem are pulled together, without being completely resolved, in its last section:

> Va anocheciendo. El viento huele a lluvia
> y su compás se altera. Y vivo la armonía,
> ya fugitiva,
> del pulso del papel bajo las nubes
> grosella oscuro,
> casi emprendiendo el vuelo,
> tan sediento y meciéndose,
> siempre abiertas las alas
> sin destino, sin nido,
> junto al ladrillo al lado, muy cercano
> de mi niñez perdida y ahora recién ganada
> tan delicadamente, gracias a este rocío
> de estos papeles, que se van de puntillas,
> ligeros y descalzos,
> con sonrisa y con mancha.
> Adiós y buena suerte. Buena suerte. [pp. 23-24]

The speaker stands out in this section, giving a unifying perspective to the different perceptions of the earlier part of the poem. By identifying himself with the "already fleeting harmony" of the paper, he pulls together in one single image the two processes seen before, the creative order and the sense of loss. He also develops further the previous juxtaposition between the representational and symbolic planes. This speaker is on the one hand part of the specific episode, a witness to the paper's flight; he is on the other a commentator who gives wider meaning to the event. His presence helps fuse (and to a certain extent confuse) the representational and the symbolic levels as well as the two different patterns of symbolism. This lets the poem leave us at the end with a bittersweet impression of a reality both specific and meaningful, both harmonious and doomed to fade in time.[20]

We can therefore conclude that the speaker is a key device, used by Rodríguez to pull together the diverse levels of the poem, and also to make us feel the tensions still present between them and to highlight the sense of defamiliarization. He at once unifies the poem and adds to the impression of an enigmatic experience that it produces—the sense that what it offers us looks like an everyday scene and a symbolic pattern, but is actually a very complex interplay of levels and outlooks which incorporates many seemingly contradictory elements and calls our attention to the paradoxical way in which they come together.

The poem has a humorous level, too. The personifications of the first part (the cardboard with silly feet, for example) are based on visual impressions (as of a piece of cardboard blowing aimlessly, jerked by the wind); but by juxtaposing an insignificant object and a human being, they produce surprise and laughter. The same effect is achieved by the final personification and by the speaker's last statement, addressed to the papers. By wishing the latter good luck, this speaker is placing the papers on the same human level as himself while at the same time mocking lightly the whole situation, confusing the literal and symbolic levels. The papers do play the symbolic role of human seekers, but this does not really justify their being treated as companions. When the speaker does so he extends the parallelism into a playful joke. All these humorous elements form a level and code which recall the ones we saw in "A mi ropa tendida." Together with the juxtapositions and the role of the speaker, they make us feel that what we have in front of us is not a "straight" realistic picture, nor even a neatly symbolic one, but rather a conscious re-creation and reinterpretation, and a mixture of different levels and perspectives. The humorous code also contributes to the impression that the representational and the symbolic levels of the poem do not combine or explain each other logically but coexist mysteriously in a scene presented from many angles and in diverse tones and perspectives.

When we come to the end of this poem we experience not so much a resolution of its tensions as the impression that the various levels somehow combine into a single enigmatic experience, in which reality reflects in somewhat puzzling fashion several wider schemes, and in which a sense of harmony is woven together with an impression of loss and fleetingness. Very much like "A mi ropa tendida," this poem makes use of juxtapositions, of its speaker, and of a humorous level to produce a defamiliarizing effect, making us feel that the reality it portrays, much as it may superficially resemble our everyday one, is in the last analysis a new creation, artistically embodying a mystery of life. Whether we consider this created reality as one total meaning with which the poem leaves us, or simply a provisional reading which will be subject to further rereadings as we and others find new dimensions to the tensions I have described, "Ballet de papel" is an example of the rich experience which Rodríguez infuses into his apparently common materials.

The enigmatic nature of the resolution we have seen in many of Rodríguez's poems is a characteristic that helps define his work. By an interplay of diverse codes, Rodríguez creates a new reality that both connects and confuses its ingredients, and offers us a perception of a meaning and an enigma. We witness a series of events, symbolic interpretations of these events by a speaker, and a variety of tensions engendered by and between the events and the interpretations, and accented by humor. All these elements come together into one experience, but an experience that can never by fully explained or resolved. Rodríguez also invites constant reflection concerning the role of poetry in combining diverse patterns, codes, and perspectives to create richer and irreducible meanings. The interplay between codes often makes the poems undercut one dimension by means of another, thus becoming self-referential and leading us to experience the enigma of poetic creation as well as of life itself.

By using and combining diverse language codes in his poetry, Claudio Rodríguez has managed to create extraordinary combinations of concrete and symbolic patterns; he has captured various aspects of experience without artificially simplifying it, and has made us feel the multiplicity, the mystery, and the coherence of human life. From the very beginning, his poetry juggles its codes and levels to this end. In his first two books the interplay occurs mainly between a representational and a symbolic plane, often modified by humor; in *Alianza y condena* and *El vuelo de la celebración,* the symbolic patterns themselves become more complicated and multifaceted. Throughout his whole poetry (but more

evidently in his later books), Rodríguez also has made us aware of the
process of poetic creation itself, and of its mysterious role within the
larger enigma of life. Like other writers of the 1960s, but in a very
unique way, he has managed to deal with fundamental issues of existence in context of the realities and shadings of ordinary life, and to
embody and recreate them in compelling works of poetry.

4 ANGEL GONZÁLEZ
Transformation and Perspective

Although Angel González is considered one of the most important Spanish poets of the late 1950s and the 1960s, his work has proved perhaps the most difficult to characterize. This is due in part to its range and variety: even though González published his first book relatively late (in 1956, at the age of thirty-one), he has written a number of volumes of poetry and dealt with a variety of subjects in very different tones. Because of that he has been characterized in different ways as critics have sought to highlight individual aspects of his work.

The themes of González's poetry seem quite varied: a sense of solitude and nostalgia, an awareness of the losses caused by time, a search for solutions based on the intensity of living on the one hand and on solidarity among people on the other.[1] In his later works González offers a negative portrayal of modern society; he also writes works dealing with the very matter of poetic composition. Despite the seeming heterogeneity of these subjects, one can discover common threads and attitudes that underlie the poet's treatment of all of them. Again and again he creates visions of duality and conflict: between a past love and present loneliness, between one's lost ideals and the harsh realities of the present, between the limits of life and time and the desire to overcome them, between the search for perfect expression and the routine clichés of modern language. But a sense of these dualities, although it helps us connect the diverse subjects treated in González's poetry, does not in itself define its uniqueness.

A study of its style and tone does offer useful insights. Emilio Alarcos Llorach has commented on González's use of gradually unfolding structures, of contrasts, and of linguistic devices to create complex experiences and capture a sense of tension and duality. He has illustrated how González, like many of his fellow poets of the 1960s, exploits everyday language in highly artistic fashion.[2] Alarcos has also noted the increasing use of irony by González, and has indicated how this irony protects the poet's expression from simple-minded sentimentality. Tak-

ing the point further, Douglas Benson has shown how irony helps
González to establish diverse relations between reader and speaker and
to communicate ambiguous experiences of both a personal and a social
nature.[3]

Yet even these studies do not fully explain the impact of González's
work, and leave us with a somewhat false impression of its
heterogeneity and of a shift from individual to social subjects and from
a direct to an ironic tone. One way of defining the continuity and unity
of González's work, as well as its uniqueness, is by studying how this
work modifies previous views, conventions, texts, and perceptions.
Again and again, González's poems are based on an outlook, a text, or
an image with which their reader will be familiar; what they present,
however, is an alteration of this familiar reality. This alteration, being
unfamiliar, will not be understood by the reader on the literal level; he
will be obligated to proceed to a second level, at which he must define
the distortion that has taken place and overcome the apparent inconsis-
tencies of the text in order to reach its full meaning.[4] He will have
established a dialectic with the text, and through it reached its significance. As we will see, González's poetry contains various types of transformations which produce such a dialectic. In some of them, a set belief,
convention, or phrase is altered to produce a new meaning; in others,
a traditional situation or poetic motif is changed by the use of an
unexpected or seemingly ill-fitted image; in others yet, a common reality is altered by being employed in unusal ways or by being seen from
an unusual perspective; at times a poem comments on its own process
to produce a totally new insight.

These transformations thus form a constant which lets us connect
seemingly varied works, from love poems to social verse. By examining
them, we will be able to see how these works embody their meanings.
Usually an awareness of the transformation that has taken place will
lead us to focus on the poem's speaker and his attitude, and thus to
discover a level of meaning beyond the superficial subject of the text.
Where the poem is ironic, the irony will be based on the alteration of
normal beliefs or attitudes by they speaker. Hence González's ironic
poems are in the final analysis not that different in strategy from his
"straight" ones, and need to be studied in relation to the general process
of transformation which underlies all of his work.

This process can already be discerned in *Aspero mundo*, González's
first book of verse. As critics have noted, this work alternates positive
views of love and illusion with a sense of the harshness of surrounding
reality.[5] At times an idealized past contrasts with a negative present or
future, triggering feelings of solitude and nostalgia. Despite the conven-

tional nature of these subjects and the traditional form and language employed, the best poems create an original impact. As Benson has pointed out, this is often due to the play of perspectives and the creation of a complex vision.[6] In "Muerte en el olvido," however, it is due to the transformation of a physical truth on the one hand and of a common belief on the other:

> Yo sé que existo
> porque tú me imaginas.
> Soy alto porque tú me crees
> alto, y limpio porque tú me miras
> con buenos ojos,
> con mirada limpia.
> Tu pensamiento me hace
> inteligente, y en tu sencilla
> ternura, yo soy también sencillo
> y bondadoso.
>   Pero si tú me olvidas
> quedaré muerto sin que nadie
> lo sepa. Verán viva
> mi carne, pero será otro hombre
> —oscuro, torpe, malo—el que la habita . . . [p. 21]

The reader first approaches the poem with his normal pragmatic belief that one's identity, one's physical stature, and one's mental properties are objective realities, independent of the attitudes of any other human being. By breaking those "rules" the text forces him to leave behind his literal view and start seeking another frame of reference in which the text's "ungrammaticality" will make sense.[7] He also approaches this poem, in all probability, with a remembrance of Descartes's "cogito ergo sum"; the first two lines of the poem, with their neat causal pattern ("existo / porque") easily bring it to mind—and also twist it. Here again the poem breaks the convention, linking man's life and existence not to his own thoughts but to the thinking and imagining of another person.

Both distortions force us to focus on the poem's speaker, and to discover some unifying principle behind his transformation of ordinary belief and philosophical convention. That principle is, evidently enough, his view of the beloved; he has attributed to her such importance that she breaks the "rules" of the world and becomes the causal agent for his life. In this sense, one can see the whole poem as a kind of extended metaphor: she is as important to him *as if* she were literally the creator of his being and his qualities. Our awareness of this principle not only helps us to see how the poem makes "sense" (i.e., is consistent) in its frame of reference, but also suggests that its true subject is not what it seemed to be. It is not so much a portrayal of the beloved, or even of the speaker as lover, as it is a metaphorical expression of his attitude to her—an embodiment of his willingness to leave behind the rules of reality and philosophy in order to assert his love and his dependence on the beloved.[8]

Various details of the text direct us through this process. The verbs used to describe the speaker's view of himself seem, in and of themselves, to stress the objective reality of that view: "sé," "existo," "soy" (used twice), "quedaré muerto." Yet that seeming reality is entirely dependent on the subjective attitude of the beloved, stressed by the verbs which describe it: "me imaginas," "me miras," "me olvidas." The contrast and interplay between the two kinds of verbs dramatizes the process through which the speaker distorts common causality and *makes* a system of rules in which subjective attitude influences reality. In the last sentence, he hypothetically allows the beloved's attitude to kill him, and also to turn him into another and to see himself from the outside. We note the use of the third person in "será otro hombre." All this makes his willingness to move to a new vision and a total dependence on the beloved for his self-definition so much more intense. In the final analysis, it raises the poem above its conventional subject. Rather than a mere restatement of the idea that the beloved makes the lover better, or a simple formulation of the conventional view that love elevates one, this text becomes a dramatization of the tremendous force which the beloved (and love) exerts on the speaker. The distortions of a literal view and a philosophic convention, by involving us in a process of rereading the poem and discovering the principle on which they operate, heighten our sense of the speaker's vision and account for the impact of the text.

One could argue that a perfectly acceptable reading of this poem can be performed without any process of rereading, or any conscious awareness of the ways in which it negates set norms. Yet at some level, conscious or unconscious, the reader of this text must sense the negation by the speaker of the ordinary physical realities of human life and characteristics. Were he to ignore this negation, he would be forced to see the text as a mere assertion of the greatness of the beloved, and to deem it naive and sentimental. It is just because we see the speaker's almost frightening negation óf "what is" that we can sense the power of his feelings and of the actions of the beloved as he perceives her, as well as the tragedy of his possible abandonment.

Somewhat similar transformations can be found in several other poems of *Aspero mundo*. In "Muerte en la tarde" (p. 20), González again changes the literal definition of death, describing as death his isolation from the world surrounding him. In another poem he inverts the normal relationship between a person and a natural element, and makes a river into a personified searcher who follows the course and rhythms of a woman (the speaker's beloved) and sees itself reflected in her:

> No vas tú por el río:
> es el río el que anda
> detrás de ti, buscando en ti
> el reflejo, mirándose en tu espalda. [p. 49]

Although not as frequent or as dramatic as those which appear in later books, these transformations already make the poems transcend a conventional presentation of the themes of loneliness, nostalgia, or illusioned love. Combined with a simple but carefully selected vocabulary, and with a very effective use of pauses and punctuation, they enable González to convey emotional meanings in such a fashion that they go beyond a personal expression of feelings and acquire wider dimensions. Yet the technique of transformation is not used as frequently as in later books, and does not involve the tone and perspective play which we will note there. (Only one work, "Me falta una palabra" [p. 19] plays with the process of creating a poem.)

In *Sin esperanza, con convencimiento,* published in 1961, we can observe a number of transformations based on unusual correspondences: by linking a mood with a seemingly inappropriate object, or an attitude with an unusual image or transformation of reality, González forces us to revise our initial vision and reading, and to reach an original perception. Similar transformations can be found in *Grado elemental* (1962), here frequently accompanied by irony and a play of perspectives.

In the following poem from *Sin esperanza,* González alters our ordinary definition of hope by presenting it as a spider:

> Esperanza,
> araña negra del atardecer.
> Te paras
> no lejos de mi cuerpo
> abandonado, andas
> en torno a mí,
> tejiendo, rápida,

inconsistentes hilos invisibles,
te acercas, obstinada,
y me acarcicias casi con tu sombra
pesada
y leve a un tiempo.

Agazapada
bajo las piedras y las horas,
esperaste, paciente, la llegada
de esta tarde
en la que nada
es ya posible . . .
                          Mi corazón:
tu nido.
          Muerde en él, esperanza. [p. 77]

The poem seems puzzling on its first reading: we find it difficult to
associate hope, a positive feeling, with an image as negative as that of
a spider. Even taking into account some correspondences developed in
the text (the persistency and patience attributed to both hope and
spider, their arrival at a seemingly hopeless moment in the speaker's
life), the comparison seems difficult to justify, and the last line, an
exhortation for the hope / spider to bite the speaker's heart, does not
seem to make much sense. How can an expectation of hope be presented
so destructively?

To move to a second level and comprehend the import of the image,
we must again center our attention on the attitude of the speaker; when
we do so, we realize that the principle on which he operates is that hope
in itself is negative, a destructive feeling which unfortunately comes
upon him just when he is ready to abandon all desire. In this sense, the
image of the spider as hope directs us to, and embodies, the incredibly
negative vision of the speaker, who considers anything that saves him
from pessimism and despair as an undersirable distraction. The poem
therefore represents a distortion—indeed, a contradiction—of an elementary principle of life, that a positive and hopeful attitude is better
than a hopeless and negative one. By facing us with an image that
seemingly breaks the rules of comprehensibility, and by thus forcing us
to discover the nature of the distortion and of the "rules" by which the
text operates, González has made us see the true subject and impact of
the poem. The latter is finally not a characterization of hope but the
dramatization of the most extreme pessimism of its speaker.

Once we have seen this, we can discover how the details of the text
contribute to its overall meaning. The reference to "atardecer" in line

2 at least hints at the end of things, and thus points ahead to the last part of the poem ("esta tarde / en la que nada / es ya posible"). The adjective "abandonado" as applied to the speaker's body also contributes to the feeling of decay, while the portrayal of the spider's weaving its web around him and the description of the spider in the last stanze ("agazapada ... esperaste") emphasize his feeling of being trapped. All of these elements operate as signs of suggestion; they are not linked explicitly to the theme of the poem, but they support its subjective mood and vision.

The distortion of a normal viewpoint in this poem and the effect it engenders are an important way of presenting one of the main themes and visions of *Sin esperanza, con convencimiento.* From the very outset, this book defines its theme as an experience of loss and disillusion. The conflict between an idealized past and a negative present, which we saw in *Aspero mundo,* is intensified and modified to place greater stress on the negative vision and the rebellion engendered by the latter. Distortions of attitude such as we have examined contribute to this vision, as do a series of unusual transformations which make literal reality give way to its subjective effects.

In "Ayer," a day suddenly changes from Wednesday to Monday:

> Ayer fue miércoles toda la mañana.
> por la tarde cambió:
> se puso casi lunes,
> la tristeza invadió los corazones
> y hubo un claro
> movimiento de pánico hacia los
> tranvías
> que llevan los bañistas hasta el río. [p. 88]

The shift from Wednesday to Monday on the same day, while breaking the "rules" of time, clearly portrays the negative attitude to the work day experienced by the people (Monday being the classic "blue Monday"), and leads to a rebellion against the system of the work week: everyone leaves work routines and goes out to enjoy the day. The rest of the poem portrays the happiness that this engenders, as we can see in this passage:

> ya veis,
> qué divertido,
> ayer y siempre ayer y así hasta ahora,
> continuamente andando por las calles

> gente desconocida,
> o bien dentro de casa merendando
> pan y café con leche, ¡qué
> alegría! [p. 88]

The poem ends as the speaker, with an almost prophetic tone, recalls the glory of that day which, unfortunately, had to give way to a more realistic "today:"

> dejadme que os hable
> de ayer, una vez más
> de ayer: el día
> incomparable que ya nadie nunca
> volverá a ver jamás sobre la tierra. [p. 89]

By transforming one day into another, and by creating a vision of universal rebellion against the rules of work, the poem in fact becomes a sort of fable which portrays not what really happens, but what one's fantasy would *want* to happen in the battle of illusions against the grim realities of petty life. Just as the presentation of hope as spider created a distortion which made us feel the horror of a pessimistic view, so the distortion of the day and its history here dramatize the desperate (and ultimately hopeless) rebellion against the negative course of things. In similar fashion, González breaks the rules of reality by making the loss of a word which defined an experience the equivalent of the destruction of that experience in "Palabra muerta, realidad perdida" (pp. 113-14); here the distortion serves to stress both the fragility and the importance of language and poetic expression.

In several other poems, González, without actually breaking the rules of reality, uses unusual images and personifications. In "Porvenir" (p. 93) the future becomes a rebellious animal; in "Diciembre" (pp. 98-99) that month is personified to present a view of the pettiness and ugliness of daily existence. When seen in context of the transformations observed in other poems, these images illustrate the way in which González takes ordinary reality, casts it in an unusual light, and thus conveys his subjective visions.

The same process can be observed in *Grado elemental,* with a greater use of parody and ironic commentary on the part of the speaker.[9] The whole book is presented as a series of elementary "lessons" about life which, with the interplay of diverse tones and ironic commentaries, point to the limitations of our world. (In "Lecciones de cosas," pp. 137-39, a supposedly serious philosophic vision is altered and undercut by pedantic parenthetical definitions and dictionary references.) At times the speaker takes a conventional form or genre and inverts it; thus in "Introducción a las fábulas para animales," (pp. 161-62), he offers to use human experiences as moral lessons for the behavior of animals, so that they can be more true to their selves. One effect of this is to invert our ordinary perspective and make the human world seem even more stereotyped and trivial than the animal world we remember from traditional fables. (Other characters who appear in the poems of this section parody a dictatorial soldier, a bumbling thinker, a trivial bureaucrat.)

A slightly different sort of transformation occurs in "Muerte de máquina" (p. 174), which presents the demise of a machine in terms more applicable to the death of a person. This forces the reader to contemplate the reversal of his normal belief in the primacy and individuality of humans, and to view a reality in which machines have higher value. By making a light ascending from the machine's remains seem like soul, by having people see it as a miracle, and by using images and words of human life in relation to the machine, González turns the whole poem into a frightening parody of both the machine age and traditional religious attitudes to death. But the main effect of the poem depends on the reversed view of man and machine, and its main impact comes from the reader's awareness that this may well portray the hierarchy of values of our modern society.

Another kind of transformation occurs in "Prueba," in which the speaker focuses on his own ability to write and to record reality in his writing.

> De todas formas, tengo todavía
> este papel,
> la pluma
> y la mano derecha que la aprieta,
> y el brazo que la liga con el cuerpo
> para que no se quede
> —tan distante y lejana—
> como un desarraigado objeto extraño
> —cinco dedos moviéndose,
> marchando
> por el suelo,
> igual que un sucio
> animal acosado por la escoba . . .
>
> Esto es algo,
> repito,
> si se tiene
> en cuenta
> esa admirable prueba de la existencia de Dios

constituida
por el perfecto funcionamiento de mis centros nerviosos
que transmiten las órdenes que emite mi cerebro
a las costas lejanas de mis extremidades.
Pienso:
> *la tarde muere,*
y mi mano escribe:
> > *la tarde*
muere,
> Ergo Dios existe [p. 148]

Although we may not have here any obvious violations of the "rules"
of reality, the poem does transform and undercut several traditions and
conventional views. On the surface of it, the speaker's assertion that his
ability to write proves his own human dignity as well as the existence
of God, fits in a long line of arguments which use man's thinking and
creative expression as proof of his transcendent value. There is also an
echo of Descartes in the last section, especially if we juxtapose "Pienso"
and "Ergo Dios existe."

But the tone and language of the passage contradict its supposed
message. The detailed and mechanistic description of the hand writing,
of the connections between parts of the body, and of the process by
which the mind causes the hand to write, all make man seem more
mechanical, denying the very transcendence that the poem asserts. The
vision of the fingers scurrying like an animal (presumably a mouse),
although denied by the speaker (the hand is not an animal because it
is tied to the arm), nevertheless makes it harder for us to accept the
dignity of the human form. The speaker's frenzied efforts to assert his
view ("esto es algo, / repito") only makes us more dubious, and the
facile connection he draws between the hand's following orders and the
existence of God seems totally unmerited. The poem so far has taken
a common view of man's worth and a traditional philosophical argument, and has turned them into a very suspect and desperate defense
against meaninglessness. Once we are aware of the transformation, we
focus on the main strategy of the speaker and see him as defending,
desperately and inadequately, man's worth; at this point the poem
becomes for us a dramatization of the inadequacy of the defense.

This inadequacy becomes even more apparent in the second half of
the poem, in which the speaker expands on the functions of his hand:

> Qué fácil es, ahora,
> integrarse en un mundo ordenado y perfecto,

cuando se dispone de una mano tan valiosa,

. . . .

Mano, frótame la cabeza!
Mano, acércame
la silla. Desabróchale
el corsé a esa muchacha
—y tú, la otra, no te quedes quieta.
Coge
todo el dinero, mano:
incendia,
mata.

Por lo tanto,
se prueba una vez más,
como decía,
el orden natural y preexistente,
la armónica hermosura de las cosas. [p. 149]

The earlier transformations now give way to broad satire, as solemn assertions of the world's order are juxtaposed to vignettes of trivial or sordid actions. The speaker's calling attention to himself ("Por lo tanto . . . como decía") highlight the absurdity of his argument and emphasize the parody of a traditional idealistic view of human nature.

Benson has pointed out how the irony functions in this poem, turning the speaker's words against him and destroying his argument.[10] But this irony must also be seen in terms of the larger question of transformations of traditional views and concepts. Where the speaker of "Muerte en el olvido" broke the rules of the Cartesian statement and of normal causation, the speaker of "Prueba" seems to be following the rules of argument and giving a traditional defense of human dignity. But in fact his own language undercuts his position and makes his seeming adherence to the rules meaningless. Where in "Muerte en el olvido" the mimetic level of the poem, the rule of reality and logic, was broken overtly, in "Prueba" it is denied more covertly, through the irony that undercuts the poem's position.[11] The final effect, however, is quite similar: both poems lead us to focus on the speakers and their attitudes, and from them to draw their final meanings. If "Muerte" made us sense the frightening and tragic force of love on its speaker, "Prueba" conveys to us the hollowness of its protagonist's defense of human values and of a whole traditional vision of the dignity of man. The use of irony as part of the process of distortion seems particularly suited to the larger, somewhat less individual issues of life which dominate *Grado elemental,* and to the negative overall vision which emerges from the book. But it is clearly one more facet of a more general pattern of transformation. The poem also reveals a metapoetic dimension, and in this sense anticipates later works of González. Its speaker, like González himself, is trying to capture meaning through language; yet he can only write the trite phrase "la tarde muere." His linguistic quest and its failure mirror the larger failure of the speaker.

Transformation through irony also occurs in "Alocución a las veintitrés," which is cast as an after-dinner speech by a pompous, cliché-ridden, and smug conservative. His message is all too clear: he advocates ignorance and complacency, and asserts that a steadfast defense of a traditional erroneous position is better than a questioning stance:

> No es que sean importantes los asuntos
> objeto de polémica:
> lo importante es la rígida
> firmeza en el error. [p. 175]

As part of his defense the speaker also asserts one of the commonplace arguments of the Franco regime, claiming that the steadfast defense of conventional attitudes will ensure decades of peace. All in all, the poem is obviously a monologue by a highly unreliable speaker, calculated to elicit in the reader a very negative reaction. The effect of the irony on the reader, and the value of the poem, depend on the way in which the speaker's attitude blatantly violates conventional beliefs. Our amazement at the fact that someone would argue that error is better than truth leads us to step back, assess the speaker, and realize that he is violating normal attitudes because of a unifying principle: the belief that order is the key value of life. To this extent the poem functions very much like "Prueba"; the difference lies in the fact that there the violation of rules and the new principle that underlies it led to our ultimate assent, where here it triggers off violent dissent. The dissent is accentuated by a variety of details which González puts in the speaker's mouth: clichés ("honorables cabezas de familia"), absurdly trivial references to the setting and to irrelevant events ("con esto / y una buena cosecha de limones"), inappropriate comparisons between the dinner and peace.

The irony of this poem, the use of an unreliable speaker, and the everyday language and setting seem particularly well fitted to the subject: they highlight the triviality and absurdity of a stagnant political and social outlook. In that sense they clearly represent the poet's discovery of techniques suited to the more "social" subjects that gain importance in *Grado elemental.* But the basic process underlying the irony and accounting for its success is still one of transformation, akin to that seen in *Aspero mundo;* this process again forces the reader to be estranged, to step back from the mimetic level of the text, and to discover a principle which leads to a new reading.

The poems of *Palabra sobre palabra* (the particular book published in 1965, as opposed to the complete works) reveal a process of transformation different from the ones we have seen so far. Through a series of five long poems, the book focuses on the search for a "tú," a search closely related to the speaker's quest for identity, to his examination of reality, and to his poetic creativity.[12] The process of discovering the word and using it to define love and reality, and thus to assert one's being, is central to the book (see "La palabra," [pp. 179-182]); the words one selects, in turn, create his reality ("Palabras casi olvidadas," [pp. 183-85]). Yet creative language cannot seize and transform fully the world or the loved one, and the speaker reverts to a more pragmatic and literal acceptance of the physical reality of the "tú," while still dreaming of the world hidden behind it ("En ti me quedo," pp. 190-92). The whole book is best seen as a unit which reveals a single transformative process, based on one metaphorical pattern. By seeing himself as a creator with words, the speaker puts himself in the role of God—either implicitly, as when he sends out the word *amor* in "La palabra", or explicitly, as when he states that if he were God he would create a being just like the beloved, in "Me basta así" (pp. 186-87). The process is complex and tension filled, as the speaker searches for diverse words to express varying impulses.

The transformation present in this book does not make us misunderstand, reread the text, discover underlying principles, and move to a new perspective, as González's earlier poems did. But its ultimate effect recalls those poems: by creating a kind of fable in which the speaker acts as poet / creator, and in which the beloved is linked with a reality examined and sought after, the book embodies the poet's vision of his search and makes us participate in it. The stress placed on the act of naming poetically as a way of discovering reality adds to the work's intensity, making us feel that in the very act of writing for us the speaker / poet is exhibiting his quest, just as he exhibits it in the act of loving the "tú."

The poems of *Tratado de urbanismo* (1967) contain transformations more like the ones we have seen in *Sin esperanza* and *Grado elemental.* The book counterposes a section titled "Ciudad uno," which gives a critical and ironic vision of a modern city, to another one called "Ciudad cero" and based on a series of nostalgic evocations. As José Olivio Jiménez has noted, each part must be seen in the context of the other: not only do they add up to a dialectical, conflictive view of reality, but

both are needed to define the outlook of the speaker and of the book:
the evocation of a lost world of childhood is his answer to and his refuge
from the negativity of the first part.[13]

In several poems of the book we find dominant images which break
the rules of normally expected correspondences, and hence lead us to
examine the speaker's premises and discover his vision. (They recall, in
this sense, "Esperanza / araña negra.") Some of them, in addition,
contain parodic transformations of conventional attitudes like the one
we saw in "Alocución a las veintitrés." "Cadáver ínfimo" does both, and
in addition turns upside down the vision offered by a well-known poem
of César Vallejo:

Se murió diez centímetros tan sólo:
una pequeña muerte que afectaba
a tres muelas careadas y a una uña
del pie llamado izquierdo y a cabellos
aislados, imprevistos.
Oraron lo corriente, susurrando:
"Perdónalas, Señor, a esas tres muelas
por su maldad, por su pecaminosa
masticación. Muelas impías,
pero al fin tuyas como criaturas."
El mismo estaba allí,
serio, delante
de sus restos mortales diminutos:
una prótesis sucia, unos cabellos.
Los amigos querían consolarle,
pero sólo aumentaban su tristeza.
"Esto no puede ser, esto no puede
seguir así. O mejor dicho:
esto debe seguir a mejor ritmo.
Muérete más. Muérete al fin del todo."
El estrechó sus manos, enlutado,
con ese gesto falso, compungido,
de los duelos mas sórdidos.
                              "Os juro
—se echó a llorar, vencido por la angustia—
que yo quiero morir mi sentimiento
que yo quiero hacer piedra mi conducta,
tierra mi amor, ceniza mi deseo,
pero no puede ser, a veces hablo,
me muevo un poco, me acatarro incluso,
y aquellos que me ven, lógicamente
deducen que estoy vivo,

mas no es cierto:
vosotros, mis amigos,
deberíais saber que, aunque estornude,
soy un cadáver muerto por completo."

Dejó caer los brazos, abatido,
se desprendió un gusano de la manga,
pidió perdón y recogió el gusano
que era sólo un fragmento
de la totalidad de su esperanza. [pp. 219-20]

The poem seems very difficult to assess until we take into account that there are behind it several realities and conventions as well as a previous text; González is both basing himself on all of them and violating their rules in order to create his own work. The first reality alluded to and denied by the poem is that death is a single transcendent tragedy, totally different from small losses such as the loss of a tooth; its seriousness is motivated by the fact that it extinguishes our most precious asset, life, and we avoid it at all costs. The poem, on the other hand, makes death something relative, a mere extension of the loss of some teeth; it also defines it as something desirable to the speaker, who seeks to finish the process begun and to prove that he is really dead. In adopting this attitude, the poem turns upside down a social and religious convention: the need to lament the passing of the dead, to console the survivors, and to pray for the soul of the departed is here applied to the small losses of teeth, toenail, and hair, and seems ludicrously inappropriate. Its speaker denies that loss of life is of a different order than the loss of a toenail, denying the cooperative principle and the maxim of truthfulness. Finally, the poem recalls Vallejo's "Masa," in which a cadaver comes to life because of the love of fellow men; here in contrast, the fellow men simply encourage death, as a process which should go faster.[14] (This goes back to the premise that death is not undesirable and not transcendent.) The intertextuality, by contrast, emphasizes the nihilistic view of González's poem. Its denial of basic beliefs is supported by making the whole scene a parody. The words attributed to the fellow men are parodies of commonplaces—first of religious prayer (God is asked to forgive the teeth, which are sinners and yet his creatures), then of common language used to encourage some action ("esto debe seguir a mejor ritmo.")

All of this of course makes the poem seem literally incomprehensible. Yet it directs us to the speaker's attitude and to his premise that the life of this modern man is (or perhaps better, is treated as) something lacking in significance. If such a premise were true, everything in the poem would be consistent: death would not be a major tragedy, the line delimiting the loss of a tooth and the loss of life would not be important, religious declarations would be totally meaningless conventions, and one might wish for the completion of the process of death just as one might desire the end of any action. Even the miracle of Vallejo's poem would be meaningless, and encouraging death would be a social act preferable to encouraging resurrection. In an incredibly perverse way, the poem's various distortions all "make sense."

But where does this leave the reader? In poems like "Muerte en el olvido," his discovery of the speaker's premise motivated his assent and his admiration. Here it has the opposite effect: we recoil with horror at the effects that the premise has on human life and behavior, at the trivialization and mechanization of man that it produces. And this of course is exactly what the poem, the section, and *Tratado de urbanismo* are conveying to us. Behind the protagonist of this poem, and behind a speaker who seems to accept the basic premise and report what happens, we feel the presence of an author who selected the transformation, manipulated the language to maximum effect, flouted the maxim of quality in the words he has made his speaker say, and guided us to feel the full horror of the vision offered. In this fashion he has created a truly significant social poem, one which instead of preaching simple concepts of justice and injustice, makes us discover within our own experience the terrible unnaturalness of a mechanized view of man.

Other poems in *Tratado de urbanismo* also use transformations of ordinary premises to highlight the limitations of the modern world. In "Chatarra," which recalls "Muerte de máquina" of *Grado elemental,* the functioning and breaking down of a machine are presented in terms of human life and death; the poem ends with hope for other machines, free of mortality (pp. 206-07). The poem accents both the perversity of a world (and a view) in which machines have taken over the roles of humans, and the limitations imposed on man when his life is equated to that of a machine.

In other poems of the book, González uses seemingly inappropriate images to form a twisted vision of surrounding reality. In "Civilización de la opulencia" (pp. 223-24), a shoe becomes the cathedral that glorifies the beauty of a foot:

> un único zapato inconcebible:
> abrumador ejemplo de belleza,
> catedral entrevista sin distancia
> cantando con su esbelta arquitectura

> un mudo "gloria a las alturas" a la
> mórbida, larga afortunada y fuerte
> pierna posible que de su horma surja.

Both the image itself and the parody of religion testify to the emptiness of the civilization described. By using and intensifying diverse types of transformation, by combining them, and by linking them with the use of irony, González has constructed in *Tratado de urbanismo* a unique and artistically successful book of social poetry.[15]

In studying the process of transformation and the uses to which it is put, one can usefully group together González's three most recent books: *Breves acotaciones para una biografía* (1969), *Procedimientos narrativos* (1972), and *Muestra, corregida y aumentada, de algunos procedimientos narrativos y de las actitudes sentimentales que habitualmente engendran* (1976 and 1977). In all of them, the ironic play which we have seen in *Tratado de urbanismo* becomes even more evident; it leads to frequent examples of literary parody and to instances in which the speaker comments or parodies his own process of writing. One of the sections of the last book is titled "Metapoesía," and commentaries on poetic creation within poems become quite common and form part of the general process of viewing oneself and one's world ironically. González now reaches beyond the issue of individual ideals and losses, and even beyond the social patterns, conventions, and problems we have just seen in *Tratado de urbanismo*. He makes us feel the conflicts and tensions present in all kinds of life schemes, and shocks us with highly unusual and irreverent visions. Much like some excellent works of recent fiction, his poems combine narrative techniques, tone, and language manipulation to create disquieting worlds which cast new light on our own and call it into question.[16] Some poems are ultimately negative in their effect, some positive, but almost all of them depend on a transformation of and challenge to things which we have come to accept.

"Eso era amor" exemplifies this poetry very well.

> Le comenté:
> —*Me entusiasman tus ojos.*
> Y ella dijo:
>   —*¿Te gustan solos o con rimel?*
> —*Grandes,*
>   respondí sin dudar.
> Y también sin dudar.
> me los dejó en un plato y se fue a tientas. [p. 261]

Part of the humor (and the reader's confusion) comes from the fact that the poem draws on and transforms several contrasting realities, perspectives, and conventions. It is set up as a casual dialogue—one that we might find in a trite realistic short story, or perhaps in a television soap opera, judging by some of the vocabulary used. (The woman's response is set in the form of a question one might be asked in a restaurant.) The speaker's initial statement, on the other hand, is a conventional romantic declaration, but one so conventional and trite that it evokes a parody of love rather than love itself. Yet even up to this point there has been a violation of rules of behavior: a potential love (or seduction) plot has been cast in terms of a restaurant scene.[17] By making mascara ("rimel") something like the equivalent of the milk we might serve with coffee or the bacon we might serve with eggs, the poem increases this sense of a merger of conflicting realities. If we were to stop our reading here and leave out the last two lines, we might say that the speaker defines himself as a materialistic cynic, and that the poem conveys to us the comic yet degrading vision of a society in which love is reduced to a base level. And this is clearly part of the poem. (To this degree it echoes some of the ones we have studied before.)

The last two lines, however, add a new dimension. By having the woman take out her eyes, give them up on a plate, and go away blind, the poem portrays an act of supreme sacrifice for love, one that we might expect in a traditional romantic play. Coming in the context in which it does, this act seems particularly ill-fitting, and disorients us. Why would the female protagonist of such a sordid world make this sacrifice? Yet here lies, precisely, the impact of her action: despite the world in which she is operating, this woman manages to give herself unselfishly. In some sense her action is as overwhelmingly intense and admirable as the vision of the speaker of "Muerte en el olvido."

Yet at least two more levels need to be taken into account. The woman's sacrifice is portrayed in rather matter-of-fact terms by the speaker (and presumably seen in such terms by us). By making her leave her eyes, like eggs, on a plate, and subsequently crawl away, the text takes a literal and cruel view of her gesture. In addition, it sets up an intertextual relationship and calls our attention to a possible literary parody: the speaker of the poem follows to the ultimate, literal consequence his metaphor of giving love as equal to a literal giving of one's eyes. This evidently parodies the conventional image of eyes given over to the lover as looks and soul placed upon him. (We could recall, perhaps, Góngora's *romancillo* "La más bella niña.")

But what is the total effect of all these levels? To my mind, the reader leaves the poem with a paradoxical sense of both the triviality and the potential ideality which coexist in our world. He is probably somewhat upset at the speaker's seeming cynicism (which the speaker, in fact, may be transcending in the title, and when he perceives the woman's sacrifice at the end). He probably admires the sacrifice, and yet laughs at the parody created. All in all, he experiences the conflicting and disquieting vision of reality which forms the basis of González's recent poetry.

Another—in part complementary—way of assessing the poem would view it as a "deconstruction" of the realities it evokes. The question of the woman, which brings together the love scene and the restaurant scene, creates seeming nonsense, a gap in the meaning of the text similar to that found by J. Hillis Miller in *Troilus and Cressida*.[18] That gap in turn motivates a series of disturbances (here perspectival rather than acoustic), and produces all of the levels and tensions we have been noting. Yet even if we place emphasis on this gap and on the impossibility of reducing the text by a neat interpretation, we are left with a general sense of our world as at once trivial and possessed of ideals.

Tensions similar to the ones we have seen in "Eso era amor" are often produced by seemingly inappropriate metaphors. Thus in "A mano amada," González presents memories of the past as bandits assaulting him in the night. He further intensifies the inconsistency by replacing the set phrases "a mano armada" with "a mano amada" and "arma blanca" by "alma blanca"—the attack by memories involves not the weapons of killing but the remembrance of a beloved:

A mano amada,
cuando la noche impone su costumbre de insomnio,
y convierte
cada minuto en el aniversario
de todos los sucesos de una vida;

allí,
en la esquina más negra del desamparo, donde
el nunca y el ayer trazan su cruz de sombras,

los recuerdos me asaltan.

Unos empuñan tu mirada verde,
                              otros
apoyan en mi espalda
el alma blanca de un lejano sueño,

y con voz inaudible,
con implacables labios silenciosos,
¡el olvido o la vida!,

me reclaman. [p. 290]

Somewhat as the inappropriate image of the spider altered the ordinary definition of hope in "Esperanza, / araña negra," so the assault portrayed here twists our ordinary view of memories. To comprehend the image we must again comprehend the attitude of the speaker: for him the memories of love are destructive, and forgetfulness a treasure of which they rob him. Past love and destruction are thus equated and very appropriately combined in the phrase ("a mano amada") which alludes to them both. The poem distorts a set phrase and creates an unexpected metaphor to give an embodiment of the suffering caused by a past.

Other seemingly ill-fitting metaphors are presented more lightly. In "Ciencia aflicción," problems are attacking dogs:

—Guau, guau,
nos dirán los problemas enseñándonos los dientes,
mordiéndonos los fondillos de los pantalones,
aturdiéndonos con sus bufonadas insolubles. [p. 280]

And in "A veces" (p. 257) a shock effect is produced by likening a poem to an orgasm, and by presenting the poet's struggle with words in terms of a detailed love-making scene ("muerdo sus senos . . . les levanto las faldas"). In these two cases and several others like them, the image serves not so much to lead us to a new view of the speaker, as to destroy the conventionally solemn attitude taken to certain subjects, and to produce a more irreverent vision of life. This illustrates how González's recent poetry is "social" in the broadest sense, by upsetting routine views and interpretations.

At times, González presents a whole scene to transform reality in an unexpected fashion. In "Dato biográfico" (pp. 327-28), for example, he reports a dialogue between himself and the cockroaches in his apartment, in which they request that he enjoy himself and stop writing so that they can roam freely. Aside from parodying various facets of life and politics, this poem again forges an upside-down world which challenges and modifies our ordinary assumptions. In a slightly different way, "Empleo de la nostalgia" (pp. 267-69) blends ironic and irreverent visions of American college co-eds with a meditation on nostalgia and on the fleetingness of memories.

On some occasions González builds poems by playing on language itself. In "Meriendo algunas tardes" (p. 260), an expression that would normally refer to his occasionally eating an afternoon snack creates the image of eating scenery. The otherwise conventional theme of the work, the memory of past events, acquires as a result a totally new dimension. In other poems previous literary works become the subjects of transformation. One example is "Poética No. 4," which plays off on a "rima" of Gustavo Adolfo Bécquer:

> Poesía eres tú,
>> dijo un poeta
> —y esa vez era cierto—
> mirando al Diccionario de la Lengua. [p. 314]

This work forms part of a section entitled "Metapoesía," which offers several contrasting views and perspectives, all of them undercutting the vacuous solemnity of traditional statements about poetics. In this particular text, González bases himself on what was, in Bécquer, a highly romantic vision, and parodies it, transforming it into a pragmatic assertion of the way in which poetry is built on language. Yet in at least one way, González's poem is in the spirit of Bécquer's. If we read the latter as addressed to the poet's muse rather than to a particular beloved, it defends, just as González's work does, the essential nature of his art.

Looking at it that way, González's poem becomes a "reading" and a modification of Bécquer's, a way of inserting oneself within the previous text and re-creating it, with attention given to both similarities and differences. This may be true in somewhat diverse ways of all poems in which González echoes other writers (we recall "Cadáver ínfimo"), as well as those which echo poetic conventions ("Eso era amor"). In all these poems González uses intertextuality to effect his transformations. The meaning of all of them emerges out of the unfolding and restructuring of a previous one, and invites the reader to see how this unfolding has taken place, to pursue its implications, and perhaps even to continue his own process of unfolding and "deconstructing."[19]

The transformations which we have observed in González's poetry vary considerably in technique, frequency, and effect. In simple terms, we can see a gradual increase of such transformations, an increasing use of violations of speech-act maxims, a more frequent presence of ironic (often "unreliable") speakers as the social dimension of González's poetry increases. All of this contributes to the disquieting visions of the last books, with their challenge to our ordinary perspectives and premises. All in all, the process of transformation which we have been

examining sheds light on what is perhaps the most significant attribute
of González's poetic work: its way of taking common themes and common language, and yet creating out of them original experiences for the
reader. By presenting the reader with an at-first incomprehensible or
contradictory reality, by forcing him to examine it, to discover its underlying premises, and to reread the poem with those in mind, González
involves him in the communicative act of the poem while also making
him aware of the issue of poetic creation and re-creation.

5 GLORIA FUERTES
Intertextuality and Reversal of Expectations

The poetry of Gloria Fuertes is marked by its colloquial tone and its resemblance to conversational address. Her works are filled with references to everyday objects and events: buses, storefronts, newspaper advertisements; any more significant themes emerge from these. Almost all her poems are written in free verse, a verse that seems to deliberately avoid rhythmic regularity and consistently break the conventions of the traditional lyric. These qualities are so patent as to suggest that the author is constructing a very special kind of poetic expression.

Noting the presence of social concerns in much of Fuertes's poetry, one is tempted to situate her in the current of social poetry that emerged in Spain after the Civil War. Yet such a view needs to be qualified: an attitude of rebellion against the injustices of the social system certainly underlies Fuertes's poetry, and one can find many negative references to war, to lack of love, to the problems of a modern industrial city. But the main impact of her poems is never didactic: rather than argue a certain stance, they make one witness and share a wide variety of human experiences which emerge from the problematic and often cruel world of a modern, industrial Spanish society.[1] Social issues are intertwined with personal ones: many of her poems deal with love, with loneliness, with attempts to define a rather unusual God. The speaker never mythifies herself as a visionary prophet or social leader, but speaks from a much more individual perspective. All of this differentiates Fuertes's work from much of the social poetry written in Spain in the early 1950s, and gives it a character all its own.

Fuertes makes effective use of common language to communicate these individual experiences that arise out of her poetry. References to objects of daily life and the use of specific tones of spoken language serve to take the poem beyond generalized didacticism, to give it its unique expressiveness. The frequent use of humor and word play, as

Margaret Persin has aptly noted, involve the reader in a different vision of the world. And for all its apparently prosaic nature, Fuertes's poetry makes use of precise linguistic techniques (paronomasias, alliterations, other word plays).[2] Seen this way, her poetry fits well with that of the other writers who became prominent in Spain in the late 1950s. Like Rodríguez, Brines, and González, Gloria Fuertes has found her own way of making artistic use of seemingly ordinary materials and thus verbally creating and conveying significant visions and experiences.

Fuertes's poetry seems even more colloquial than that of these other writers. While Brines and Rodríguez use everyday language and make poetry out of ordinary scenes, their works are not so full of slang expressions and idiomatic language as those of Fuertes. This profusion of everyday elements could lead us to consider her work less creative, less significant; if we examine it with some care, however, we will see that in its colloquialism lie the seeds of its originality and its value.

Again and again, a poem that deals with a significant theme of human life or with a conventionally poetic subject will jar us by using seemingly inappropriate language (which may include slang, advertising slogans, references to trivial events). In each case, this inappropriate language introduces, as it were, a new and different "text," at odds with the one we have come to expect in light of the poem's subject.[3] The meaning of the work emerges from the confrontation and the weaving together of the two texts. This may occur explicitly (when two easily identifiable modes of expression clash in the poem) or implicitly (when the language merely suggests a conflicting convention or form of expression). In either case the poem deliberately disorients its implied reader. The latter finds that the attitude which she expected to take toward the serious subject of the poem has been undermined by the presence of the second text; she must then grope for some new way of organizing and resolving the materials of the poem.[4] In some cases, she will be left with an apprehension of the problems and discords of modern life. In all cases, however, she will have become involved in a complex play of perspectives between the two texts and will have obtained, as a result, a whole new vision. The process parallels and yet differs from that observed in Angel González's work: where in González's poems we saw the gradual restructuring of previous conventions, in Fuertes's we will witness drastic irruptions which destroy traditional visions and produce new perspectives.

As we examine various cases of textual irruptions in Fuertes's poetry, we will see that they take different forms; in some cases the second text appears as a symbol which the poet applies to the poem's literal level, in others as a specific literary allusion, in others as a single word that brings in a different form of expression, in yet others as a whole system (or code) of words and expressions that evoke a different reality.[5] The concept of intertextuality will allow us to see how all these function in similar fashion—how they serve, in the final analysis, to undermine the initial text, to modify the expectations of the implied reader, and to produce significant meanings in a novel way.

This process is present, if not dominant, in Fuertes's early works. Her first book, *Isla ignorada,* has practically vanished; the few poems that are available and the comments of critics indicate that it contained traditional nature descriptions with *modernista* echoes, and did not show the characteristics of her later work. But in *Antología y poemas del suburbio, Aconsejo beber hilo,* and *Todo asusta,* such intertextual irruptions already appear, if not as blatantly as they do later on. Nevertheless, they are significant in determining the meaning of many poems. A good example is "El vendedor de papeles o el poeta sin suerte" from *Antología y poemas,* which uses the language of commercial advertisements:

> Vendo versos,
> liquido poesía,
> —se reciben encargos
> para bodas, bautizos,
> peticiones de mano—,
> ¡aleluyas a diez!
> No se vaya,
> regalo poesía,
> llévese este cuarteto
> que aún no me estrené! [p. 52]

The implied reader comes to this poem with a preconceived, traditional vision of poetry as a serious and dignified occupation, removed from the triviality of everyday life. Fuertes plays against this vision and this conventional text in developing her poem. By presenting poetry as something which can be marked down and sold cheap, or produced for practical reasons, and in adopting the specific language of commercial exchange ("liquido," "se reciben encargos," "no me estrené"), she sets up an opposing text—a colloquial poem. This destroys our premise that poetry and everyday life stand well apart from each other. The reversal of expectations, especially when seen in context of the whole book from which this poem comes, makes us attentive to the meanings that the poet can find in seemingly ordinary circumstances and to the possibility that poetic insights can arise from daily life.

Another weaving together of two texts occurs in "Oración," from
Antología y poemas. Here the original language of the "Our Father" and
our traditional views of God as a transcendent being and of prayer as
a solemn activity are undercut by the tone and attitude of the speaker:

> Que estás en la tierra Padre nuestro,
> que te siento en la púa del pino,
> el el torso azul del obrero,
> en la niña que borda curvada
> la espalda mezclando el hilo en el dedo.
> Padre nuestro que estás in la tierra,
> en el surco,
> en el huerto,
> en el mina,
> en el puerto,
> en el cine,
> en el vino,
> en la casa del médico.
> Padre nuestro que estás en la tierra,
> donde tienes tu gloria y tu infierno
> y tu limbo que está en los cafés
> donde los burgueses beben su refresco.
> . . . .
> Padre que habitas en cualquier sitio.
> Dios que penetras en cualquier hueco,
> tú que quitas la angustia, que estás en la tierra,
> Padre nuestro que sí que te vemos,
> los que luego te hemos de ver,
> donde sea, o ahí en el cielo. [pp. 47-48]

By taking the first phrase of the "Our Father," altering the word order,
and substituting *la tierra* for *los cielos,* the speaker reveals her break with
the view of a superior and remote God. She continues repeating and
modifying her version of that phrase to stress God's worldliness and
earthly presence, and finally to suggest that our ultimate union with
God may not be the grandiose rising to Heaven traditionally anticipated.
The colloquialism of the last line ("donde sea, o ahí en el cielo") elimi-
nates any grandiloquent vision of such a heaven, while the mention of
specific places of our world stresses that it is in them that God and
religion must be found.

Just as "El vendedor de papeles" related poetry to everyday life,
"Oración" suggests that religion and our relationship with God emerge
from the circumstances of daily existence. The poet's tactic of setting

her text against the conventional one of the "Our Father," destroying
the implied reader's expectations regarding prayer, and presenting her
with a colloquial address and a commonplace God makes the vision
emerge gradually and vividly from the poem.

In "Me crucé con un entierro" from *Aconsejo beber hilo*, a contrast
to our ordinary way of seeing deaths and funerals is used to communicate an experience of despair (although that only becomes clear at the
end of the poem):

> Me crucé con un entierro
> —el de la caja iba muerto—.
> —¿A dónde vas?—me decía—.
> —Adonde tú—respondiendo—.
> Se marchaba muy tranquilo,
> me quedaba sonriendo.
> ¿Quién va más muerto que vivo,
> quién va por mejor sendero,
> el de la caja o yo misma,
> que todavía te quiero? [pp. 90-91]

This poem again sets itself against the reader's "horizon of expectations," which dictates that the subject of death and funerals be approached with reverence. The colloquial way of describing the dead
man ("el de la caja iba muerto") indicates a flip irreverence that clashes
with the serious tone normally used on such occasions. The conversation with the corpse not only contradicts the rules of reality but also
takes on a casual tone that contrasts with the solemnity with which the
dead are usually approached in our culture. The denouement of the
scene, with its calm parting of the protagonists, adds to the sense of an
ill-fitting improbability. All of this makes the poem the opposite of any
traditional poem about the dead. The implied reader must notice how
this text sets itself against others with which she is familiar—a serious
report, a lament on someone's death, perhaps even a poem addressed to
the dead. Until the last four lines of the poem, the reader is left wondering where this intertextuality is going to take her.

In these last lines the speaker finally reveals her theme, suggesting
that her continued love for a "tú" (who presumably scorns her) makes
her more dead than the corpse. This hyperbole, which would probably
seem unacceptable were it to stand alone, is much easier to accept in the
context of the whole poem. We do not, for one, have to see it as grimly
serious: the speaker of the poem has already revealed a colloquial tone
and a critical posture with respect to traditional texts, which suggest
that she can see her own predicament in matter-of-fact fashion. In

addition, the way in which the first part sets itself against conventional writing suggests that the whole poem may be a parody of another conventional text, a romantic lament for a love lost.

This becomes clear when we recall the characteristics of such romantic poems, in which images of death, graveside laments, and hyperbolic complaints abound. Fuertes undercuts these stock images of an abandoned lover's lament and the stock setting of a funeral procession by turning them into an abrupt street scene. (The dialogue in lines 3-5, for example, seems more fitting to a casual encounter between neighbors running errands.) Even the form of the poem may contribute to this sense of parody. It is a *romance* in e-o, a form employed to recount heroic deeds in the traditional *Romancero* and often used later on by romantic poets; here it is utilized by a contemporary poet (who normally writes in free verse) to give a very colloquial twist to a traditional theme.

It is hard to define with certainty the final experience produced by this poem: should one read it as a broad parody of a romantic lament, or as a modern and somewhat ironic, yet partly serious, restatement of such a lament? The latter reading seems more convincing to me: the last line suggests real suffering, though one tempered by a very modern awareness of the world around us. By setting her text against others—conventional reports of death, romantic poems—Fuertes has woven within her reader's mind and experience a new and complex vision, a product of the interplay between all these texts.

A similar undercutting of conventional texts and attitudes occurs in two other poems which refer to the dead, "Los muertos" from *Aconsejo beber hilo* and "Mis queridos difuntos" from *Todo asusta*. Both present the dead as much happier and better adjusted than the living. In the first work, (pp. 99-100) they go about daily activities in the cemetery in matter-of-fact fashion; in the second (p. 123) the speaker expresses regret at having to leave the harmonious world of the dead and return to the discord of the living, cautioning the dead not to be resurrected. Fuertes does not describe the dead as being in Heaven or in a glorified afterlife: they are happier simply because they are away from the world. This denial of life as worthwhile highlights one theme of Fuertes's poetry, the limitations of our world and our society.

A somewhat different kind of intertextuality is engendered by "Guía comercial" (p. 115), a work made up entirely of sentences that imitate typical advertisements. By thus introducing previous texts which we normally consider highly antipoetic, Fuertes contradicts our expectations of what is proper to poetry and what is proper to everyday life. This not only satirizes and denigrates the prosaic world which the poet is confronting but also reopens the question of the relationship of poetry to the everyday forms of expression of this world. A similar effect is produced by "De los periódicos," (p. 127), which lists a number of haphazard objects supposedly found in an ostrich's stomach, as reported by a newspaper. Neither of these poems is a simple message regarding the relationship of poetry to popular culture and forms of expression; both refer to the texts of this culture to raise the issue of this relationship and to invite us to reexamine its implications in new ways.

In all of the poems we have seen so far, Fuertes has constructed internally consistent pictures or stories which nevertheless oppose previous texts which they evoke, and consequently alter the implied reader's preconceived attitudes. In most cases this serves to destroy conventional notions regarding the value of human life and of social order, the independence of poetry, or the grandiloquence of religion. All of these poems depend on the reader's "horizon of expectations" to furnish these conventional notions, making the reader anticipate attitudes which are then dramatically undercut within the text.[6] This procedure ultimately engenders an irreverent view of our world, based on the problems of the reality surrounding us. By making that view emerge within the implied reader as she gropes with the contradictions between her expectations and the text she is reading, Fuertes has made a vivid poetic experience out of what could have been otherwise no more than a didactic message.

These poems also demonstrate how, in order to convey the problems of the modern world, Fuertes creates intertextual weavings which engender a variety of tensions, destroy conventional visions, and produce a new form of expression. Fuertes actually states this as a conscious goal of her work on several occasions.[7] It also emerges from the way in which she draws the *persona* of her speaker. In "Es obligatorio," the speaker pictures herself as rebelling against the hypocritical niceties of society and polite language in order to achieve real communication:

> Es obligatorio tener mitos
> y yo gustosa desobedezco,
> gustosa me plancho las blusas,
> cuando tengo tiempo,
> porque antes es hablar con los amigos. [p. 136]

The colloquial expressions and the clash with previous texts present in Fuertes's early work, far from indicating expressive inadequacies, convey the poetry's subjects in a new and effective fashion.

Three books of poetry published by Gloria Fuertes in the 1960s, *Ni tiro, ni veneno, ni navaja, Poeta de guardia,* and *Cómo atar los bigotes al tigre,* reveal an even more creative use of everyday language and common-place materials. As Francisco Ynduráin has noted, individual episodes and personal themes now point even more clearly to larger questions of the value of human life, of basic emotions and feelings, of the role of God, of poetry.[8] Fuertes exploits colloquial expressions, Madrid slang, and specific allusions to create unique perceptions and to embody her themes in novel ways. Her humor jars the reader, recreating within her a new vision of the poem's subject. As she does all this, Fuertes makes even greater use of intertextual correspondences and contrasts to create rich experiences. Frequently the other texts alluded to are now more specific; where in the earlier poems we could discern general echoes of advertisements or romantic laments, we now see detailed evocations of an automobile accident, a Madrid store, or a poem by Saint John of the Cross. This produces works which are on the one hand more com-plex and more jarring to our expectations; it leads on the other to more frequent and more elaborate relationships between the specific subject of a poem and some larger theme. The intertextual relation-ships make the reader see these themes in unusual and compelling ways.

All this is perhaps most apparent in *Poeta de guardia,* published in 1968. As Ynduráin has noted, this book is not only one of the most extensive written by Fuertes, but also perhaps the most significant.[9] The title and several poems in the work assert the author's role as viewer of and commentator on reality. The book deals with a wide range of themes, encompassing universal issues such as social injustice, the meaning of life, and the impact of death, and more personal subjects such as love, the monotony of daily life, the problems of a writer. None of them are in themselves novel or unusual. What makes their treatment unique, however, is the way in which Fuertes uses intertextuality to set these themes in the modern context and give them new dimensions. We can see how this occurs in "Galerías Preciadas":

> Todo te viene pequeño
> —o demasiado grande—,
> ni siquiera lo que escojes te va,
> todo te viene pequeño.
> Con el alma desnuda por una cosa u otra
>   imploramos el Tendero.
>
> Y si llegas a encontrar . . .
> quien bien te quiere te hará llorar . . .
>   —¡Vaya consuelo¡
> (¡Qué suerte ser eremita o farero!) [p. 192]

The title contains a pun, immediately perceived by any resident of Madrid. In titling the poem with a modified version of the name of Madrid's best known middle-class department store (Galerías Preciados), Fuertes calls to mind a very specific second text, which we immediately associate with prosaic shopping trips, with bargain hunting, and perhaps with shoddy merchandise. All these associations clash with the poem's theme, the larger question of what is valuable in life. ("Preciadas" is obviously rooted in "preciado"— that which is valued or esteemed.) This clash is continued in the body of the poem, in which the common happening of not finding an article of clothing that fits is linked to and contrasted with the question of finding something meaningful in one's existence. The first four lines stress the anecdotal event; the next two, in contrast, point to the wider question. By referring to the soul and capitalizing "Tendero," Fuertes obviously creates an allusion to man's questioning of God.

In a conventional reading, we might say that Fuertes has done no more than construct a symbol, making the search for clothing stand for a quest for some deeper meaning. This is of course technically true; but the effect of this "symbolism" depends almost entirely on its surface inappropriateness, on the conflict between texts, and on the jarring effect it produces. The activity of hunting for clothes that fit in an inexpensive store turns the larger quest for something meaningful into a pedestrian activity. We are tempted to stand back with the speaker and mock this quest a little, or at least to realize that we live in a world in which grand searches get mixed in with very trivial activities, and in which it is hard to be uniformly significant and heroic.

It might be best to see this poem as a combination of two different codes, in the sense attributed to that term by Roland Barthes. Fuertes has violently joined a representational code referring to a shopping expedition (a code formed by the colloquial expressions "te viene pequeño," "[te viene] grande," "te va") to another symbolic one referring to a deeper, seemingly religious quest (a code formed by "alma" and the capitalization of "Tendero"). In line 5, both codes appear almost simultaneously, as a reference to the soul is followed by the colloquial "una cosa u otra," and as the storekeeper and God become fused in "Tendero." All in all, the two codes interfere with each other and thus jar the reader into feeling the inappropriateness of their conjunction. This leads, in the final analysis, to a paradoxical vision of our world in which larger questions emerge in trivial ways, and yet in which daily happenings also become tied to deeper issues.

The second stanza defines the large quest more specifically: it becomes the search for someone, presumably a beloved. By indicating that this search would only lead to suffering even if it were to succeed, the speaker adds another dimension to the earlier pessimism. The wish to be a lonely hermit or lighthouse keeper dramatizes her final hopelessness of finding meaningful union or communication.

It is important to note that the allusions to the second text (the store) and the resultant conflict of codes are not continued in this second stanza. Once the poem defines its particular quest, it no longer maintains the tension between perspectives which it set up at the beginning. That tension nevertheless affects our evaluation of the second stanza. Aware that for the speaker of the poem larger questions are mixed with, and seen in the terms of, the most prosaic reality, we will not read her final lament as a repetition of romantic clichés but as the complaint of someone who realizes the tensive mixture of the serious and the petty, the grand and the trivial, in the world in which we live.

In the light of this, we can see a new intertextual play taking place in the second stanza. In evoking hermits, lighthouse keepers, and a love doomed to suffering, the speaker calls to mind the tragedies and conventions of sentimental fiction. That intertextuality, however, serves mostly to underline a contrast: unlike the heroines of such fiction, this poem's speaker has taken everyday reality into account and has not fallen into conventional lamentations. In this sense, the intertextuality of the first stanza has played a crucial function: it has set up a perspective which now lets the speaker present a romantic complaint without seeming trite or naive. In a larger sense, it has allowed Fuertes to treat the old theme of the hopelessness of finding love in a new and acceptable way.

Another poem in the same book is titled "Extraño accidente":

> En aquella primavera se le aflojaron los tornillos;
> en unas curvas peligrosas
> se le rompió la dirección.
> Los testigos afirmaron que se lanzó al bello, precipicio
> —como a sabiendas—.
> Murió de corazón roto
> a tantos de tantos, como tantos,
> aunque continúa yendo a la oficina. [p. 195]

Here the words and images suggest and juxtapose two distinct realities and two texts. The description of the first four lines, as well as the specific references to "tornillos," "curvas peligrosas," "precipicio," and the loss of direction, evoke an automobile accident. Less evident at the beginning, yet nonetheless present, is the suggestion of a disorienting romance. "Aflojarse los tornillos," is of course an idiomatic phrase for losing one's senses, and may recall the phrase "aflojarse(le) las rodillas," a cliché reference to the timidity of a lover. "Curvas peligrosas" covertly alludes to the figure of a woman, and the adjective "bello" in line 4 suggests that the precipice is a metaphor for a dangerous woman rather than a literal chasm. This second reality or second text of the poem becomes explicit in line 6, which makes the reader go back and see more clearly what she probably only felt or suspected when she first read the poem's beginning. Fuertes has offered us a very evident text and code which allude to an accident, and initially less evident ones which suggest a romance and gain importance in the poem's ending.

In one sense, this process makes the poem function like "Galerías Preciadas": it lets Fuertes present an old subject in a novel way, avoiding the dangers of conventionalism and sentimentality. (The last three lines of the poem, were they to stand alone, would give a grim and almost moralistic vision.) In addition, its way of setting up two simultaneous texts and codes, playing with the meaning of words, and thus producing a lighter tone, suggests that the catastrophes of modern life, while serious, are also somewhat petty and comical. The scorned lover is not a noble figure but a miserable middle-class victim of something resembling a foolish automobile accident. The presence of the "accident text" imparts an air of mechanization to the love affair. In this fashion, the intertextual play suggests a second tragedy, in some ways larger than that of the protagonist; our world offers but a limited and mechanized version of archetypal catastrophes. At the end, the protagonist who keeps going to the office but is a mere shell of himself seems (somewhat like T.S. Eliot's Prufrock) a bureaucratic parody of a romantic hero. Fuertes has again woven together two texts to portray a limited tragedy of the modern world.

Whether we talk of the interplay of codes or of the presence of two texts in discussing "Galerías Preciadas" and "Extraño accidente," we end up stressing the same effect.[10] By setting up two frames of reference and pointing in two directions at once, Fuertes has modified our normal expectations and ways of seeing old subjects (the hopelessness of finding love, a lover's catastrophe). By creating an interplay between a text and a code focused on modern reality and another focused on love, she has conveyed to us her sense of a world in which perennial human problems occur, but in ways that are peculiarly down-to-earth, comical, and fitted to the characteristics and limitations of our everyday lives.

In "Mi suerte," Fuertes creates an intertextual conflict that goes in the opposite direction from the ones we have just seen. The poem begins by focusing on the universal questions of one's fate in life; then sud-

denly it shifts to the petty "fate" of winning a saucepan in a lottery. In
this fashion it undercuts and modifies its basic philosophic text by
inserting into it the everyday text of petty chance (rather than Fate):

> En la vida
> ya he hecho un poco,
> pero me queda mucho.
> En el amor,
> ya he hecho mucho,
> pero me queda un pozo.
> En la Rifa,
> todo lo perdí . . .
> —pero me tocó un cueceleches. [p. 177]

The focus on the universal (as well as the capitalization of "Rifa" and
the sweeping statement "todo lo perdí") makes us see the lottery as a
cosmic metaphor for life, and tempts us to read the whole poem as a
grand pronouncement.[11] When Fuertes then shocks us by the petty,
everyday image of the "cueceleches," we again sense that larger questions come to the speaker (and to us) in the context of our immediate
lives. This in no way destroys the symbolic level of the poem: the
"cueceleches" is, in fact, a good image for the limited successes that life
offers. But it functions in a dramatic and earthbound way, not in the
grandiose manner we had been anticipating. A similar break in expectations occurs in " . . . Y me tengo todavía," in which a serious presentation of the monotony of life is undercut by another text—by a petty
self-portrayal of the speaker: "bebo, fumo, escribo cartas / y meo una
siempreviva" [p. 222].

"A San Juan de la Cruz" creates a different kind of intertextuality,
setting the language and tone of the poem against those of the poetry
of Saint John of the Cross:

> Querido Juanito:
> No,
> si poseer poseo
> el entendimiento del amor;
> lo que no alcanzo
> ni con amor ni con oración ni con bondad ni con poesía,
> es ser por el amado correspondida.
>
> Está mi alma cautiva
> y al paso está cautivada
> por una esquiva, mirada,
> que ni miro ni me mira.

Y si salgo de vuelo
o me voy por las ramas,
sólo es para dar a la Caza caza,
me remonto y bajo rauda,
porque aún es la tierra mi sitio,
mientras que me quede un ala. [pp. 220-21]

The colloquial tone stands, of course, in stark contrast to the elevated one of Saint John's verse. This contrast corresponds to a thematic and attitudinal one: where Saint John speaks of an idealized love, the speaker here deals with a much more ordinary one; where Saint John paints a picture of elevated lovers in perfect communion, the speaker expresses her annoyance at not being loved in return. All of this not only lets us see the difference in kinds of love and attitudes to them, but makes us feel very strongly the conflict between the whole vision of reality that underlies Saint John's work and that which is present in this poem (and, by extension, in our own everyday world).

That conflict is heightened by the use of specific words and images that echo Saint John's work but that here carry quite different meanings and implications. The references to the speaker's captive soul allude to an infatuation rather than a transcendent love; the word "esquiva" (which appears in Saint John's "Llama de amor viva") here describes a scornful lover; the image of the hunt (the main metaphor of Saint John's "Tras de un amoroso lance") seems to refer to a very earthly love chase. "Salgo de vuelo" echoes specifically the phrase "voy de vuelo" used by the Amada in Saint John's "Cántico espiritual," but it is undercut by the prosaic "me voy por las ramas," which evokes a literal picture of a bird, and at the same time is a colloquial idiom for disorientation. Other prosaic lines also help undercut any mystic echoes: the long list of efforts to move the lover in line 5 makes the quest desperate rather than significant, and the speaker's view of herself in line 15 ["me remonto y bajo rauda"] is jarringly physical.

The final effect of this textual interplay and apparent parody may be harder to define. The poem does make us feel that in this earthly reality love is very different from that described by Saint John. Yet the speaker is cognizant of the latter's transcendence, and may be expressing some desire for elevation, especially in the last line—even as she realizes that in the world in which she lives any idealism is quickly undercut. Like many other poems in *Poeta de guardia,* this one engenders a conflict which offers a complex and unusual view of a larger theme, the quest for love, set in modern prosaic circumstances. (A similar

conflict occurs in "Empeoro y mejoro" [pp. 181-182], where the
speaker's seemingly private striving for serenity is suddenly rendered in
a quotation from Fray Luis de León.)

In "El camello (auto de los Reyes Magos)" (pp. 240-41), Fuertes
takes the biblical scene of the adoration of the Magi and gives it an
entirely new focus. The poem dwells on the plight of the kings' camel,
ignored and scorned by the Magi and yet finally treasured by the child
Jesus, who rejects the cold gifts of gold and incense and starts playing
with the camel. Fuertes here evokes a second text, the original story of
the Magi in the New Testament, and uses it to create a contrast as well
as a parallel. Unlike the Christ in the Bible, her child Jesus scorns the
rich gifts and turns to the lowly camel—suggesting a critique of earthly
values in religion. On another level, however, Fuertes's version of the
story conveys in a new way what is essentially a traditional vision of
Christ as interested in love rather than material possessions.

In "El lo sabe," a religious subject is handled by another textual
interplay. God's control over our lives is presented as if it were a petty
accountant's keeping track of statistics. This not only reduces any notion of God's grandeur (fitting the book's general view of God as a very
human being with whom the poet is engaged in a debate), but also
captures the tedium and the lack of transcendence of our lives. Events
which we normally judge individual and central become mere statistics
in a file controlled by an impersonal statistician:

> Porque Él lo sabe todo de antemano,
> ÉL o ELLA, quien sea, se lo sabe.
>
> Hay Alguien que recita de noche tu futuro,
> que escribió antes del parto tu estadística . . .
>
> Fecha de muerte tal, fecha de nacimiento . . .
> Balance de besos dados . . . recibidos . . .
> Total que faltan . . .
> Número de amores . . .
> Litros de llanto . . .
> . . . .
> En infinito archivo están nuestros "papeles";
> en carpetas de hule nuestro expediente escrito;
> marionetas somos,
> . . . .
> Y ni Dios con ser Dios puede rectificarse,
> desdecirse,
> borrar, tachar, [pp. 207-08]

An additional complexity is introduced into the poem at the end, when the speaker wonders if this is reality or simply a perspective adopted "para calmarme." The main effect of the poem, nevertheless, lies in its dramatization of a skeptical view of reality and religious meaning.

Ni tiro, ni veneno, ni navaja is much shorter than *Poeta de guardia,* containing only thirty-two brief poems. Many deal with the theme of death and the subject of God, although the task of the poet, the issue of love, and the sterility of modern life are also touched on. The irruptions of other texts are often brief and result from the appearance of an unexpected detail, rather than from the more sustained interplays of texts or codes which we saw in *Poeta de guardia.* In "Zoo de verbena," for example, a list of unusual animals in a zoo of freaks suddenly takes an unexpected turn: "En la jaula se exhibe lo nunca visto, / fue muy difícil atraparlo . . . / ¡A peseta le entrada vea al *hombre feliz!"* (p. 163). The appearance of the "happy man" brings in a whole new level and text: what seemed to be a descriptive poem turns into a philosophic statement on the impossibility of human happiness.

"La vida a veces es un río frío y seco . . ." exemplifies another kind of intertextuality. Here Fuertes evokes the traditional *carpe diem* image of life as grapes, only to give it a different value from the one normally attributed to it:

> Robemos los racimos,
> los han puesto al alcance de la mano
> —y la Esperanza tiene más alcohol que la uva—.
>
> Para pasar el río frío y seco
> "¡Venga alegría
> señores venga alegría . . .!"
> ¡Emborrachémonos
> para la travesía! [p. 149]

By turning a traditionally serious and positive image into an invitation to drunkenness as a solution to the problems of life, the poem undercuts not only the value of this solution but that of the whole *carpe diem* vision of joyous affirmation of life. By alluding to, and turning upside down, an old image and text, it dramatizes a pessimistic rejection of a traditional and easy optimism.

Several poems in this book contain a type of intertextuality that we have not yet seen in Fuertes's poetry. They are cast in the form of other kinds of writing—telegrams, letters, file cards, examination questions. The reader is obligated to take into account her view of the kind of writing involved and somehow relate it to her view of poetry; in every case this produces disorientation, since the other writings evoked differ radically from conventional poetry in their goals and language. In most cases, this kind of intertextuality makes us feel that a superficially "anti-poetic" form can in fact best fulfill the communicative goals of some poetry.

"Telegramas de urgencia escribo" offers a good example of this kind of textual interference:

> Escribo, más que cantar cuento cosas.
> Destino: La Humanidad.
> Ingredientes: Mucha pena
>   mucha rabia
>   algo de sal.
> Forma: ya nace con ella.
> Fondo: que consiga emocionar.
> Música: la que el verso toca
>   —según lo que va a bailar—
> Técnica: (¡Qué aburrimiento!)
> . . . .
>   Y nace sólo el poema . . .
>   Y luego la habilidad
>   de poner aquello en claro
>   si nace sin claridad. [p. 141]

This is the first poem in *Ni tiro, ni veneno*. Like the title poem of *Poeta de guardia*, it constitutes a kind of poetics, stressing the poet's attempt to convey significant meanings rather than to follow certain formal rules or to produce decorative writing. The evocation of another kind of text, the telegram, supports its meaning perfectly. The very notion of a telegram of course contradicts the notion of an idle, profusely decorative work. In addition, the features of this particular work—its condensation, its brief disconnected sentences and phrases, its outline form—all contradict the view of poetry as a rich verbal exercise. The reader who holds this view sees her expectations reversed and is led to the poem's message. The starkness of the work and the reference to the telegram text embody and convey Fuertes's defense of a nondecorative, nondiscursive, yet profoundly meaningful poetry.

Another poem in this book, "Sociedad de amigos y protectores" (p. 145), is cast in the form of a public address to a society of friends of ghosts, asking them to take care of a phantom that disturbs the speaker's equilibrium. The cliché form of a speech clashes with the rather poetic image of one's problems and anxieties as a ghost; the poem also seems to allude to the view of society as a menacing protector during the Franco regime. All of this engenders a tensive view of safety and order.

Similar uses of other kinds of texts to give form to her poems can also be found in Fuertes's other books: even as early as *Todo asusta* the tragedy of a worker is evoked in a poem written as a file card in a hospital admissions office:

> *Ficha ingreso Hospital General*
>
> Nombre: Antonio Martín Cruz.
> Domicilio: Vivía en una alcantarilla.
> Profesión: Obrero sin trabajo.
> OBSERVACIONES: Le encontraron moribundo.
> Padecía: Hambre [p. 135]

Apart from any intertextual effects, the stark and apparently prosaic form of the file card captures summarily the impact of the man's tragic life, making it emerge right from the work and without any didactic commentary which would weaken its effect. The reference to another kind of text, the file card, makes us explicitly conscious of the fact that this sparse writing may capture modern tragedies better than a conventional lyric poem. As in the poems that evoke or imitate other kinds of texts, Fuertes here draws on an unexpected and seemingly antipoetic form of writing to give impact to her subject and to suggest the need for new forms of poetry.

Cómo atar los bigotes de tigre does not differ radically from *Poeta de guardia* and *Ni tiro.* The social implications of many poems are more evident, and personal happenings and themes acquire, as Ynduráin has noted, more collective implications—the speaker's dilemma echoes or presages those of others.[12] Fuertes uses humor even more frequently than before, and makes more allusions to everyday scenes, events, and phrases. The juxtapositions in this book are more often formed by brief vignettes, images, and verbal twists than by the more sustained interpolations of different planes of *Poeta de guardia,* although we can find some examples of the latter. Fuertes seems to be expressing a vision similar to that of her previous book in a slightly more terse and playful way.

One poem is presented as a letter to God, filled with the prosaic clichés of middle-class letter writing and cast in a conventionally respectful tone. The insertion of this highly antipoetic text, when combined with the religious allusions, produces a parody of traditional religious images:

Muy Señor mío:
Hace mucho tiempo que debía haberle escrito,
espero que sabrá perdonar y comprender mi tardanza
cuyo motivo,
            Usted bien sabe.
Deseo que al recibo de estas líneas
se encuentre bien en compañía de su Sagrada Familia
y demás Santos de la Corte Celestial. [pp. 287-88]

Fuertes has used the letter-writing form to shock the reader out of conventional postures taken to religion and to evoke the picture of a worldly and bourgeois divinity, fitted to our modern society and caught in the same daily dilemma as "his" people.

In "La excursión" we find another kind of intertextuality, somewhat similar to ones we have seen in earlier books. Here a text referring to the coming of death is inserted into another which apparently describes the preparations for a very ordinary trip:

Habrá que madrugar, eso sí.
Sin saber
            a qué hora
                        poner
                              el despertador.
Preparar la tartera, el bocadillo,
las botas o el termo de café;
y abrigarse,
            hará frío,
—cuatro tablas de pino no calientan—.
Es mejor hacer una fogata con el ataúd,
iluminar la Excursión con la Esperanza
o quedarme durmiendo hasta la cita. [p. 255]

The poem unfolds very slowly, using a profusion of details to describe the preparations needed for the early start of an expedition. This immerses the reader in a seemingly common happening (although she may wonder why one doesn't know what time to set the alarm for). In this fashion, the indication that the planned trip is in fact death causes a shocking break in expectations, accentuated by the indirect nature of the revelation (there is no heat in a coffin).

By forcing us to approach death as though it were a petty trip, Fuertes jars us out of our conventional solemnity in dealing with the subject. She also takes the traditional metaphor of life as a trip and gives it a completely new "realistic" dimension. Far from weakening the effect of the poem's subject, this procedure intensifies it: the coming of death is no longer an old subject, as seen in many poems we have read, but a shockingly real experience, akin to things that happen to us in our own lives. The jarring effect of this poem leads us right into the last stanza, making more credible the speaker's decision either to take an attitude of violent rebellion or to ignore and block out the coming event. This poem stands as another excellent example of how Fuertes makes inter- textualities embody basic themes in new and expressive ways.

In *Sola en la sala,* Fuertes continues to deal with a variety of themes in colloquial language. She continues noting her vocation for poetry and the way in which her poems emerge from daily life ("Carta explicatoria de Gloria," pp. 293-94), but she places greater stress than before on the spontaneity of the process and on the variety of the resulting works ("Este libro," p. 294). This stance corresponds to the nature of the book itself: it contains many brief poems and tends to aphorisms and epi- grams. Even more than Fuertes's earlier work, it is filled with references to modern subjects and events that range from boxing and bullfights to man's landing on the moon. Quick but penetrating psychological per- ceptions alternate with unusual visual images and with metaphors that capture emotional states. The intertextualities that we find in the work fit very well its epigrammatic nature, and are in almost all cases brief and unusual metaphors or unexpected combinations of image and idea. Most often they are used to describe states of emotion, as in "Nunca se sabe":

> Si no tuviera esperanza,
> me tiraría por la ventana;
> pero . . .
>
> ¿dónde está la esperanza y la ventana,
> si vivo en un sótano? [p. 347]

The first stanza sets up a stock image and makes us think that we will have a traditional (maybe trite) poem about hope, presumably one with a positive ending. When the speaker switches to a more literal perspec- tive and brings in a very different kind of text, a matter-of-fact state- ment that she cannot jump because she lives in a basement, she forces us to witness the undercutting of both our expectations and a poetic image and convention. All this helps highlight the poem's theme—the real frustration of a modern person who is set in such a petty world that she cannot even act with romantic desperation.

In another brief poem, Fuertes inserts a second text—an old propa- ganda slogan of the Franco regime—, remaking it to assert Spain's need to rise above its limitations: "Para conseguirlo, / pagarás la cuota de veinticinco o cincuenta / años de paz y riñones" (p. 355). Undeniably, however, intertextualities do not have as significant a function in this book as they did in several of Fuertes's previous ones. The more elaborate relationships between texts and the more complex visions that we found in *Poeta de guardia* are simply not a feature of *Sola en la sala*.

As Yndurain has indicated, Gloria Fuertes is very conscious of her poetic stance and goals. In every book we find some poems that deal with her poetics, and she has not hesitated to make prose statements about her work.[13] She talks about the need to write clearly, to make one's poetry deal with the main issues of life, to use it in order to convey one's emotional insights and also to help others gain such insights. Apart from any value they may have in defining poetry in general, such statements make clear the author's devotion to her art and her consciousness of her goal of creating a new and significant kind of expression. Keeping them in mind, we can see her novel use of the everyday and her way of juggling texts and producing reversals in reader expectations as a way of reaching this goal.

This becomes even clearer when we observe how Fuertes's statements about poetry and the poet give increasingly greater importance to the creative use of everyday language in poetry. "Nota Biográfica" from *Antología y poemas del suburbio,* for example, stresses the speaker's ordinary life and occupations: poetry is part of that life as well as an effort to express oneself in ordinary settings ("he publicado versos en todos los calendarios"). In the title poem of *Poeta de guardia* (p. 167), the speaker's role as poet has acquired greater transcendence: she is now the observer of and commentator on life. This vision culminates in Fuertes's view of poetry as underlying life and of her task as unearthing it, expressed in a poem from *Cómo atar los bigotes del tigre* (p. 283): "No te tapes Poesía / te reconozco en las cosas pequeñas / y en las casas grandes, / allí donde estés, daré contigo." At the same time, Fuertes stresses her need to avoid hollow forms: "no me tientes a retóricos sonetos, / vamos a hablar como siempre, / ¡o te mando de paseo!"

At about the same time, Fuertes ascribed a very high function to the writing of poetry. Answering José Batlló's 1968 questionnaire, she wrote: "Hoy mas que nunca el poeta debe escribir claro, para todo el mundo, que se le entienda, y si no le sale, que lo rompa y vuelva a la carga—de paz. Necesitamos un estado poético en el corazón y en los países."[14] This lets us see that Fuertes's decision to use colloquial language and everyday events in her verse is no accident, but rather the result of a conscious and growing impulse to exploit such language and such events in poems both significant and accessible to all readers. The intertextualities and modifications of reader expectations are key elements in the creation of such poems. Through these techniques, Gloria Fuertes has made original and artistic use of seemingly trivial materials, and opened new directions for contemporary Spanish poetry.[15]

6 JOSÉ ANGEL VALENTE
Reading and Rereading

Author of both poetic and critical works of major importance, José Angel Valente has articulated with precision the poetics and the attitude to art which underlie the works of his generation. In his essays Valente constantly stresses the goal of poetry in seizing and coming to know reality. Opposing the notion (so prevalent in the immediate post-Civil War period) that poets should communicate previously existent philosophic and social outlooks, Valente defends their role in discovering, through language, realities which would otherwise remain unexplored. This attitude is most evident in his frequently cited essay "Conocimiento y communicación": "Todo poema es, pues, una exploración de materia de experiencia no previamente conocido que constituye su objeto. El conocimiento más o menos pleno del objeto del poema supone la existencia más o menos plena del poema en cuestión. De ahí que el proceso de la creación poética sea un movimiento de indagación y tanteo en el que la identificación de cada nuevo elemento modifica a los demás o los elimina, porque todo poma es un conocimiento 'haciéndose.' "[1]

On several occasions, Valente indicates that the full meaning of a poem does not exist prior to its composition, but rather emerges in the process of bringing together its materials and embodying them in words. If one sees poetry as mere communication of set meanings, one ignores this fact and deprives poetry of its role in uncovering new dimensions of reality. Valente therefore condemns the attitudes of writers who stress theme to the exclusion of form and language, pointing out that they fall into a new formalism of sorts: "un formalismo de la peor especie: el de los temas o el de las tendencias." Such writers cannot make their works instruments of discovery: "Parecen los poetas más preocupados por vocear ciertos temas que por descubrir la realidad de que esos mismos temas pueden ser enunciado ideológico. . . . Por eso, mucha de la poesía que se escribe entre nosotros carece de esa raíz última de necesidad que da existencia el estilo: la conversión del lenguaje en un instrumento de invención, es decir, de hallazgo de la realidad."[2]

At times Valente's view of the poem's meaning as emerging in the process of its composition motivates in him some skepticism regarding the poet's control. If the writing of a text is a progressive act of discovery, and if a work's meaning is evolving gradually, then language is never fully in the author's power and the process of writing is a dialectical confrontation between poet and language. In the first poem of *Poemas a Lázaro*, Valente talks of himself as "culpable / de las mismas palabras que combato," and makes the work transcend its creator.[3] (This view at least implicitly suggests that a poem could keep evolving on successive readings.)

Valente's view of the poem as evolving gradually gives us a clue to the understanding of his own work. The common vocabulary of his first three books, their references to everyday events, and their avoidance of preciosity of expression have led critics to deem them realistic.[4] This is helpful in highlighting their sobriety and lack of empty rhetoric, and in distinguishing them from the overblown existential verse then being published in Spain. Yet we must not confuse the sparseness and sobriety of these books with lack of creativity; they are in no way limited to reporting ideas or describing real objects. In all of them the representational or mimetic level serves as the basis for the creation of an original vision or experience which emerges gradually. In Valente's more recent poetry, this creation of a new vision also takes place but is achieved somewhat differently, often growing out of literary allusions and intertextual patterns.

To understand this process of creation in Valente's poetry, we must generally undertake a second reading of the text, oriented at perceiving signs and linguistic codes which are not at first evident, but which nevertheless underlie its full significance. This significance is often not apparent at a poem's basic or representational level, but emerges when we pay attention to verbal patterns which redirect our reading and help us to see a new focus and unity.[5] We have already seen the importance of such a second reading in the poetry of Angel González, in which diverse transformations of commonplace objects and events lead us to the work's significance. In Valente's poetry, unlike González's, the second level does not depend on distortions which force a search for a new principle to account for the apparent "ungrammaticality" of the work. It emerges, instead, when we follow a clue given in a seemingly comprehensible text, discover unexpected patterns of language, imagery, or intertextual allusions underlying it, and are forced to go back and reassess the whole text. Our second reading does not erase or change the poem's representational level (as often occurs with González's poems), but offers a new perspective and new meanings. Since it leads us to find these meanings in the very process of our reading, it allows us to duplicate and perhaps even continue the task of discovery which Valente attributes to poetry.

A modo de esperanza, Valente's first book of poems, is centered on the themes of death and loss. Again and again the poem's speaker focuses on episodes of death, and in doing so raises questions regarding his place in the scheme of things and regarding the human condition in general. Yet these subjects and this existential perspective, which led other contemporary poets to a neoromantic stance and rhetorical expression, are handled in an understated manner. Valente evokes specific episodes and realistic scenes; his poems retain a vivid particularity, and wider questions emerge from this particularity as we reread the text. Thus his poems maintain a unique combination of immediacy and significance, and also involve the reader in a process of discovery.[6]

"El espejo" furnishes an excellent example of this process:

> Hoy he visto mi rostro tan ajeno,
> tan caído y sin par
> en este espejo.
>
> Está duro y tan otro con sus años,
> su palidez, sus pómulos agudos,
> su nariz afilada entre los dientes,
> sus cristales domésticos cansados,
> su costumbre sin fe, sólo costumbre.
> He tocado sus sienes: aún latía
> un ser allí. Latía. ¡Oh vida, vida!
>
> Me he puesto a caminar. También fue niño
> este rostro, otra vez, con madre al fondo.
> De frágiles juguetes fue tan niño,
> en la casa lluviosa y tranjinada,
> en el parque infantil
> —ángeles tontos—
> niño municipal con aro y árboles.
>
> Pero ahora me mira—mudo asombro,
> glacial asombro en este espejo solo—
> y ¿dónde estoy—me digo—
> y quién me mira
> desde este rostro, máscara de nadie? [p. 15]

The scene, the theme of the poem, and the speaker's attitude are clear from the outset. The speaker sees his image in a mirror, feels the effects of age, recalls his youth, and finally contemplates the loss produced by time and comes to a negative vision of his image and of himself. All this fits very well with the view of time and mortality which pervades the book, and seems to make the poem an excellent example of a straight-forward and "realistic" rendering of one of the main subjects of *A modo de esperanza.*

Yet this description does not give a sufficient account of the experi-ence produced by the process of rereading the poem. In some fashion, repeated readings lead us to stress less and less the protagonist's individ-ual dilemma and to feel more and more intensely negative about human nature and the human condition. Two images in the last stanza may explain this reaction. There the image of the speaker's face in the mirror as "máscara de nadie," as well as the image-adjective "glacial" applied to his amazement, de-individualize that face and make it lifeless. Once we have read this stanza, we can easily go back through the poem and find other elements that point, though more covertly, to the same view. The adjectives "ajeno" of line 1 and "otro" of line 4 underline the speaker's alienation from his mirror image; seeing the eyes as "cristales domésticos" dehumanizes this image; the use of the third person in-creases the distance. A strong contrast is created between the impersonal mirror image in the present and the vignette of the speaker as a lively child in the past (stanza 3). (The juxtaposition of "fue niño / este ros-tro" dramatically contrasts the living being of the past with the objec-tified part of the body in the present.) See in this way the poem turns out to be much less "realistic" than it seemed. It becomes an artfully constructed (and ultimately symbolic) portrayal of the depersonaliza-tion and loss of identity of a human being in time. The depersonaliza-tion takes the emphasis off the speaker as an individual, since the objectified mirror image can evoke an alienated version of any one of us, and calls attention to the larger process of alienation rather than to the speaker's particular concern with his mortality.

All the elements I have been noting seem to form, in fact, a code pointing to man's loss of individuality. This code stands against, and overwhelms, a code of vitality engendered by the image of a child playing in the past, and by the words "árboles," "parque," "niño," and "madre." The two codes come together (or clash) right in the middle of the poem, when the speaker touches his temples and still feels life in them ("aun latía / un ser allí."). His self, as it were, stands at a crossroads between the lively child of his past and the lifeless image in the mirror of the present. Our awareness of that scheme, in fact, may add to the poem's effect, since it highlights the dramatic view of man at the cross-roads between vitality and petrification.

My analysis of the text seems to make this pattern so clear that it may leave us wondering why (or whether) it should not have been apparent on first reading. Yet it was really not apparent. The language, the immediacy of the situation, and even the use of the commonplace scene and of the theme of a speaker witnessing his aging, all helped immerse us in the poem's representational level and in the conventions of a "realistic" text during that first reading. There were no "ungrammaticalities" or puzzling features to suggest its incompleteness and to make us look quickly for a governing principle that we were missing. It was only after seeing the images of the last stanza that we were inclined to look back and seek a reading based on other principles—ones which would account more fully for the general depersonalization produced at the end. Then and only then did we abandon the realistic view of the text as straight narrative, identify the codes and their grouping within the text, and move to the second vision of the poem.

A similar experience is produced by "El adiós":

Entró y se inclinó hasta besarla
porque de ella recibía la fuerza.

(La mujer lo miraba sin respuesta.)

Había un espejo humedecido
que imitaba la vida vagamente.
Se apretó la corbata,
el corazón,
sorbió un café desvanecido y turbio,
explicó sus proyectos
para hoy,
sus sueños para ayer y sus deseos
para nunca jamás.

(Ella lo contemplaba silenciosa.)

Habló de nuevo. Recordó la lucha
de tantos días y el amor
pasado. La vida es algo inesperado,
dijo. (Más frágiles que nunca las palabras.)
Al fin calló con el silencio de ella,
se acercó hasta sus labios
y lloró simplemente sobre aquellos
labios ya para siempre sin respuesta. [p. 40]

Cano, quite justifiably, uses this poem as an example of realism and simplicity of narrative which nevertheless conveys emotion. Santiago Daydí-Tolson notes its understatement.[7] For all the work's simplicity, however, it conveys an impact which only emerges on second and subsequent readings. Much of this is due to a certain ambiguity on the plot level, an ambiguity developed and partly resolved in the last line. Until we come to that line we see the poem mainly as a description of alienation and lack of communication between lovers or spouses. The realistic description, the details of daily life, the common vocabulary and unemphatic tone, and even the distanced third-person narration all tempt us to see this as the portrayal of an unremarkable if painful breakup. (The title, read literally, confirms this interpretation.) Some elements may seem puzzling: we are surprised that the woman offers no comment at all, not even an explicit rejection. But such a reaction is not impossible, and we keep reading the poem "realistically." Even at this level, the stress on the man's fervor and the woman's lack of response creates a sense of loss and frustration.

When we come to the last line ("labios ya para siempre sin respuesta"), we have to consider a new interpretation: perhaps the woman is not only detached in thought but literally dead. This adds a more fundamental meaning to the episode, shocking us into the realization that the alienation we have been witnessing was in fact final and tragic. (The shock is intensified by the contrast between this realization and the understated tone of the poem.) We then have to go back and reread the poem in a rather different way.

Before undertaking such a rereading, though, we must consider the last line further. Does it *necessarily* refer to death? "Para siempre sin respuesta" could simply indicate that the beloved has blocked out her lover's questions with absolute finality. (She does look at him without responding in line 3, which suggests that she is then alive but uncommunicative.) The explanation based on her death, while it seems most likely, is not inevitable, leaving a small uncertainty in our minds and a small gap in the explanation offered by the poem—one that reminds us of the incongruities found by J. Hillis Miller in his study of *Troilus and Cressida.*[8] Yet this gap and this incongruity, to my mind, are highly creative ones, and central to the experience of the poem. By leaving us in some uncertainty as to whether the woman is dead or simply impassive, the text forces us to see those two possibilities together, and even to consider them as alternative versions of the same thing. Total rejection would, from the man's point of view, be similar to the attitude she would take to him were she to die; an absolute separation of lovers would be a kind of death. The dichotomy and the confusion created by the poem's ending become, in this sense, a means of leading us to a new awareness of its subject: we come to see rejection, loss, and literal dying as different versions of the larger concept of the end (death) of all things.

The awareness of death, in any event, invites us to reread the poem. We now notice the sharp contrast between the man's activity and the woman's passivity. The man's activity is highlighted by a series of verbs in the preterit ("entró," "se inclinó," "se apretó," "sorbió," "explicó"), which underline his participation in the detailed activity of daily life. (These preterits also suggest that the speaker, set in the present, maintains distance from the episode.) The woman's passivity is marked by the lines in parentheses, set aside and isolated from the rest of the text; by the use of verbs in the imperfect, which contrast the continuity of her silence to the abrupt actions of the man; by the adjective "silenciosa" and the phrase "sin respuesta." We could therefore speak of contrasting codes of activity and inactivity, polarized around the two characters and serving to organize the work structurally. They are connected by the man's past dependence on the woman for inspiration and motivation. By expressing this dependence in traditional, almost cliché terms ("de ella recibía la fuerza"), Valente calls our attention to it and underlines the dimensions of the loss. At the end, the man's activity is both literally and symbolically overcome by her passivity: instead of moving or acting, all he can do is be silent and cry. His collapse is presaged to some extent by the earlier line "para nunca jamás." The image of the mirror in lines 4-5 also seems related to the loss of life and activity—the mist on it is merely an imitation of life.

In light of this rereading, the poem turns out to be not so much a direct narrative as a pattern of oppositions between activity and inactivity, culminating in the collapse of the former under the impact of the latter. It is also the embodiment of an experience of loss as a condition of human life, an experience emerging from the surprise ending and from the ambiguity which confuses—and finally fuses—abandonment and death into a single subject. This experience unfolds progressively as we reread the poem: we might even speak of the poem's theme and vision as coming into form ("haciéndose," in Valente's words) as we do so—just as they did, presumably, in the process of its being written.

In other poems of *A modo de esperanza* a "second level" appears in a slightly different way. "Serán ceniza . . .," for example, is symbolic even on first reading: the speaker's crossing of a desert and traveling onward stands for the course of his life in time:

> Cruzo un desierto y su secreta
> desolación sin nombre.
> El corazón
> tiene la sequedad de la piedra

y los estallidos nocturnos
de su materia o de su nada.
. . . .
Toco esta mano al fin que comparte mi vida
y en ella me confirmo
y tiento cuanto amo,
lo levanto hacia el cielo
y aunque sea ceniza lo proclamo: ceniza.
Aunque sea ceniza cuanto tengo hasta ahora,
cuanto se me ha tendido a modo de esperanza. [p. 13]

If traveling through the desert represents living, the touching of the beloved's hand evokes a search for love and union in the course of that living. The poem's anecdote is therefore but a means of presenting a whole view of life, and does not stand by itself like the stories and scenes of "El espejo" and "El adiós." (This is undoubtedly related to the poem's function in the book: it comes at the very beginning and introduces the work's main themes of the fleetingness of life and the loneliness and losses of the individual.) Yet the symbolic story of this work is presented with the same attention to detail as the more literal stories of the other poems: Valente anchors his text in specific reality, using concrete elements and exact sensations to give it all immediacy.

Since a symbolic meaning is already clear on a first reading of this poem, we might expect subsequent rereadings merely to confirm that meaning. Nevertheless, new dimensions do become apparent as we keep delving into the text: certain words and phrases gradually acquire importance as we go back over them. On our initial reading, the desert seemed mainly part of the symbolic landscape. As we reread the poem, however, we recall the many traditional and literary associations of the desert image, its connotations of sterility, abandonment, loss of hope.[9] Similarly, the word "ceniza" recalls its frequent use in religious evocations of man's temporality; this makes us see the speaker's path as part of man's tragic fate, and his final assertion as an acceptance of that fate combined with a declaration of life's value in the face of it. The images of the desert, of stone, and of "ceniza" therefore form a code which extends the poem's range significantly. By echoing other texts, they set the speaker's quest in the frame of a much larger tradition. They operate, as Santiago Daydí has so well shown, as a system of "resonances" outside the text, but these "resonances" function mainly as clues to a rereading of the poem that greatly increases its significance.[10]

In "El ángel" (pp. 17-18), Valente combines detailed references to a game of dice with a symbolic vision of the protagonist's battle with an angel. By a process of reading and rereading, we come to see the connections between the two levels; the protagonist's action of taking apart a flower and the angel's wielding of his sword of light embody contradictory yet complementary impulses to keep living and to discover the clear principles of things. The patterns thus emerging become more ambiguous and more complex as we keep going over the text and seeing the shifts in focus from the literal details of the dice game to the more fantastic images. Rather than lead us to any neat resolution, the poem leaves us with a sense of the mystery and multiplicity of the basic scheme of life.

In spite of the differences between them, all of the poems from *A modo de esperanza* which I have examined reveal a common thread. In each of them Valente offers a clear and seemingly "realistic" vision or narrative, which in itself holds meaning: "El espejo" conveys the speaker's awareness of aging, "El adiós" the drama of a separation, "Serán ceniza" a quest for life. Yet each of them also leads us, on subsequent readings, to perceive new dimensions created by hitherto unsuspected codes and patterns. Thus the particular awareness of the process of aging becomes, thanks to the code of loss of individuality, a whole sense of the alienation of human life; the drama of separation of the second poem similarly turns into a vision of the tragedy of loss and death. In each case, our double reading allows us to experience these larger visions without losing touch with the specific world from which they emerge.[11]

The theme of death remains important in *Poemas a Lázaro,* written between 1955 and 1960. The book's speaker identifies himself with Lazarus, who comes to stand not only for a man reborn but also for someone immersed in life and dealing with its temporality, its suffering, and its mysteries.[12] In the introductory poem (pp. 61-62) he examines his "history" and tells it in order to deepen his vision and to fit his own life into the larger scheme of human life, poetically seen. The book therefore becomes a portrayal of the patterns of human existence as they emerge from the episodes of one's life.

Again Valente makes use of common objects and specific events. Many of the poems in this book are more discursive than those in *A modo de experanza;* the speaker comments more frequently and more explicitly on the realities presented. Symbolic patterns are more evident, and a "second level" of significance becomes partly discernible from the outset. These shifts do not make the book radically different from the earlier one; rather they intensify the process of making meaning grow gradually from the poem's representational level.

References to art and to poetry are more frequent in *Poemas a Lázaro*, suggesting Valente's increasing concern with his craft. Poems dealing with art and poetry also depend on patterns which motivate rereadings; this procedure, as we shall see, is especially suited to make the reader feel how poetry creates significance and to involve him in the poetic process.

"La llamada" exemplifies Valente's use of language patterns and symbolism to invite rereadings:

> Temprano, en la mañana, la llamada.
> Tal vez es el teléfono que avisa
> y me levanto a ciegas,
> tentando el despertar sin ver su rostro.
>
> Tropiezo en los residuos de la víspera,
> cuanto hay de ayer en hoy me sale al paso,
> y con torpeza y sumisión recojo
> la llamada en el alba, tan temprana.
> "Quién es, quién, quién",
>   Silencio.
> Alquien dice mi nombre y calla luego.
> El despertar se rompe en nueva sombra.
>
> "Quién, quién—repito—, quién tan pronto".
>
> En mil pedazos salta la mañana.
>
> Desde el umbral me llega, tibia y sola,
> la voz de la mujer envuelta en sueño,
> caída aún en la última caricia,
> ("quién era, quién, quién era . . .")
>
>   Se deshacen
> lentamente la luz y las palabras,
> la voz de la mujer resbala lejos,
> muy lejos, más allá
> que la otra voz—allá—de la llamada. [p. 77]

The poem can be read exclusively on the literal level, right up to the last section: it refers to a familiar occurrence, a confusing early-morning telephone call answered by a sleepy protagonist. Valente, however, inserts signs throughout that lead us to expect some further dimension. The "tal vez" in line 2 indicates uncertainty as to what really is happening, while lines 5 ("tropiezo en los residuos") and 8 ("la llamada en la alba") adopt a nonliteral perspective and suggest some symbolic meaning, although there is no way of telling exactly what this meaning might be.

The last nine lines answer our expectations and allow us to undertake a rereading. By making the telephone call a shattering experience that leads the speaker to fade away from the literal reality in which he has been placed, the poem makes this call a summons from beyond—be it from God, from death, from destiny—which obliges him to leave his normal perspective and existence.[13] Once this symbolic dimension is clear, many elements present in the earlier parts of the poem fall into place within it. Margaret Persin has aptly commented on what she terms a "code of uncertainty" in this poem, composed of all the elements which create disjunction and suggest an inability to conciliate the realities of the setting and of the phone call.[14] Behind that disjunction and justifying its presence, however, lies the gradual process of alienation from the real world experienced by the speaker. His uncertainty as to the nature of the event ("tal vez"), his stumbling in the darkness while only half awake (stressed by the image of himself as a blind man), and his general clumsiness all evoke this alienation, and make us see him as moving symbolically away from reality. By connecting "torpeza" and "sumisión" in line 7, Valente links the man's clumsiness and alienation to his obedience to a higher order. Overcoming the impediments of his real past (line 6), the speaker accepts the symbolic call which seems related both to a premature end ("tan temprana") and to the transition to a new vision or life ("alba"). Having been called away from his real existence, he finds himself more and more remote from his setting and from the woman who has been accompanying him: the last two stanzas portray this process of separation, as the woman's inquiry and voice fade into the background and the speaker leaves his past reality behind. The parallel between the woman's fading inquiry and the speaker's earlier question while first answering the call underlines the estrangement produced by the whole experience.

Other patterns support the symbolic scheme I have been noting. The words "temprano," "temprana," "alba," "despertar," "luz" and "mañana" form a code pointing to a new beginning, which of course stands in opposition to the reality being left behind. The verbs of action in the present ("me levanto," "tropiezo," "dice," "repito," "se rompe") stress the speaker's progression from the one to the other. Once the symbolic scheme has become evident, everything in the poem fits into it and supports the theme of transition from the world of reality to one beyond it.

Like the poems studied before, "La llamada" describes a seemingly realistic event which acquires a deeper dimension; also like those poems, it invites a rereading which clarifies and heightens this dimension, making us apprehend and understand the speaker's transition from one perspective and one reality to another. It differs from the other poems, however, in that it offers early clues to the significance of the episode, creates an air of mystery which radically transforms the scene, and turns out to be explicitly symbolic. Like many other works in *Poemas a Lázaro*, "La llamada" seems to charge its representational level with meaning in a more obvious fashion than did "El espejo."

This all seems related to another dimension of the poem, already examined by Persin.[15] As she has indicated, the reader's struggle to understand the reality of the poem reflects the speaker's struggle to understand the mysterious call; in this fashion the reader participates in the poem's process. Extending this interpretation and relating it to the rereading that we have been studying, we might say that the text first offers us a representational level which parallels the representational level of the speaker's experience: he answers a phone call and we witness the event. Yet just as the call seems enigmatic to him, so its real meaning is made enigmatic to us by the clues I have noted; and just as his constant questioning reveals, finally, its symbolic import, so our rereading of the poem reveals its symbolic nature. This makes the reader something of a collaborator of the poem's speaker, and hence a dependent of the poet who is portraying this speaker's experience and creating (as well as discovering) its meaning.[16]

"El sapo" also has a symbolic dimension which is intensified in the process of rereading:

> El sapo melancólico
> de húmeda palabra,
> con pulso de agua humilde,
> transparente y remoto que vibrara
> para llenar el sueño de frescura,
> asesinado yace a mediodía,
> a medio mundo en luz.
>
> Luz breve fue su canto.
>
> Bajo el poder oscuro,
> que acaso presintiera,
> de tanta luz reposa.
> Y ya no puede el aire
> o la memoria de su flauta tenue
> refrescar su garganta.
>
> Mediodía:
> ansiada luz que acepta y que devora.

Un cadáver gravita, pesa sordo
contra la tierra.
Más pesa su silencio.

Pobre muerte mortal de sapo claro
que cae desde su música ligera,
pesadamente muerto para siempre. [p. 108]

Like the other poems we have seen, this one is built on a common and
seemingly trivial scene. Yet the dead toad here portrayed evokes what
at first seems a disproportionately strong emotion in the speaker, who
sees its life and demise in human terms (the toad used words, its killing
was an assassination, it was endowed with memory and forethought).
All of this makes us think of the toad in other than literal terms, and
anticipate a symbolic level. When we come to the end of the work, two
different symbolic strands have become clear. The toad's death has been
presented as the loss of a singer whose art was all too fleeting, and it
has also been made to suggest the tragic finality of human life.

Once these dimensions are clear, we can see how the poem's language leads to and reinforces them. The image of the toad's "humid
word" in line 2 develops into a metaphor of its song as water, which in
turn makes us see this song as a natural art too quickly lost. Valente
creates an opposition between the "brief light" of the toad's song and
the harsh light of noon which reveals its corpse. This opposition is
reinforced by the contrast between the expressions "sueño de frescura"
and "refrescar" on the one hand, and the heat and heaviness of noon
and of the scene of the corpse on the other. These counterpositions
accent the sense of loss, in both the artistic and the more generally
human dimension. Although these patterns can be discerned to some
extent on a first reading of the poem, they become much more significant in successive rereadings, as we take fully into account the larger
tragedy of death stressed in the poem's ending ("pesadamente muerto
para siempre") and move further and further beyond the anecdotal
level.

Although this poem does not involve us in its process the way "La
llamada" did, it refers to the theme of poetic creation. Especially in view
of the many references to the poetic act in *Poemas a Lázaro,* its allusions
to the fleetingness and mortality of song also apply, by extension, to
poetry. "El sapo" thus reinforces the connections between the values
and limitations of life and those of poetry which Valente draws in
Poemas a Lázaro.

The theme of art dominates "El cántaro," which seems very
straightforward in its meaning:

El cántaro tiene la suprema
realidad de la forma,
creado de la tierra
para que el ojo pueda
contemplar la frescura.

El cántaro que existe conteniendo,
hueco de contener se quebraría
inánime. Su forma
existe sólo así,
sonora y respirada.
            El hondo cántaro
de clara curvatura,
bella y servil:
el cántaro y el canto. [p. 104]

The jug here described quickly acquires a symbolic meaning and comes
to represent the fusion of form and function, of aesthetic and practical
value, which the poem envisions as an ideal. But the last stanza brings
in a new dimension and forces a rereading. Suddenly the jug is equated
to a poem, and we must realign the text's message to take this into
account. One might argue that this hardly changes the text's meaning,
since the concept of a work both beautiful and functional applies easily
to poetry. Yet the awareness that it *is* being applied to poetry gives new
significance to specific images and words: "sonora y respirada" calls to
mind the sound of a poem being recited, while "clara curvatura" applies
to the way a poem is printed as well as to the shape of the jug. All of
this, as Persin suggests, involves the reader in a creative process during
the course of a series of rereadings and reappraisals of this seemingly
simple text.[17] And the very fact that we discover new dimensions and
get drawn into the creative process in these rereadings makes the poem
a kind of "tour de force," a demonstration on Valente's part of what a
poet can do with a seemingly simple reality, and of what creative activities can take place in the process of writing and of reading.

One evident characteristic of *La memoria y los signos,* written between 1960 and 1965, is the poet's concern with the historical and social
context in which he grew up and lives. One whole section of the book
focuses on reminiscences of the Civil War and its effects on a number
of people; individual poems of various sections deal with human relationships in the light of social circumstances, with patterns of life and
death in one's family, with specific episodes of the speaker's biography.
But we are constantly made aware that this material is being seen and
interpreted from a poetic perspective: what is important is not just its
evocation but its interpretation and transformation by means of poetic

language. Valente prefaces the volume with a poem titled "La señal," which ends: "Aguardo sólo la señal del canto. / Ahora no sé, ahora sólo espero / saber más tarde lo que he sido" (p. 139). Reality will be discovered as it is remade poetically in the book.

This process of discovery seems to depend on perspective and "resonances" more than on imagery, as Daydí has noted.[18] Valente makes frequent use of a first-person speaker whose interpretation of a scene produces its meaning. He also casts traditional themes in a new light, engendering resonances and intertextual perceptions. The book therefore marks a further step in the increasing use of the speaker as a poetic device which we noted in *Poemas a Lázaro*, and also of the increasing stress on the poetic process and on the involvement of the reader in that process. In *La memoria* intertextual echoes are more frequent than in the previous volume, and the transformation of the poem's representational level is more extensive and more extreme.

Rereading is often crucial to a perception of a poem's meaning, precisely because it clarifies the transformation which occurs and introduces the theme of re-creation. Again and again, the latter part of a poem will contain references to the poetic act which will send us back through the text, making us reinterpret its "story" in the light of this theme. In this fashion Valente leads us to repeat the process of verbal reelaboration, making us participate, as it were, in the discovery of meanings through the poetic act. "Rereading" becomes, even more than heretofore, a form of "rewriting."

"El moribundo" seems to be a description of a dying man's thoughts:

> El moribundo vio
> pasar ante sus ojos signos
> oscuros, rostros olvidados,
> aves de otro país que fuera el suyo
> (mas en un cielo extraño).
>
> Por la ventana abierta entró el terrizo
> color de la tormenta.
> Oyó el rumor de los olivos
> lejos, en su infancia remota,
> azotados ahora.
>
> Quebróse el aire en secos estallidos.
> Vio los campos, el sol,
> el sur, los años, la distancia.
>
> Opaco cielo se extendía
> sobre una tierra ajena.

                                        Y con voz lenta
            reunió lo disperso,
            sumó gestos y nombres,
            calor de tantas manos
            y luminosos días
            en un solo suspiro,
            inmenso, poderoso,
            como la vida.

            Rompió la lluvia al fin el cerco oscuro.
            Dilatóse el recuerdo.
                                        Pueda el canto
            dar fe del que en la lucha
            se había consumado. [p.170]

The last three lines surprise us, interrupting a seemingly "neutral" description of the dying man's recollections with the speaker's hope that
this man's life can be seized in the poem. This invites us to reread the
poem in a totally new light, focusing not so much on the man's recollections in themselves as on their representation in poetry; the poetic
process, rather than a biography, now becomes the subject of the work
and our main concern.

     Once we adopt this perspective, we realize that the man's recollec-
tions have been presented in the fashion of a text and not just as an
anecdote. The poem first refers to these recollections as "signos / os-
curos" (lines 2-3). Later on, the man's recall of his past is presented
as a gathering ("reunió lo disperso") and a process of addition ("sumó
gestos y nombres")—active transformation rather than passive recall.
This leads him to a sigh as powerful as life, a grand and desperate effort
at total expression. From this perspective, the dying man seems to be
a poet organizing the "signifiers" of his life into a newly created text.

     Once we see this, we also pay more attention to the interplay
between the dying man's thoughts and the neutral setting. In stanzas 2
and 3, the sight of a coming storm starts the man's process of recollection; by the end of the poem, the actual arrival of this storm signals its
ending and his death. ("Cerco oscuro" may refer both to the scene
before the storm breaks and to the dying man's confinement on his
deathbed.) Just as the tension in nature is released in the storm, so the
man's re-creation of his memories is released and extended beyond him
at his death. The verb "dilatóse" suggests that his recollections do not
so much end as transcend the limits of his consciousness. This parallel
between the man's process and the natural pattern gives greater significance to his recollections, and intensifies our view of him as a "poet"
recreating his life in harmony with the world surrounding him. And if

the man's dying recollections become a poetic quest, then the whole episode turns into a poem dealing with the conversion of life and memory into poetry.[19]

In other works, the process of re-creation is based on intertextualities and literary allusions. "El sacrificio" (pp. 213-14), for example, portrays a new version of the biblical episode of Abraham and Isaac. Valente dramatically changes the ending, making the son's salvation from death at his father's hand depend not on God's angel but on the boy's wrath and his defeat of the father. Much of the work's effect depends on our awareness that it is a reversal of the traditional story, which not only remakes the plot but also reverses the "moral" and shows us a world in which a god counsels evil and a man must save himself from a sadistic father. After we finish our initial reading of the poem and realize the extent to which it departs from the biblical story, we are forced to go back, to keep rereading the poem and seeing how many details emphasize the reversal. (The facts that Abraham is "furtive," fools his wife, and is obsessed with his power, for example, highlight the change from the positive to the negative.)

"El canto" deals directly with poetic creation and portrays the speaker/poet's high goal of finding an expression that will transcend limited verbal play, redress the major problems of the world, and offer an ideal vision:

> Un canto.
>   Quisiera un canto
> que hiciese estallar en cien palabras ciegas
> la palabra intocable.
>   Un canto.
> . . . .
> Un canto nuevo, mío, de mi prójimo,
> del adolescente sin palabras que espera ser nombrado,
> de la mujer cuyo deseo sube
> en borbotón sangriento a la pálida frente,
> de éste que me acusa silencioso,
> que silenciosamente me combate,
> porque acaso no ignora
> que una sola palabra bastaría
> para arrasar el mundo,
> para extinguir el odio
> y arrastrarnos. [p. 221]

At the end of this long poem, however, the speaker suddenly stands back and questions his whole enterprise: "¿Por este sueño he combatido?" (p. 222). This ending totally denies our expectations. Having seen the speaker assert idealistically the goals of his art, we had come to expect that he would end with some final assertion of his goal. When instead he questions (perhaps even denies) its achievability, we must reread the poem in a new light, this time seeking evidence for the excessive idealism of the vision that was developed, for the clues that made it ultimately impossible. We can find them in the speaker's expectation that one word alone will change the world, in the absolutely clear-cut opposition between the purity of the imagined song and the corruption of the world, and maybe even in the apocalyptic tone. As a result of the reversal at the end and of the subsequent rereading, "El canto" becomes not a clear statement of poetic goals but rather the embodiment of conflict between these goals and the possibility of their fulfillment. The poem's organization and procedure cast us right into the midst of that conflict.

José Olivio Jiménez has studied the theme of a quest for poetic expression in *La memoria y los signos,* noting that the author/speaker sees himself as a poet involved in that quest. (Even the concern with his past and his circumstances is related to his efforts to capture them in verse.) That search, as he indicates, motivates a series of tensions and doubts which add richness to the book.[20] Through the rereading that I have been examining, we are drawn right into those tensions and into the very process of the poet's search, becoming at least partially his collaborators in it and in the examination of human life that it entails.

In each of his first three books of poetry, José Angel Valente presents common scenes and events in such a way as to make us "read" them more than one time and perceive them on more than one level. This not only imparts greater significance to seemingly common subjects, but increasingly involves the reader in a process of discovery and creation being undertaken by the poem's speaker. This involvement is intensified even more in Valente's more recent poetry, which depends primarily on intertextuality to motivate rereading of the text.

In several books published between 1967 and 1970, Valente deals more discursively and in more complex fashion than before with a variety of themes ranging from the alienation of the individual to the ills of social structures. In the process he moves away from the surface realism of his earlier work.[21] His poems now depend even more frequently on allusions and intertextual patterns to lead us through a series of readings and rereadings. By making us recall other texts and by forcing us to counterpose their meanings to those of his work, Valente involves us in complex plays of perspectives. This interplay often makes us create within our own experience some resolution to the tensions we

face in the texts, and makes Valente's more recent poetry even more
dynamic than his earlier work.

   In some poems Valente uses specific allusions to a single given text.
The book *Siete representaciones,* for example, consists of reelaborations of
the "seven deadly sins"; the poem devoted to anger uses references to
the Bible to construct its own vision of this sin and its effects. The very
first lines of the poem evoke the end of the world very much as it is
portrayed in Saint John's Revelations, and more specificially in its
eighth and ninth chapters, in which the angels' trumpets signal the Last
Judgment:

> El día en que los ángeles
> fuercen en las redondas
> esquinas no soñadas de la tierra
> sus ácidos clarines
> y no encuentren respuesta, [p. 243]

Other references to the Bible appear intermittently throughout the
poem: the dead rise as the world ends, only to die again (recalling
Revelations 20:11-14, in which the dead rise up again at the Last Judgment and those condemned suffer a "second death"); lambs attack and
devour wolves (twisting the prophecy of the lamb and the wolf in
harmony with each other at the time of God's Judgment in Isaiah 11:6,
and suggesting a more negative reversal of normal life patterns than
Isaiah envisioned); the images of a banquet and of a "traje impuesto"
evoke the parable of the Last Judgment in Matthew 22:1-14, in which
the wedding guests who do not wear proper attire are condemned. All
these references invite the reader to see the poem as a reelaboration of
the biblical view of the Last Judgment, and to anticipate that the portrayal of God's anger will follow and will presage a final reordering of
the world. The image of lambs devouring wolves may make the reader
question this anticipation, but is not sufficient in itself to destroy his
expectations.

   At the end of the poem the reader is faced by a surprising reversal
—the day described will bring not God's anger and final judgment but
rather man's anger and the destruction of the world: "el día en que la
cólera del mundo / destruya el mundo, el día de la ira" (p. 244). The
phrase "día de la ira" recalls the words and motif of "dies irae," God's
anger in the Last Judgment (see Romans 2:5-8), but redirects it to an
image of human vengeance and destruction. By counterposing this
emerging image to the biblical view of God's anger and judgment,

Valente shocks his reader into the vision of a much more negative universe, the injustices of which can only lead to a purely destructive response on the part of man. All the biblical references and echoes in this poem have served to set up a false expectation of a traditional "healing anger" of God, and finally to break that expectation and leave us facing a universe in which God does not bring justice, and in which the end of the world is a meaningless destruction rather than an ordering judgment. Faced with this surprising ending, we are led to reread the poem from a different perspective, to see all the signs portrayed as clues to the world's collapse in anger, and to develop an ironic attitude toward the prospects of a healing last judgment.

Another specific literary antecedent underlies "Reaparición de lo heroico" from *El inocente* (pp. 370-71). [22] Here Valente recalls books 21 and 22 of *The Odyssey*, in which the returning hero confronts the suitors of Penelope and finally kills them. Valente's poem begins with a speech by the suitor Antinuous, who is portrayed as a cautious, "civilized," and pragmatic being, advocating attention to practical matters and telling his listeners to forget the fantastic deeds of a heroic past. In itself this attitude seems to make sense. Yet when in the middle of the poem we become aware that the speaker is Homer's villain and that the unreal past he is dismissing refers to the heroic deeds of Odysseus, we must modify our reactions and turn against him more than we otherwise would. This awareness may even force us to reexamine our own standards of judgment, to make us wonder if our own tendency to value practicality and reasonableness may not be as reprehensible as those of the suitors.

As the poem develops, it shifts to a third–person perspective and gradually distances us from the suitors' attitudes. Odysseus is presented in a superficially negative fashion as a ragged beggar; yet our knowledge of *The Odyssey* makes us aware that this is the hero with whom we will side. As he prepares to take his vengeance and slay the suitors, the poem's language becomes more illusioned and the third-person narrator describes the battle in more heroic terms, making us abandon any identification with the common-sense suitors and immerse ourselves in Odysseus' act of vengeance. All in all, the shifts in perspective and the intertextual play between this work and *The Odyssey* serve to make us change our attitude to the pragmatic and the heroic, creating within us a dramatic conflict between two attitudes to life.

Our reading of "Reaparación de lo heroico" therefore depends on a blend of Valente's text and the Homeric text that it recalls. The final vision we are offered emerges from the interplay of the two, supporting

Gustavo Pérez Firmat's notion that in cases of intertextuality two texts modify each other and create a whole new text in the reader's experience.[23]

In other cases Valente does not relate his poem to one specific previous work but echoes several possible ones. In "Mar de Muxia" from *Breve son* (p. 262), he evokes traditional Spanish poetry as well as some poems of Rafel Alberti's *Marinero en tierra,* leading us to reread his poem as a new version of a traditional poetic motif, the desire to walk on top of the water. In "Tres canciones de barcas" (pp. 265-66), also from *Breve son,* he combines echoes of traditional sea poems with references to the crossing of the river Styx, counterposing different visions and ultimately making us feel the power of poetry in fusing and recreating diverse motifs. In these poems, as well as in the ones which evoke a single identifiable source, Valente's use of intertextuality involves the reader in the very process of creating the work's meaning. Different as they may appear from Valente's seemingly realistic earlier works, these poems also lead us to a series of readings and rereadings through which we obtain a rich vision of human life. And they illustrate equally well the poet's ability to immerse the reader in a gradual process of discovery that corresponds to his own beliefs about poetry.

7 JAIME GIL DE BIEDMA
The Theme of Illusion

Jaime Gil de Biedma's poems come across on first reading as clear and "realistic." Many of them comprise detailed evocations of specific episodes, narrated by a first-person speaker who gives commentaries and conclusions. Quite often these commentaries offer philosophic insights; at times, especially in the later books, they contain social or political ideas. All of this has led some critics to characterize Gil de Biedma as a realistic poet proccupied with ethical and social issues.[1] The very clarity of his work has caused readers to miss its depth and originality.

Several critics have begun to modify such interpretations. Pere Gimferrer has indicated that the specific details present in this poetry create subjective meanings and experiences, and allow Gil de Biedma to embody such meanings effectively, avoiding hollow generalizations. Gimferrer has also pointed out that Gil uses natural language artistically. Approaching the poetry from another angle, José Olivio Jiménez has observed that it is based on a dialectic between reality and unreality: despite all the realistic details present in them, Gil's poems transform or evade a literal perspective. At times, a description is transformed by an inquisitive commentary; at others, it dissolves or turns into a dream. More often than not, Jiménez suggests, these poems convey the unreality of our lives.[2]

Taken together, these studies belie the notion of Gil's poetry as simple, stressing its value as an artful exploration of significant issues. They also make clear that subjectivity and illusion are in the final analysis key elements of this poetry. Yet they leave basically unanswered the question of how this poetry transforms and transcends its realistic materials. To deal with this issue, I will examine carefully individual poems, paying particular attention to the ways in which specific scenes, images, and details are presented and modified. This will let us see how Gil de Biedma uses language and perspectives to create subjective experiences which often differ significantly from the overt subject of the poem.

In examining closely the poems of Gil de Biedma, we will notice
that the very theme of illusion, its relation to apparent "realities," and
the complicated relationships between illusion and reality emerge again
and again in poems which seemingly deal with other subjects. The role
of illusion is an underlying theme in poems which seem to describe
social classes and in works that apparently narrate specific love episodes
or everyday events. Although in many cases the theme of illusion is
related to the view of life as unreal, it also has other dimensions and
appears in a wide variety of works with differing visions and emphases.
Illusions also become, at times, significant realities in their own right,
and the power of illusion a positive force.

Gil de Biedma's first major book of poetry, *Compañeros de viaje,*
contains works written between 1952 and 1958. The theme of time
passing dominates this book, fitting it into a general current of Spanish
poetry of the late 1950s.[3] Most of the poems of this volume focus on
specific episodes, and from them derive wider perceptions regarding
temporality: childhood remembrances evoke an awareness of loss in
some poems, a sense of the limitations of middle-class existence in
others; a chance encounter suggests an idea of mortality. The real originality of the book, however, may lie elsewhere. Its philosophic insights
on time and on life's values do not stand as neat messages but form part
of very paradoxical experiences. At times the final "meaning" of the
poem is different from the apparent "message"; often it emerges from
a conflict between diverse attitudes which undercut each other. By
selecting words and by handling perspective, Gil de Biedma produces
rich visions in poems of apparent simplicity. Again and again the subject
of illusion turns out to be central to the poem's meaning, although its
presence may not be apparent at first.

This is the case in "Idilio en el café," a seemingly simple work which
describes the speaker's attitude as he sits in a café, feels a sense of
strangeness, and goes out in the night with his loved one. The scene of
lovers on a starlit night, with which the poem ends, is so conventional
that it tempts us to see the work as a romantic portrayal of love and
union. Yet the poem offers instead a paradoxical view of reality and
illusion:

> Ahora me pregunto si es que toda la vida
> hemos estado aquí. Pongo, ahora mismo,
> la mano ante los ojos—qué latido
> de la sangre en los párpados—y el vello
> inmenso se confunde, silencioso,
> a la mirada. Pesan las pestañas.

No sé bien de qué hablo. ¿Quiénes son,
rostros vagos nadando como en un agua pálida,
éstos aquí sentados, con nosotros vivientes?
La tarde nos empuja a ciertos bares
o entre cansados hombres en pijama.

Ven. Salgamos fuera. La noche. Queda espacio
arriba, más arriba, mucho más que las luces
que iluminan a ráfagas tus ojos agrandados.
Queda también silencio entre nosotros,
silencio
        y este beso igual que un largo túnel. [p. 38]

The title in itself suggests some tension: a café is not the usual
location for an "idilio." Any sense of confusion produced by this is
reinforced throughout the poem by the speaker's own confusion, as he
keeps questioning the experience he is undergoing ("ahora me pregunto," "no sé bien de qué hablo"). This places the "event" in a puzzling
and subjective frame, and leads the implied reader to stand back, to
examine the speaker's statements rather than be carried away by them,
and to seek wider dimensions to the event—preparing us for the emergence of the poem's final meaning.

Looking at the work as a whole, we notice a disproportion between
the amount of space and emphasis devoted to the café scene and to the
scene of the lovers in the night. The former really dominates the poem:
most of the details given describe the speaker and his surroundings,
before the beloved is even mentioned. When love does emerge in stanza
3 it is dealt with quickly and with little descriptive detail. Despite the
title, the "idilio" actually occurs *outside* the café, after and in opposition
to the scene described at length in the first two stanzas.

Taking this into account, we begin to pay attention to the contrast
between the dominant coffee house scene and the subsequent love
scene. Focusing on the contrast, we notice its paradoxical features. Despite the length of the description and the profusion of details accorded
to it, the coffee house scene comes out distorted and unclear, and produces confusion in the speaker. By observing his eyelashes and the
magnified hairs on his hand as he holds it in front of his face, he actually
blocks out any objective perception of the scene. In stanza 2 he sees the
people in the café as if they were in a dream: their faces are watery
reflections and the scene ends with a never-explained evocation of bars
and pajama-dressed men which seems to confuse the literal scene of the
café with some fantasy. The sentence "No sé bien de qué hablo" underlines the subjectivity and confusion of this whole picture. For all its

detail and despite the space devoted to it, the café scene ends up being enigmatic and meaningless.

Conversely, and despite its brevity and lack of detail, the love scene at the end acquires a clear meaning. Although the outdoors is devoid of the specific objects and figures present in the café and is described only in terms of space, of silence, and of the beloved's eyes, it embodies a sense of union between the lovers: it is here that the "idilio" can actually take place. Lack of detail, silence, emptiness—these are the characteristics that provide the setting for the love to occur and for the poem's meaning to emerge.

This paradoxical contrast lies at the heart of the poem. Immersion in details did not offer clear meanings; the speaker's attempts to gain insight by examining the café and his physical self only led to greater confusion. It is only when he goes out into a world of space and silence that he focuses on the beloved and obtains a positive vision, and that we can see the "idilio" take place. (Its occurence at the end is underlined by the mythic picture of the loved one's enlarged eyes illuminated by the stars.) What seemed most literally and specifically concrete (eyebrows, eyelashes, faces, bars, men) turns out to be a meaningless, dreamy illusion; what was most illusive (lovers in silence and space) emerges as real.

José Olivio Jiménez has used this poem as an example of Gil de Biedma's way of dissolving reality. But it is more than that.[4] In the final analysis, "Idilio en el café" explores the whole theme of reality and illusion, creating a vision in which the illusory is fundamentally real and the superficially "real" is but a confusing, meaningless dream. Through language and perspective Gil de Biedma has constructed, out of a simple vignette, a vivid representation of this vision.

But illusions are not always so positive, and their relationship to reality and meaning vary. In "Infancia y confesiones," Gil de Biedma deals with different kinds of illusions while examining his middle-class social background:

> Cuando yo era más joven
> (bueno, en realidad, será mejor decir
> muy joven)
>   algunos años antes
> de conoceros y
> recién llegado a la ciudad,
> a menudo pensaba en la vida.
>   Mi familia
> era bastante rica y yo estudiante.

> Mi infancia eran recuerdos de una casa
> con escuela y despensa y llave en el ropero,
> de cuando las familias
> acomodadas,
>   como su nombre indica,
> veraneaban infinitamente
> en *Villa Estefanía* o en *La Torre*
> *del Mirador*
>   y más allá continuaba el mundo
> con senderos de grava y cenadores
> rústicos, decorado de hortensias pomposas,
> todo ligeramente egoísta y caduco.
> Yo nací (perdonadme)
> en la edad de la pérgola y el tenis. [p. 47]

On first impression, the poem seems pure anecdote. Its speaker begins by calling attention to himself and recalling his youth, making us expect typical reminiscences of youth. His way of "correcting" himself in lines 2 and 3 intensifies this impression, and by addressing his readers as friends whom he met some time ago, he makes us adopt the perspective of people listening to a friend reminisce. All of this seems calculated to make us expect a casual narration of ordinary realities.

Our expectations seem to be fulfilled as the poem unfolds. The facts mentioned by the speaker reveal a typical middle-class childhood, and even his thoughts ("a menudo pensaba en la vida") illustrate typical adolescent concerns. The rhythm of the poem also accents the impression of an ordinary narration. Using free verse, caesuras, and run-on lines, Gil de Biedma creates an interrupted, conversational flow. In places he alters normal word order ("Mi familia / era bastante rica y yo estudiante"), creating a sense of casual meandering. The style corresponds to a very ordinary telling of a very ordinary upper middle-class life, with no illusions on the part of either the speaker or the people portrayed. (The emphasis on the "despensa" and the locked closets suggests this society's primary concern with material property.)

Yet the last part of this section introduces a different note. The names and descriptions of the summer places suggest a certain kind of grasping at illusions, pedestrian though they might seem. "La Torre del Mirador" indicates an attempt to turn the villa into a castle; the garden paths and decorations suggest a certain pretentiousness, and perhaps the social climbing instincts of the "nouveau riche." The reality of this middle class contains its own quite unimaginative and unpoetic seeking of illusions. The speaker's attitude to this, we notice, is far from objective. By referring to the families as "acomodadas, / como su nombre

indica" he stresses their materialism; by using the adjective "infi-
nitamente" he underlines their idleness and the emptiness of their life
and "ideals"; at the end of the section he emits a direct judgment
("ligeramente egoísta y caduco") on this society. As a result of all this,
what started out as a factual portrayal turns into a critical assessment
of the cheap illusions of a society by a speaker who, at least by implication, holds higher ideals.

The theme of illusions is underlined by a clear reference to a poem
of Antonio Machado and by possible echoes of Machado's work in
general. Line 10 ("Mi infancia eran recuerdos de una casa") almost
paraphrases the beginning of Machado's "Retrato": "Mi infancia son
recuerdos de un patio de Sevilla."[5] The intertextuality sets this poem of
Gil de Biedma's in the context of Machado's meditative poetry and of
his constant concern with ideals lost and recalled. Gil's poem, unlike
Machado's works, recalls a rather limited life and limited illusions. (The
contrast is heightened by the difference between the positive images
and the affirmative tone of "Retrato" on the one hand, and the anecdotal
perspective of "Infancia y confesiones" on the other.) Yet the speaker's
implied desire for some ideal higher than those of the vacationing bourgeois would fit the spirit of Machado's work.

The last part of this description, and the speaker's evaluation, constitute of course a commentary on society and justify this text as a
"social poem." But their meaning goes beyond that of a simple message
on the idleness of the upper middle class. In the context of the poem's
beginning and of the echoes of Machado, they make us aware that some
sort of illusion inevitably intrudes into the most factual reality and the
most factual description. The "familias acomodadas" display their limited illusions in the summer estates; the speaker asserts his illusions in
condemning their idleness and their "cursilería" and in apologizing for
having been born into that world.

This impression of the inevitable intrusion of illusions is confirmed
in the last part of the poem:

> La vida, sin embargo, tenía extraños límites
> y lo que es más extraño: una cierta tendencia
> retráctil.
>   Se contaban historias penosas,
> inexplicables sucedidos
> dónde no sé sabía, caras tristes,
> sótanos fríos como templos.
>   Algo sordo
> perduraba a lo lejos

y era posible, lo decían en casa,
quedarse ciego de un escalofrío.

De mi pequeño reino afortunado
me quedó esta costumbre de calor
y una imposible propensión al mito. [pp. 47-48]

In the most obvious sense, this section marks the failure of the escapist illusions of the upper middle-class world. Their carefully created pseudoparadise of villas and garden paths cannot hide sorrowful and tragic happenings which the speaker soon comes to discover. (By finding in their life a "tendencia / retráctil," the speaker dramatizes the intrusion of the past, or the way in which the present focuses back into it.) In that sense, cheap illusions cannot hide past realities.

In another sense, we can see this irruption of the past as the irruption of new illusions for the speaker. The stories of past sufferings offered him mysterious visions which seem to have given him a welcome relief from the bourgeois world in which he had been living. Negative though they may have been, the "historias penosas" clearly contained an element of romance lacking in his daily world. This becomes clear in the last stanza, in which the speaker notes that he brought with him "una imposible propensión al mito." One might argue that such a "propensión" occurred in reaction against the pettiness of his surroundings; but it must have been fueled, inevitably, by the undercurrent of mysterious stories from the past. His very mention of "caras tristes" and "sótanos fríos como templos" indicates his ability to recall those stories and the effects they have had on him. (Here again he resembles the speaker of many poems of Machado.)

How can we pull together these varied impressions of realities and illusions irrupting on each other? Rather than try to find a logical scheme for their resolution, we can step back and mark one constant which underlies the poem. Throughout its development it undercuts each "reality," and perhaps also each "illusion," with another one. The "reality" of the literal-minded bourgeois world turns out to be filled with its own petty illusions, and is attacked by the implicit illusions of a better society in the speaker's critical comments; the bourgeois illusions are undercut by the tragic stories of the past—which serve, in turn, to give the speaker some basis for his myths and illusions of the future. All this finally conveys the impossiblity of disentangling a single "reality," or perhaps a single clear perspective on what is "real" beyond illusions. One person's reality may be another's illusion; different realities and illusions succeed and modify each other in a chain of shifting perspectives. The reference to Machado's "Retrato" extends this chain further, making Gil de Biedma's whole poem part of a tradition of searching for illusions in poetry.

The speaker's bourgeois background is again evoked in "Ampliación de estudios." This poem, too, is centered on the issue of realities and illusions. Looking back at his past, the speaker realizes that what then seemed most significant turned out to be a falsification of what was going on; his past ideals were perhaps no more than escapist pleasures:

> esa efusión imprevista, esa imperiosa
> revelación de otro sentido posible, más profundo
> que la injusticia o el dolor, esa tranquilidad
> de absolución, que yo sentía entonces,
> ¿no eran sencillamente la gratificación furtiva
> del burguesito en rebeldía
> que ya sueña con verse
> *tel qu'en Lui-même enfin l'éternité le change?* [p. 54]

A critical view of the middle-class world dominates this poem. Yet as so often occurs in the work of Gil de Biedma, as in that of other poets of this generation, a philosophic issue underlies the social theme. (Possible echoes of "Institución Libre de Enseña" contribute to the impression of a philosophic reassessment in progress here.) And the resolution of the poem is at least somewhat ambiguous. Although the contented feeling of the past seems to be the "illusion," and the socially critical posture of the ending the "reality," the poem ends with a question, leaving room for doubt.

A number of poems in *Compañeros de viaje* contrast past and present perspectives, suggesting that the realities of the past are twisted into illusions which give some value to the present. This idea emerges clearly in "Aunque sea un instante":

> el eterno temor que tiene nuestro rostro
> nos asalta, gritamos invocando el pasado
> —invocando un pasado que jamás existió—
>
> para creer al menos que de verdad vivimos
> y que la vida es más que esta pausa inmensa,
> vertiginosa,
> cuando la propia vocación, aquello
> sobre lo cual fundamos un día nuestro ser,
> el nombre que le dimos a nuestra dignidad
> vemos que no era más
> que un desolador deseo de esconderse. [p. 39]

In similar fashion, in "Recuerda" (p. 40), past illusions are an attempt to overcome the destruction which the speaker fears time will inflict upon him. The theme of the battle between realities and illusions is inextricably linked to the theme of time in this book.

It would be impossible to find a single scheme for the play of realities and illusions in *Compañeros de viaje*. Rather than offer a clear view or message on this topic, Gil de Biedma forges different ways in which these elements play against each other in human life. He uses specific scenes and recollections, carefully manipulated by language and perspective, to involve the reader in a complex vision of reality and illusion.

Moralidades contains poems written by Gil de Biedma between 1959 and 1964. The book creates a greater impression of objectivity than *Compañeros de viaje:* it refers to specific episodes in the speaker's life, there are fewer reflective commentaries, and sensorial perceptions are more integrated into the presentation of events.[6] This is not to say, however, that the meanings of these poems are any less subjective or original than those of the earlier ones. Even more than before, Gil de Biedma uses his language to endow the episodes described with significance.[7]

The theme of illusion pervades the whole work. Again and again, the speaker evokes a present or past episode which involves his illusions and stands out against the limiting realities of his life. Although in some poems illusions are merely a way of escaping unpleasant matters, in most cases they are seen more positively. Often they allow the speaker to create a more compelling vision than would be possible otherwise. Again and again, Gil de Biedma uses his imagery and his perspective to make his reader feel the tensions and interplays between realities and illusions, and to suggest that they underlie the very essence of life.

"De aquí a la eternidad" reaches beyond its seeming subject, an evocation of Madrid, to portray realities and illusions coming together in the perspective of its speaker. As he arrives in the city, this speaker looks at various places, evokes various memories of his youthful life, and combines past and present into an illusioned view. The work begins with a closeup of his feelings:

> Lo primero, sin duda, es este ensanchamiento
> de la respiración, casi angustioso.
> Y la especial sonoridad del aire,
> como una gran campana en el vacío,
> acercándome olores

de jara de la sierra,
más perfumados por la lejanía,
y de tantos veranos juntos
de mi niñez. [p. 91]

By focusing on the sensations produced in him at the moment of arrival
in the city, the speaker immerses us in a specific happening. Its specificity is heightened by the mixture of sensations—smells and sounds
become fused, producing something akin to synaesthesia—and related
to memories of the past. As a result, what could otherwise have been
a sterotypical commonplace, the recall of one's past as one returns to the
native land, becomes a very immediate experience.

As the speaker sees various parts of the city come into view, he
interprets them:

Luego está la glorieta
preliminar, con su pequeño intento de jardín,
mundo abreviado, renovado y puro
sin demasiada convicción, y al fondo
la previsible estatua y el pórtico de acceso
a la magnífica avenida,
a la famosa capital.

Y la vida, que adquiere
carácter panorámico,
inmensidad de instante también casi angustioso
—como de amanecer en campamento
o portal de belén—, la vida va espaciándose
otra vez bajo el cielo enrarecido
mientras que aceleramos. [p. 91]

All the specific elements of the scene are transformed by the subjective
perspective, and reveal something about the speaker. Seeing the
"glorieta" as a "mundo abreviado," he demonstrates his interest in a
limiting order: using the adjectives "magnífica" and "famosa," he shows
his awareness of the traditional values and myths of the capital and
seems to view them as he might have done in his childhood. A note of
irony intrudes here, and continues throughout the poem. The illusions
of the past are negative as well as positive, and fuse with reality as the
speaker enters Madrid.

The last part of this section seems more puzzling. The sense of life
opening up and stretching out is appropriate enough, but why select
the images of a camping and a creche or birthplace? The explanation

must lie within the speaker: his return to the city and the illusions of his youth brings forth the theme of births and deaths, beginnings and ends. We notice that this instant is called "angustioso," echoing the "ensanchamiento / de la respiración, casi angustioso" of stanza 1. The anguish can only be the speaker's, based on his perception of life's limitations and problems. In the light of this, the sense of acceleration and of life spreading may refer not only to the specifics of the trip but also to the speaker's awareness of the larger issues of life.

This becomes even clearer in the next section of the poem, in which the speaker evokes scenes from his past:

> Porque hay siempre algo más, algo espectral
> como invisiblemente sustraído,
> y sin embargo verdadero.
> Yo pienso en zonas lívidas, en calles
> o en caminos perdidos hacia pueblos
> a lo lejos, igual que en un belén,
> y vuelvo a ver esquinas de ladrillo injuriado
> y pasos a nivel solitarios, y miradas
> asomándose a vernos, figuras diminutas
> que se quedan atrás para siempre, en la memoria,
> como peones camineros. [p. 92]

His contemplation of Madrid and the illusions and insights it engenders have led him fully into his past, stylized into a cliché scene and yet fundamentally and perennially true. The speaker again focuses on the present in the poem's ending; yet even when he does so, illusions of a past, fanciful Madrid of *zarzuela* days intrude:

> Cuando el rojo se apague torceremos
> a la derecha,
> hacia los barrios bien establecidos
> de una vez para todas, con marquesas
> y cajistas honrados de insigne tradición.
> Ya estamos en Madrid, como quien dice. [p. 92]

The overt subject of this poem, the speaker's feeling on arriving in Madrid, has turned out to be merely the backdrop for an interplay between present observations of reality and illusioned remembrances of the past. By first immersing us in the speaker's experience on seeing the city, and then revealing his interpretation of these experiences in the light of childhood memories, the poem has exemplified an interplay between observation and recall which leads finally to a deeper awareness of life. When, at the end, it leaves us with the speaker witnessing the present and yet weaving his memories into it, "De aquí a la eternidad" makes us feel that observation, remembrance, and transformation have become all bound together. The final "reality" (and subject) of this poem is not just Madrid observed, nor Madrid remembered from childhood, nor Madrid recreated to fit its traditional image, nor even a philosophic message, but rather an interplay between various perspectives coming together in the experience of one human being.

"París, postal del cielo" describes the way in which another city becomes an illusion. The title focuses on Paris not as a real place but as a transformed version of the imagined beauty portrayed by postcards. The speaker calls attention to himself and makes us see his trip to Paris as a romantic adventure.

> Ahora, voy a contaros
> cómo también yo estuve en París, y fui dichoso.
>
> Era en los buenos años de mi juventud,
> los años de abundancia
> del corazón, cuando dejar atrás padres y patria
> es sentirse más libre para siempre, y fue
> en verano, aquel verano
> de la huelga y las primeras canciones de Brassens,
> y de la hermosa historia
> de casi amor. [p. 89]

By referring to the love affair he is about to describe as "casi amor" while dwelling on the setting and on a traditionally romantic epoch of youth, the speaker evokes an illusioned romance rather than an intense love. This is borne out by the ensuing description of the affair: the beloved is a student from the United States who finds Paris "too romantic," and the motivating factor for the affair seems to be the city's beauty and vague romantic longings.

Given all this, the poem's denouement seems surprising: the speaker first imagines his beloved, now old, recalling the affair; he then describes his own memory and dream:

> Como sueño vivido hace ya mucho tiempo,
> como aquella canción
> de entonces, así vuelve al corazón,
> en un instante, en una intensidad, la historia
> de nuestro amor,
> confundiendo los días y sus noches, [p. 90]

As a dream recalled, the love affair acquires an importance which it did not have when it took place. It is now "nuestro amor" rather than merely "historia de casi amor"; it maintains its intensity (or gains intensity) across time; it becomes an ideal memory for the speaker. He has transformed a limited past into a significant illusion, making it much more compelling. In this sense, we could say that the real theme of the poem is the significant role that illusion plays in determining the meanings of life and memory, and the way in which it is woven inextricably into apparently factual "realities." The focus on the speaker and the dramatic change within this text make us discover this theme as the work unfolds.

A similar view of illusion underlies "Canción de aniversario," in which the speaker sees the value of his marriage increasing because of the illusions developed over time. After noting all the negative aspects of their life together, he says to his wife:

> La vida no es un sueño, tú ya sabes
> que tenemos tendencia a olvidarlo.
> Pero un poco de sueño, no más, un si es no es
> por esta vez, callándonos
> el resto de la historia, y un instante
> —mientras que tú y yo nos deseamos
> feliz y larga vida en común—, estoy seguro
> que no puede hacer daño. [p. 106]

In several other poems, illusions are willfully created and asserted in order to combat the dreariness of everyday existence. In "Albada" (pp. 84-85), for example, the speaker makes love to a woman and ignores the limitations of the experience in an effort to find something more positive than the routine work that awaits him.

The value of art as a creation of illusions is dealt with in "Trompe l'oeil," subtitled "A la pintura de Paco Todó," and obviously based on a contemplation of Todó's painting:

> Indiscutiblemente no es un mundo
> para vivir en él.
>
> Esas antenas,
> cuyas complicaciones, sobre el papel, adquieren
> una excesiva deliberación,
> y lo mismo esos barcos como cisternas madres
> amamantando a los remolcadores,
> son la flora y la fauna de un reino manual,

> de una experiencia literal
> mejor organizada que la nuestra.
>
> Aunque la vaguedad quede en el fondo
> —la dulce vaguedad del sentimiento,
> que decía Espronceda—, suavizando
> nuestra visión del tándem y la azada,
> de todos cuantos útiles importa conocer.
>
> (Como aquellos paisajes, en la Geografía
> Elemental de Efetedé,
> con ríos y montañas abriéndose hacia el mar,
> mientras el tren, en primer término,
> enfila el viaducto junto a la carretera,
> por donde rueda solitariamente
> un automóvil Ford, Modelo T.) [p. 93]

The poem begins with a paradox: although this world portrayed in the painting is literally unreal and not to be lived in, it offers something superior to our reality. By using animal imagery to describe the ships in the painting, Gil de Biedma suggests that they are in some sense more alive than "real" ships, in addition to being better formed (line 10). Art may be an illusion, but it is also more "real" than everyday reality.

Stanze 3 carries this idea further: if art softens the objects of our life, it endows them with something more than literal value, making them appeal to sensations and emotions rather than just to our practical sense. (A diluted picture of a bicycle for two gives us something interesting to look at, not just an inexpensive means of transportation to our next appointment.) The reference to Espronceda not only evokes the emotive vision of the romantics but at least indirectly makes us connect the creative process of painting with that of poetry, and makes the poem a commentary on the stylization and subjectification of all art. And even the poet's selection of a bicycle for two as an example of a "reality" seems more than accidental: such a bicycle already strikes us as unusual and is linked with memories from the early part of this century. Gil de Biedma seems to be emphasizing the fanciful and the imaginative.

By evoking, parenthetically, a childhood geography text, stanza 4 connects the illusion produced by the painting with one created in grade school long before. The details recalled not only stress the neatness of the scene but also portray it in motion (the scene opens out, the train and the car move). The speaker is not recalling the literal static picture in the book but rather the sense of real life and motion that it once produced in him. Hence the details of the book, like those of the painting, are more "alive" than literal reality. The reference to a model T Ford not only places this book in the past but gives it a quaintness which increases its imaginative appeal (much as the bicycle-built-for-two did).

All in all, the poem has made us feel the power of illusion (in art and in memory), its ability to create experiences more exciting than literal reality. Although our illusions may come from worlds in which we cannot live pragmatically (lines 1 and 2), they create a life of their own in our imaginations and memories. This becomes explicit in the ending of the poem:

> Que la satisfacción de la nostalgia
> por el reino ordenado, grande y misterioso
> de la tercera realidad
> no sólo está en el vino y en las categorías:
> también hacen soñar estas imágenes
> con un mundo mejor.
>
> Las lecciones de cosas siempre han sido románticas
> —posiblemente porque interpretamos
> los dealles al pie de la letra
> y el conjunto en sentido figurado. [pp. 93-94]

Dreams of illusions recalled or artfully created offer a depth (a third dimension) better than objects, facts, or ideas, and lead us beyond our limits. Although the details of those illusions are very tangible (we interpret them literally), they add up to an overall reality made larger by the imagination.

Since "Trompe l'oeil" deals with illusions created by painting, it implicitly reflects on the role of art as a way of building idealized visions and expressing the human imagination. But the poem should not be reduced to a conceptual statement on the power of art: its declarative ending merely ties down the experience previously engendered in the reader, who through the poem's images has come to feel the vividness of illusions.

The view of illusion which dominates *Moralidades* is intensified by a notion of Gil de Biedma that the imagination (dream, memory) actually transforms and governs our real lives. This is made explicit in "En una despedida":

> acaso resucite un viejo sueño
> sabido y olvidado.
> El sueño de ser buenos y felices.
>
> Porque sueño y recuerdo tienen fuerza
> para obligar la vida,
> aunque sean no más que un límite imposible. [p. 127]

Illusions, far from being an escape, are a way of putting into action insights that raise us above our limitations. And poetry, as is apparent in "El juego de hacer versos," can be a means of engendering these illusions and highlighting the best of life: "La manera que tiene / sobre todo en verano / de ser un paraíso." (p. 136). By forging such a vision of poetry and illusion in his very images, Gil de Biedma has made it "prove itself" and come alive within the reader of *Moralidades.*

If in *Compañeros de viaje* the theme of illusion appeared indirectly and at times enigmatically, in *Moralidades* it becomes much more evident and central. The value attributed to illusion is also simpler and clearer. Where in the earlier book illusions and realities interplayed to form an enigmatic and complex vision, in the latter one illusions become the means of asserting a significant view of life and liberating oneself from the confines of the matter-of-fact. And just as the theme of illusion becomes more dominant, so the poems become more forceful in asserting its value. Yet this book, like the earlier one, still transforms ordinary scenes and episodes into subjective experiences which convey this value.

In *Poemas póstumos,* Gil de Biedma's most recent book of verse, the subject of illusion is less dominant, more intertwined with other themes. The book is even more meditative and philosophic than the earlier ones and contains many works in which the speaker considers the passing of time and his own aging, and in the light of these examines himself and the values of his life.[8] Illusions appear as part of this process of self-examination; they are often viewed more pessimistically than heretofore, since they represent past hopes which did not materialize, or desperate desires to overcome limitations. In the most compelling poems of the book, however, we find an interplay of realities and illusions which recalls *Compañeros de viaje,* and offers rich and surprising perspectives on life. These poems are, even on first impression, less "realistic" than Gil de Biedma's earlier works. A close reading of them, with special attention to the theme of illusion, still reveals how the poet uses language and perspective play to enrich his overt meanings.

In "Contra Jaime Gil de Biedma," the poet divides himself into two characters and has one side of himself, a sober protagonist, adress the other, a playful bohemian:

> De qué sirve, quisiera yo saber, cambiar de piso,
> dejar atrás un sótano más negro
> que mi reputación—y ya es decir—,
> poner visillos blancos
> y tomar criada,

renunciar a la vida de bohemio,
si vienes luego tú, pelmazo
embarazoso huésped, memo vestido con mis trajes,
zángano de colmena, inútil, cascaseno, [p. 142]

As the monologue unfolds, the speaker attacks his "other self" more and more violently, arguing that his youthful casualness does not fit an aging man; the other merely replies that the speaker is getting old. The conflict between the two embodies an internal strife between youthful impulses and a melancholy awareness of time and age. And although the speaker, by taking the "serious" role, seems to give greater weight to the latter, he has to confess that he too is weak and confused at times when his other self is strong. The ending, in which the two go to bed together, makes us witness their joining in a paradoxical mix of love and hate.

The technique of this poem makes the debate between sobriety and fantasy, and by implication between disillusion and illusion, a dramtic event witnessed with some puzzlement by the reader. No clear resolution is offered, nor does one seem called for: the work's value resides in its way of embodying the issue.

The poet again splits himself in two in "Después de la muerte de Jaime Gil de Biedma," and has one side meditating about the life of his now-deceased other self. The events he recalls are replete with youthful illusions and happy episodes from the past:

Y las noches también de libertad completa
en la casa espaciosa, toda para nostros
lo mismo que un convento abandonado,
y la nostalgia de puertas secretas,
. . . .
Fue un verano feliz.
                    . . . *El último verano*
de nuestra juventud, dijiste a Juan
en Barcelona al regresar
nostálgicos, [p. 161]

He then recalls in some detail the disagreeable death of the other, presenting it in literal terms. In the last part of the poem he focuses on his own survival through the writing of poetry:

Yo me salvé escribiendo
después de la muerte de Jaime Gil de Biedma.

De los dos eras tú quien mejor escribía.
Ahora sé hasta qué punto tuyos eran
el deseo de ensueño y la ironía,
la sordina romántica que late en los poemas
míos que yo prefiero, por ejemplo en *Pandémica* ...
A veces me pregunto
cómo será sin ti mi poesía.

Aunque acaso fui yo quien te enseñó.
Quien te enseñó a vengarte de mis sueños,
por cobardía, corrompiéndolos. [p. 162]

The puzzling interplay of the two selves does not lead to an easy resolution.[9] Yet we note distinctions between the survivor and his other self: whereas the latter provided poetic inspiration, dreams, and illusions, the former taught him how to corrupt dreams—clearly the survivor seems less of an idealist. (In light of this, the death of his other self can be linked to a loss of youthful ideals and illusions.) Nevertheless, it is this less idealistic survivor who saves himself from destruction through poetry—and who has gone on to write this very poem in which his other self's values and illusions are now preserved.

By dividing the speaker into a living and a dead poet, by distinguishing between them, and by the metapoetic suggestions within the text, this poem has involved us in a play of perspectives which juggles positive and negative visions, illusions and disillusions. At least implicitly, it makes us feel that while youthful illusions are subject to an inevitable death, it is poetry's task somehow to keep them alive.

An ambiguous view of youthful illusions also underlies "Himno a la juventud" (pp. 151-152). Youth is presented as a hope which attracts all men; yet it is represented as a sexually attractive female and described in physical detail ("nalgas maliciosas," "sonrosados pechos diminutos"). This undercuts any possible solemnity and introduces an ironic level, making us see youthful glory as attractive yet clearly limited. The speaker adopts an ironic posture at various points in the text; at the very end he has all beings following this seductive youth / nymphette: "que te siguen los hombres y los perros, / los dioses y los ángeles / y los arcángeles / los tronos, las abominaciones ..." (p. 152). The heterogeneous catalogue, and the twist in the list of angels (the traditional category "dominaciones" becomes "abominaciones") turns all into comedy. While this does not completely destroy the view of youthful ideals as positive, it emphasizes its limitation from the perspective of an ironic, world-weary witness, and leaves us with a mixed view of illusions. More importantly, it embodies this mixed view in a set of surprising images and perspectives which make for compelling poetry.

By examining the ways in which the theme of illusion emerges in diverse poems and books of Jaime Gil de Biedma, we have seen how dominant this theme is in his work, and how the interplay between illusions and realities underlies all of it. More importantly yet, the tracing of this theme in various poems has enabled us to see how Gil de Biedma manipulates vocabulary, imagery, perspective, and intertextual references to expand apparently simple poems, giving them dimensions which are not apparent on their "plot" level.[10] Like the other salient poets of his era, he offers us a work richer and far more artful than its external form would indicate.

8 CARLOS SAHAGÚN
Metaphoric Transformation

Carlos Sahagún's poetry calls less attention to itself than that of most other Spanish writers of the 1960s. We do not find in it the novel use of colloquial expressions that characterizes Angel González and Gloria Fuertes, nor the surprising changes and reappraisals typical of José Angel Valente, nor the alternation of linguistic codes used by Claudio Rodríguez. The language of Sahagún's verse seems ordinary but never blatantly colloquial; his works often consist of easy-to-understand evocations of past experiences, expressed in a low key.[1] They contain many visual images and make use of some metaphors, but these tend to be conventional and unsurprising. Yet Sahagún manages to use seemingly unremarkable images and metaphors to transform the scenes he describes and the subjects he deals with. Again and again a seemingly common metaphor leads the reader to a new and surprising way of viewing reality; this view extends on through the poem or group of poems, and produces a compelling experience. By studying metaphors and metaphorical transformation in Sahagún's poetry, we will be able to explain more precisely its artfulness, the way in which it weaves significant meanings out of rather ordinary materials.

The process of metaphorical transformation is already apparent in Sahagún's second book, *Profecías del agua,* published in 1958. Like most of Sahagún's poetry, this volume is dominated by remembrances of youth: the speaker evokes a positive view of his childhood, setting it against later discoveries of the limitations and tragedies of life. This view comes to exemplify an idealistic vision of life and nature in general, and one subject to attack by time and circumstances. In the prefatory poem of the book, the speaker evokes such a positive view and links it with pure poetry:

> el agua contraía matrimonio con el agua,
> y los hijos del agua eran pájaros, flores, peces, árboles,
> eran caminos, piedras, montañas, humo, estrellas.
> Los hombres se abrazaban, uno a uno,

como corderos, las mujeres
dormían sin temor, los niños todos
. . . .
(Aquí quisiera hablar, abrir un libro
de aquel poeta puro que cantaba:
"El mundo está bien hecho, el mundo está
bien hecho, el mundo
está bien hecho"—aquí, en este instante sólo—.) [p. 16]

The quotation is from Jorge Guillén and makes us aware that this vision fits a poetic as well as a human tradition—but one that is now in the past and that can only be evoked in certain moments and while focused on a past time. (By repeating Guillén's line and changing its original rhythm, Sahagún may also be making it sound strident and undercutting its original positive impact.)

This prefatory poem provides a frame into which succeeding works are fitted. Its almost mythic vision of human existence becomes the backdrop for various evocations of childhood, and for the awareness that childish happiness and innocence were destroyed by life's ills, by suffering and by war. In several poems the speaker describes himself as water and as a river, thus picking up and developing an image of the prefatory poem (in which all beings were "hijos del agua"). Yet these images now acquire new meanings and help construct a new perspective on life and reality, as we can see in "Río":

El río adolescente se perdía en el llano,
gozosamente triste, como el corazón
Hölderlin

Le llamaron posguerra a este trozo de río,
a este bancal de muertos, a la ciudad aquella
doblada como un árbol viejo, clavada siempre
en la tierra lo mismo que una cruz. Y gritaron:
"¡Alegría! ¡Alegría!"
                    Yo era un río naciente,
era un hombre naciente, con la tristeza abierta
como una puerta blanca, para que entrase el viento,
para que entrase y diera movimiento a las hojas
del calendario inmóvil. Castillos en el aire
y aun estando en el aire, derrumbados, los sueños
hechos piedra, maderas que no quieren arder,
rayos de sol manchando los cristales más puros,
altísimas palomas ya sin poder volar . . .

¿Lo estáis viendo? Vosotros, los que venís de lejos,
los que tenéis el brazo libre como las águilas
y lleváis en los labios una roja alegría,
pasad, miraos en mí, tened fe. Yo era un río,
yo soy un río y llevo marcado a fuego el tiempo
del dolor bombardeado. Mi edad, mi edad de hombre,
sabedlo bien, un día se perderá en la tierra. [p. 24]

The traditional metaphor of a river for human existence underlies
this poem. Here the river is equated with a period of history in stanza
1, and with the protagonist's unfolding life in the rest of the work. In
both cases, we should note, Sahagún has defined a time in terms of a
place. The relationship between time and place is in each case metaphorical: one dimension of life is expressed in terms of a different one
based on their common characteristic of being parts of larger wholes.[2]
(The post-War period is a piece of historical time just as a section of a
river is a piece of its total space; a part of the protagonist's life is a
fragment of time, just as a part of the river is a fragment of space.)
Although the metaphor used here is not striking or novel, it achieves
an important effect: by making time come across as place, it concretizes
it and makes us look at it in an unusual way. The period of time alluded
to acquires a specific identity, a reality of its own comparable to that of
any physical place; it stands out from the mere narrative sequence of
events. In this sense, we could say that Sahagún has used metaphor in
exactly the way described by Paul Ricoeur: by means of it he has
suspended an ordinary perspective (in which time is an abstraction) and
given a model for reading things in a new way (in which time has the
tangibility of a concrete object).[3]

    This interpretation may seem to place too much emphasis on a
conventional image; its conventionality, however, in no way limits its
way of fixing our perspective on both the period of time and the
protagonist's life. In each case, once it has done so, the river leads into
other metaphors and similes which expand that same perspective. Thus
the post-War period is related in stanza 1 to a plot in which the dead
are buried, and also to a city twisted like a tree and nailed like a cross.
All of these not only continue the description of a time in terms of a
place and reinforce the sense of concreteness already produced, but also
delineate it more specifically. These subsequent images evoke decay, the
withering of life in time, and sacrifice, thus embodying various facets
of the post-Civil War era. They carry forward the process of modifying
our outlook on time and freezing this period into a tangible experience

of stagnation and loss. The use of a chain of metaphors and similes ("posguerra" is a city like a tree and a cross) further intensifies the effect.

Technically speaking, all these images constitute the real plane of the first stanza; the term "posguerra" is but the name given to all by an unspecified "they." Sahagún has reversed the real and the imaginary planes of his metaphors and similes, thus giving greater emphasis to the imaginary. This not only accents the negative effects produced, but highlights even more the sense that time has acquired the tangibility of a real place.

The river metaphor in the second part of the poem likewise fans out into other images which intensify its effects. Once he has described his youth in this post-War time as a river, the speaker metaphorizes his feelings and attitudes as concrete objects: his sadness is like a door which lets the wind enter, his dreams are destroyed castles, pieces of wood, doves that can't fly any higher. Although these images no longer convert time into place, they do make intangible feelings associated with a period of time into concrete objects, and thus function much as the earlier images did. The evanescent emotions of a period of the speaker's life acquire, thanks to them, a variety of dimensions as well as greater specificity. For example, the image of dreams as stone castles which crumble vividly combines feelings of impossiblity, of calcification, and of loss of youthful ideals.

The procedure we have been observing is central to the effect of this poem. By creating and developing these images, Sahagún has worked us into a metaphorical perspective in which a period of history and of the speaker's life is evoked as a concrete reality, as a specific experience of loss and stagnation.[4] This perspective overcomes both our natural inclination to view past time as an abstraction, and the disposition of the "otros" of stanza 1 (whom we might associate with conventional historians) to classify a period of the past through one term ("posguerra"), to shout happiness, and to leave it behind. Thanks to poetic metaphor, a past time has come to life.

In another sense, the metaphor explains the speaker's advice in the last stanza to those who did not experience this past. If past time can be evoked as a place and an object, it can also be left behind as any place can. The speaker's final hope is that, indeed, it will at some point be left behind by generations no longer oppressed by the destructive sensations which he has experienced.

The image of the river reappears in succeeding poems of this first section of *Profecías del agua.* In "Agua subterránea" (p. 25), the speaker contrasts an ideal society of the future with a negative past through the images of a beautiful underground river as opposed to a contaminated one. In "Otra vez río" (pp. 26-27) he identifies himself with a river seeking a more positive existence. The river images in these poems not only continue to embody, concretely and spacially, the speaker's judgments on a past time and society, but also make us relate all these poems to each other. By observing the pattern that unfolds by means of river images, we can read the whole section as a coherent dramatization of a single vision of past losses and of hopes for the future. In the last poem of the section, "Llegada al mar," the river's envisioned arrival at the sea suggests both death and fulfillment, a final loss as well as a final act of transcendence:

> Llegas a tiempo. El mar, como un gran campo, espera
> que caiga tu semilla, tu corazón. A tiempo
> llegas, a tiempo dices con los ojos cerrados:
> "El mar, el mar . . ." Inclinas hacia el sueño tus ojos.
> . . . .
> No hay barcas ya, ni luna, ni pescadores vivos
> con las manos huyendo tras los últimos peces.
> Muchacho, acércate. Tienes el mar delante
> y una tarde cualquiera te hundirás en sus brazos. [pp. 28-29]

The meaning of this poem cannot be reduced to a conceptual message: the ending represented by the river's arrival at the sea holds within it the ambiguities with which we can view the culmination and the end of human life. Yet the dominant metaphor of river and sea gives coherence to the work and to the whole section, making us feel that all the varying feelings expressed form part of a single human experience, and embodying that experience in one image and one spacial scene.

The remaining sections of *Profecías del agua* are not constructed around one metaphor. Individual images nevertheless function in a fashion similar to the one we have been observing, metaphorically transforming the subject described to produce a new perspective. In "Aula de química" the speaker's recollection of a scientific lecture on water evolves into a sustained image of water as a purifying and redeeming element, one which makes man aware of the basic beauty of life and lets him transcend the limitations of daily life and pedantic learning:

> El mercurio subía caliente hasta el fin,
> estallaba de asombro el cristal de los tubos de ensayo,
> se alzaban surtidores, taladraban el techo,
> era el amanecer del amor puro,

> irrumpían guitarras dichosamente vivas,
> olvidábamos la hora de salida, veíamos
> los inundados ojos azules de las mozas
> saltando distraídos por en medio del agua.
>
> Y os juro que la vida se hallaba con nosotros.
>
> Pero ¿cómo decir a los más sabios
> . . . .
> que ya habrá tiempo de aprender,
> decid conmigo: vida, tocad
> el agua, abrid los brazos
> como para abrazar una cintura blanca,
> romped los libros muertos? [pp.33-34]

Technically speaking, water is here not a metaphor (it is not linked to any other specific element or plane) but rather a "visión" in Carlos Bousoño's definition of that term—a sensorial image which embodies and objectifies a whole attitude and emotional state (here the state of natural happiness and acceptance of the basic patterns of life).[5] But its function with respect to the reader duplicates that of the river metaphor in "Río": it makes an elusive feeling concrete, it converts a recollection of a past attitude into a specific object and space. We can notice that just as the river became the real plane of "Río" while the abstract subject ("posguerra") was relegated to the background, so the "visión" of water is here foregrounded while the subject of the chemistry class once taken by the speaker is set into the background. This technique of reversing the importance of the poem's literal subject and of the image by which this subject is modified not only adds immediacy to the image but also suggests that what is important about past events is their sensorial and emotional impact—not the fact that they took place. The value of the past lies in the subjective experiences which it evokes and which can be rescued and re-formed by the poet.

Other images in the book function in similar fashion. In "Montaña nevada" (pp. 44-45) a white mountain and whiteness in general evoke various feelings connected with parting, with death, and with transcendence. In "El preso" (pp. 35-36) the images of soil ("barro") and blood, taken from Miguel Hernández's poetry, embody the struggle and tragedy of that poet's life, imprisonment, and death. In all these cases, as well as in the ones I have examined in detail, Sahagún has used metaphor and simile to impose a new perspective upon his subjects, to objectify and heighten the emotional attitude taken toward them, and to make a created reality supercede the literal reality on which the works are founded. Metaphorical transformation is an underlying device of his poetry, one which allows him to fictionalize and dramatize an outlook and to make us share it.

Sahagún is remarkably effective in using conventional metaphors. In one sense, of course, commonplace metaphors and ordinary language underscore the bond between the implied author and reader; they eliminate any tendency to view the former as an exotic seer, and they define him as someone who shares the reader's vocabulary and concerns. In this sense, they support the "co-operative principle" in the communication between author and reader and the effectiveness of the poem as communicative act.[6] They also bring in intertextual echoes and set Sahagún's book within the whole tradition of poetry which evokes and reflects upon the passing of time.

Yet the use of conventional imagery presents a danger: if this imagery is totally unremarkable, the poem will seem to lose its originality; it will break the convention that poetry should be linguistically novel in order to be significant. Sahagún avoids any such danger by using his commonplace metaphors and language to create very uncommon perspectives. Turning time into space in "Río" exemplifies such a perspective, and constitutes, in fact, a fictional premise of the sort discussed by Samuel R. Levin in his study of metaphor. As Levin explains, a poet who posits such a fictional premise is inviting us to conceive a world in which it (rather than the rules of our reality) holds; the poem's meanings emerge from the premise and from our assent to it.[7] By means of his fictional premise of time as space, Sahagún has involved us in a whole new vision in which past happenings live on in our emotions.

Remembrances of childhood are even more central in *Como si hubiera muerto un niño,* Sahagún's next book of poems. The poet's attitude is similar to the one pervading *Profecías del agua:* he sees his youth as a period of happy illusions and hopes, but also as the beginning of a process of discovering the sufferings of life. The evocation of the past therefore combines a nostalgia for youthful innocence with remembrances of the disillusionment that followed. The second section of the book constitutes a unit in which childhood is recalled and actualized. A pattern of metaphors creates a whole "story" out of it, one which points to its underlying meanings and gives them immediacy as well as unity. The process begins in a poem titled "Hacia la infancia":

> Pero su cuerpo inolvidable y joven
> ¿dónde se ha ido, para qué se ha ido?
> A la puerta hay un niño, madre, ahora
> es el momento, no le dejes nunca
> crecer. ¡Aquel caballo de cartón

que no galope, aquellos ojos míos
que sólo miren las estrellas! Pienso
que nada más tu caridad, tus manos
candeales de madre me podrían
salvar. Fácil sería abrir las puertas
de mi infancia y entrar a aquel jardín.
Las puertas ... Y las abro, y veo un niño
con los zapatos rotos en la arena,
aprendiendo a sumar. Cierra sus libros,
dile que hizo mal las cuentas, pero
que no importa, que el oro de los árboles
se ha derramado porque él es un niño.
¡Que no llegue a saber nada, que el alma
la tenga intacta siempre y siempre a prueba!
Ya la ciudad del niño queda a mucha
distancia, y todo lo que he anadado ha sido
mortal y poderoso. Pero es pronto.
Aún podría volver yo allí y mirando
—a la hora del jardín—la flor de entonces,
la que creció sobre mi propia historia,
olvidaría, sé que olvidaría. [p. 79]

An awareness of and a lament for the loss of youth is immediately followed by an impulse to move back to childhood and to stop time. From the beginning the speaker takes a dual attitude to his youthful self; he stands outside and sees it as "un niño," and yet also fits himself into the child's outlook ("aquellos ojos míos"). By asking his mother to stop time and save the child from the future, he combines a childish dependence with an adult's insight into the world. All of this makes the speaker an adult straining to return to his youthful self and perspective, fighting against logic and reality to deny the course taken by time and to regain a lost illusion.

Beginning with line 10, the speaker finds a way of figuratively moving back into his past. He constructs the metaphor of his youth as a garden, the doors of which can be opened to allow him to reenter it. This metaphor serves as a base for the rest of the poem, and allows the speaker to envision breaking the constraints of reality and to see himself as though he were literally back in his childhood. Like the metaphor of the river previously examined, this one of the garden converts a time (the speaker's youth) into a place (the garden). This again allows the speaker (and the poet) to evoke the past more concretely, giving it the immediacy of a scene which we might be witnessing right now. It also immerses us in a fictional view of the world in which past *is* convertible to present. Such a view underlies this poem and is used by Sahagún to involve us in the speaker's quest. By drawing this view out of a common scene and image, Sahagún again creates an extraordinary perspective from ordinary materials.

The rest of the poem expands the garden image and the view of past time as place. The natural beauty of the garden is juxtaposed to the artifacts of human life; by interrupting the child's arithmetic and encouraging him to enjoy natural beauty, the speaker sets the innocence of a basic existence above the value of educating oneself and moving into an adult civilization. The contrast between the beauty of the "oro de los árboles" and the routine nature of an arithmetic assignment justifies and reinforces this choice, and leads us to accept the speaker's final desire to return, to contemplate "la flor de entonces," and to forget his adult life. The image of childhood as a flower covering history again stresses its natural beauty in opposition to the limitations of growing up. In the middle part of the poem, the speaker seems to have immersed himself completely in the view of his childhood time as a place to which he is returning—he speaks in the present tense, contemplates the child-version of himself as if he were right there, gives him advice.

In the last part, however, he seems to hesitate, noticing that the past is spacially removed from him, and using his basic metaphor to indicate that life's experiences have taken him away from his youth (line 21). He nevertheless asserts his desire to go back into that youth and forget the present, but we feel that his initial sense of loss has returned and that he is having difficulty sustaining the metaphor and the fictional reentry into his past. Sahagún has developed and expanded his spacial metaphor of youth as a remote garden to make us follow the speaker's path from lament to immersion into his fictional return, and then to an awareness of the present and an as-yet unresolved struggle against it.

Unlike "Río," this poem uses only images directly related to its central metaphor. The flowers, the trees, and the action of interrupting an arithmetic assignment in order to enjoy nature all extend out of the basic image of youth as a garden (whereas in "Río" Sahagún introduced unrelated subordinate images). This gives "Hacia la infancia" greater cohesion and unity of focus. It also makes the poem develop like a narrative: the initial picture of the protagonist entering a garden is followed by his seeing a child in that garden, whom he advises to stop studying and enjoy nature so that he may remain innocent of adult cares. (All these steps are related by contiguity, and form one single metonymic process.[8]) By molding this metonymic pattern out of his basic metaphor, Sahagún builds a continuous, linear "story" that makes sense anecdotally. This enables the reader to accept his metaphor of youth as garden; the metaphor, in turn, adds concreteness and visual impact to the developing narrative. The poem's combination of metaphor and metonymy makes credible fiction out of an image that contradicts the "real" difference between time and place.

We should note, however, that the speaker plays a double role in this poem. On the one hand he is a protagonist who goes back to his childhood and identifies himself with an image of a child which he evokes. On the other hand, he also stands outside the child-version of himself and gives the latter (and the reader) advice on how he should develop his life naturally and avoid growing up. Here the speaker seems less a protagonist and more a version of the poet who composed this work and who is conveying a vision of youth and age to the reader. Although the poem never becomes explicitly metapoetic, this commentary by the speaker on the theme of the poem adds an important dimension. By alternating the roles of a protagonist who longs for and recreates his childhood and of a commentator who meditates on that longing, Sahagún suggests that the longing and the act of thinking about it may be inseparable. By implication at least, longing, thinking about it, and writing poems about it are all linked—and the attempt to relive one's past may be inseparable from the impulse to rethink it and the drive to rewrite it.

This last perception leads us to an overview of the poem. "Hacia la infancia" creates a fictional story and view of life out of its central metaphor and at the same time comments on this process of creation. By expanding metonymically his metaphor of youth as a garden to which he may return, the speaker embodies his wish to go back to an innocent existence, gives reality to that wish, and makes us partake of it; by also taking on the role of commentator he makes us see that wishing to change reality and go back in time is related to and perhaps equivalent to writing about it.

In the next poem of this section, titled "Niño en peligro," we witness the failure of the speaker's quest to move to his youth. At the outset, the adult speaker is contemplating a return to the place in which he spent his early years:

Volveré a esa colina desde donde
abrazaría mi ciudad, sus playas,
mi infancia azul y azul con golondrinas
al despertar. Y volveré. Tal vez
en algún niño súbito que pase
(polizón en un coche de caballos,
sin que el cochero llegue a saber nada),

encontraría yo mi puesto. Nunca
debí salir. Hubiera sido siempre
niño en peligro, pero nunca hombre
que sabiendo el peligro lo esperaba.
Y estarán las palmeras. Volvería,
si supiera que estaban volvería.
¡Que alguien me diga que aún están y nadie
me ha prohibido sus frutos! Volveré.
Todos los niños volverán conmigo. [p. 80]

Technically speaking, this poem is not based on a metaphor and does
not continue the transformation of time into place we saw in "Hacia la
infancia"; the trip here described is simply the return to one's native
city, not a fictitious going back in time. But if we read the work in
context of the preceding poem, we necessarily connect this literal return
to the figurative return to childhood described there. (Even the language
supports this connection: we note that "podría volver" was the main
verb of the previous poem's last sentence, and "volveré" the main verb
of the first sentence of this one.) The longing now expressed therefore
seems a more "realistic" and more matter-of-fact version of the one
stated previously. Although he no longer transforms time or breaks its
sequential rule, the speaker continues to express his wish to return to
the world of his childhood. The way in which this speaker envisions the
city and the boy with whom he identifies makes clear that he is attracted
by the elemental innocence of that world. It is one in which a child can
play, can stow away on a carriage, can enjoy the free fruit of a palm tree
and the beauty of swallows at dawn, in which he can live an "infancia
azul y azul."

We notice that when he is fantasizing himself into this existence the
speaker expresses himself mostly in the conditional and the subjunctive
("tal vez . . . encontraría," "hubiera sido," "volvería"), suggesting a
hypothetical wish—and again making this poem a feebler version of
"Hacia la infancia," written predominantly in the present tense. At
times the speaker does switch to the future ("volveré," "volverán"),
which suggests greater immersion in his hopes and makes us see him
hesitating between doubt and assertion. Most of the expressions in the
future tense, however, could refer to a literal return to the city rather
than to a return to childhood, and hence do not indicate the willingness
to step back fictitiously into the past of "Hacia la infancia." All in all,
the first part of "Niño en peligro" suggests the speaker's diminished
ability to rewrite his life, his return to a more literal perspective, and a
fading of his hope for childlike innocence.

The second part of the poem reveals a complete loss of this hope:

> Oh fatal población, la de la infancia.
> Un desear a ciegas lo invadía
> todo: la fuente, el mar y sus cantiles,
> la tierra, el aire apenas . . . Nunca, nunca
> debí salir de allí. Ya la alegría
> no volverá aunque vuelva yo, los niños
> no volverán. Desmesuradamente
> mis manos—aunque vuelva yo—crecieron
> para el amor, para el dolor. Volver,
> y para qué volver a esa colina. . . . [p. 80]

The speaker now adopts a fully realistic perspective, and sees that a literal return to the city will not permit a figurative return to childhood. Much as he may regret his leaving, he knows that he no longer fits the emotive outlook of childhood. The metaphor of hands grown too big for love, in contrast to the underlying metaphor of childhood as place, graphically embodies his physical and biological unsuitability to that outlook. In this sense, the ending of "Niño en peligro" marks the end of a quest and an effort; having attempted to challenge the rules of time and growth through his metaphorical vision of childhood in "Hacia la infancia," the speaker now has to confess defeat and realize that while he can desire the innocence of youth he cannot simply go back to it.[9] The metaphors we have observed in these two poems, organized in a metonymic pattern and made into a consistent "story," have immersed us in that experience and in its poetic expression.

If the first two poems of this section embody the speaker's quest to return to his childhood and then make clear its impossibility, the succeeding seven examine various facets of childhood illusions and of the ways in which these were destroyed. The speaker, having come to grips with his past and its loss, can now explore further the emotional implications of the issue. He does so through a variety of metaphors and an underlying metonymic pattern, all of which nevertheless grow out of or connect with the images of the first poem. In this fashion the theme of illusion and its loss extends into a rich vision of the speaker's life.

"Entonces" uses several metaphors to juxtapose the innocent and natural joys of childhood with the more negative state of the adult:

> ¿Y para qué aprendí a escribir
> la palabra abandono . . .? Entonces no era
> posible que la primavera
> tuviera intención de morir.

Niño yo entonces, ¿dónde ir?
Iba al reino de la madera
—juguetes, pinos—y a la era,
para ver el trigo crujir.

Ahora llevo las manos llenas
de recuerdos vivos aún.
Larga es la noche y largo ha sido

este viaje. A duras penas
paso entre niebla, como un
niño mayor que se ha perdido. [p. 81]

The initial question links learning to loss, and makes the learning of writing "abandono" stand for the awareness of time, death, and the sufferings of adult life. This is contrasted to childhood, in which spring seemed endless and life joyful. By making the latter a "kingdom of wood," the poem stresses its naturalness, which encompasses both playing with toys and enjoying the landscape, and also involves an awareness of life's basic process of growth (lines 7 and 8). By placing this evocation of the past in the imperfect tense, the poem accents its continuity—a continuity later broken by adult learning.

The tercets focus on the contrasting state of adulthood, introduced by "ahora" and embodied in the image of hands full of memories (which obviously recalls the excessively large hands of the adult in the previous poem, and echoes the view of the adult as physically unsuited for childhood illusions). Live memories of the past, pleasant as that past may have been, are ironically negative: they only stress the loss and the "abandono." The negative view is supported by images of night and of mist, which contrast with the spring and the bountiful fields linked with childhood, and which make the adult's present the obverse, the destructive side of existence. The metaphor of life as a trip in the last stanza takes us back to the view of time as space; the image of the speaker as a child wandering in the mist of adulthood heightens the main contrast of the poem and emphasizes loss.

This poem recalls some works from *Profecías del agua* by its use of several different metaphors, and also by the way in which it foregrounds the metaphorical plane rather than the real one. (The last section specifically mentions the hands, the night, and the trip; the reader must surmise the time passed and the feeling of loss.) Yet these metaphors are here closely related to the main metaphor of time as place, and form part of a neat contrast, giving the work a tightness and precision not apparent in the earlier book. The use of the sonnet form and of consonant rhyme emphasizes such precision. Furthermore, its speaker, like the one in "Hacia la infancia" (but unlike those of *Profecías del agua*), is conscious that he is writing. By wondering why he learned to write the word "abandono," he links the act of writing to the act of learning the tragedies of life. In "Hacia la infancia" reliving was related to rewriting; here writing is discovery. We sense a metapoetic dimension in this whole section, and connect the speaker's desires to go back to his youth and to understand time's losses to the poet's impulse to unearth the meaning of temporal patterns through his writing. (This awareness that the speaker is a writer is also heightened by the sonnet form.)

The next work of this section, titled "Ciudad" (pp. 82-83), picks up the image of the lost child with which "Entonces" ended, and out of it constructs a metaphorical story of the child coming to a hostile city, losing hope there, and wishing to recover a natural existence. This poem verges on allegory: the city is linked with adulthood, nature with childhood, and the boy's wanderings evoke the process of growing up. Yet Sahagún does not reduce the vision to a simplistic pattern, and incorporates in it several paradoxes: the child wishes to find refuge in a river, and yet the city wets him with loneliness ("te mojó los brazos / de soledad"); his dreams of the river only lead to a menacing sea, "el mar total de tu desgracia." Based on an underlying pattern of childish and natural illusion destroyed by time, by growing up, and by civilization, the poem makes us feel some of the irony of a life in which quest often produces loss.

In the following poem, "La casa," Sahagún makes the images of a destroyed childhood home and of a child's death and burial embody the loss of hope and the loneliness that come with age (pp. 84-85). In "Fotografía de niño" he deals with the contrast between childlike and adult outlooks and the impossibility of bridging the gap (pp. 86-87). The whole tragedy of growing up and losing one's youthful illusions is condensed and dramatized in "Cita en el mar," where the search for life leads to shipwreck: "¿Recuerdas? Una noche salimos a la vida. / Te llevé con dulzura entre mis brazos. Hijo / mío. Salvajemente nos esperaba el mar" (p. 89). Splitting himself into child and adult, the speaker makes both his innocent illusions and his wider perceptions lead only to loss. The next poem, "Jardín" (p. 90), describes the death of a child shot by a firing squad, and can be read as a final image of the destruction of ideals by the world into which he grew up.[10]

In all of these works, Sahagún employs metaphors to give concrete embodiment to his rather abstract subject of illusion and disillusion. The individual metaphors which I have noted, as well as many others, turn the idea of loss of innocence into a set of specific emotional experiences, while at the same time stressing underlying patterns—the naturalness of childhood, the artifice of adult society. In some poems these metaphors have allegorical overtones; in all of them they relate to the central metaphor of time as a place, as well as to the speaker's underlying quest for his past, and the failure of that quest. The image of the child which appears in all of the poems extends out of the speaker's recall of himself as a child in the first work of the series, and all that happens to the child protagonist of any poem (whether or not that child be seen as the speaker's alter ego) reflects the losses undergone by this speaker in time.

I have already indicated how the first poem of the section develops a metonymic pattern out of its metaphor of youth as garden, and thus starts making a sustained fiction out of its basic image. Something similar occurs in the third through the ninth poems. Poem three ("Entonces") ends with the metaphor of growing up as a trip on which the child was lost; this metaphor is picked up in "Ciudad" in its description of the child wandering through the city, is evoked in "Fotografía de niño" when the speaker sees the child following him as he moves away (p. 87), and underlies the view of the child traveling to sea and death in "Cita en el mar" and being executed in "Jardín." (The title of this whole book, *Como si hubiera muerto un niño,* makes death a metaphor for loss.) All these references to the metaphor of life as a trip constitute a metonymic chain, a progressive narration of the stages of man's "travels." This of course imparts unity to the series. Since in every poem the metaphoric plane is stressed and "foregrounded" over the real one, this chain increases the sense of specificity and of drama: we are witnessing a very real "fable" unfolding before us. Again this gives us the feeling that rather ordinary metaphors, and the explicit story woven out of them, have served as a means of creating an original and creative vision.

Metapoetic references add another dimension to this "fable": we are made aware that examining life's illusions and their loss is linked to writing about them. They also support the idea that metaphor serves a heuristic function in Sahagún's verse. The process of constructing a fable out of metaphors and of making this fable explore and embody a view of life is a way of solving a problem. The speaker, a poet who weaves this metaphorical fable, is working out an explanation of his life, constructing a verbal embodiment and interpretation of that life and its meanings. All in all, the language and the techniques of the second section of *Como si hubiera muerto un niño* mark a step forward in Sahagún's creation of a cohesive world of metaphor and metonymy to embody poetically his theme of childhood illusions and their loss.

The first section of *Como si hubiera muerto un niño,* like the second, forms a cohesive unit; it centers on a love relationship. The speaker recalls its beginning in the first poem of the section, and then devotes succeeding ones to various aspects and implications of the relationship. Metaphors play an important part in all these works, although there is no single sustaining metaphor which holds it together. Within individual poems Sahagún organizes his meanings around fictional premises rather than around single images. These premises, however, function like the metaphors of the second section. We can see it in "Claridad del día":

> Te digo que ésta ha sido la primera
> vez que amé. Si la tierra que ahora pisas
> se hundiera con nosotros, si aquel río
> que nos vigila detuviera el paso,
> sabrías que es verdad que te he buscado
> desde niño en las piedras, en el agua
> de aquella fuente de mi plaza. Tú,
> tan flor, tan luz de primavera, dime,
> dime que no es mentira este milagro,
> la multiplicación de mi alegría,
> los panes y los peces de tu pecho. [p. 62]

We cannot read the speaker's assertion that he has been looking for his beloved since his childhood as literally true, since it contradicts basic life patterns. Seen metaphorically, however, it embodies the speaker's view of the beloved as an ideal toward which his life has been directed and as the culmination of his search for harmony in nature. This in turn justifies his use of the metaphors of flower and light in describing her, and relates to his view of their meeting and his happiness as a miracle comparable to Christ's act of multiplying the loaves and the fishes in the New Testament. This passage illustrates very well Sahagún's way of superimposing a fictional and metaphoric reality on a literal one, foregrounding it, and making it the basis for the meaning of the poem. Whether that fictional reality be a metaphor (as in most poems of part two), or a metaphorical transformation of events (as is the case here), it imparts both unity and concreteness to the work, turning an idea into an experience.

Another fictional premise that operates as a metaphor underlies "Sobre la tierra" (pp. 64-65); here the idea that the speaker has to believe in God in order to name his beloved evokes both the transcendent nature of his love and the difficulty of understanding and naming her essence. The religious reference also motivates a paradox: the speaker wonders about his belief in God while affirming the salvation offered him by the beloved, making his faith in her a human substitute for religious faith. And in "Canción de infancia" (pp. 67-68), the speaker fictionally invents a meeting with his beloved when they were both children to represent his desire for a world of innocence in which they could live together. In both of these poems Sahagún again sets up a fiction to objectify an emotional attitude. Together with various individual metaphors, these fictions help develop the view of the beloved as imparting meaning to life, and of the speaker's striving for a more ideal existence through love. Again, a poetic device serves a heuristic purpose.

Como si hubiera muerto un niño ends with a poem titled "Y es de día" (pp. 97-98) and set apart from the two sections that I have discussed. This poem is addressed to an undefined "tú," related both to the speaker's memories and to his inner feelings. This "tú" could be either a lost beloved or a lost version of the speaker's self; identifying it, in any case, does not seem essential. More importantly, we come to see this being as the embodiment of the speaker's past striving for meanings and ideals. In that sense, this last poem pulls together the two sections of the book, letting the volume end with an overview of the speaker's quest as well as of its failures and its impossibility. Although it is neither metaphor nor a metaphorical fiction, this "tú" plays a role similar to those elements, objectifying the speaker's attitudes. And when the latter sees the "tú" as a source for the creation of a poem rather than a lasting and objective part of himself and his world, he highlights the poetic process and lets the book reflect back on itself: we realize that *Como si hubiera muerto un niño* portrays not only a quest but also the poetization of that quest, and blends both into a single act of search and discovery. Undoubtedly this book marks the high point of Sahagún's process of metaphorical transformation. The sustained metaphors and the metaphorical fictionalizations that I have examined, while not novel in themselves, produce unique transformations of reality and mold the striving after illusions into a powerful experience.

Estar contigo, Sahagún's next book of poetry, is both longer and more varied than *Como si hubiera muerto un niño.* Many poems deal with memories of childhood; rather than a nostalgic longing for lost innocence, however, they stress the discovery of suffering and of the ugliness of the world. Almería, the city in which Sahagún spent his youth, is drawn as a sordid and lifeless place in which the child learned about the poverty and the tiredness of life in the post-Civil War period. Other works allude to love: the second section is dominated by nostalgic evocations of the beloved, and was clearly motivated by the poet's longing while he was away in England (the dedicatory poem to the book

makes this clear). In addition, *Estar contigo* contains several poems motivated by historical circumstances, such as the Cuban revolution (specifically Ché Guevara) and the war in Vietnam, three works evoking César
Vallejo, Antonio Machado, and Pablo Neruda, and several that deal
with social issues. An awareness of the problems and limitations of
Spanish society, already observable in Sahagún's earlier work, becomes
more evident in this one; works primarily focused on childhood memories, on love, and on the speaker's son also bring in the social dimension
of life. (Love, for example, is at one point a consoling and purifying
element for someone living in an unjust society.)

The volume is quite varied in style and form. It includes prose
poems, most of them page-long vignettes of scenes from Sahagún's
childhood which capture the atmosphere of a decaying city. The book
contains long poems in free verse, divided into several parts each; it also
includes brief ones based on traditional Spanish poetry, and short,
tightly constructed works that recall baroque verse. This variety of
forms and an accompanying variety of tones make clear Sahagún's
maturity as a poet, his ability to control and modify language to fit his
needs.

Neither in the book as a whole nor in any of its sections do we find
the sustained development of one underlying metaphor, such as we saw
in *Como si hubiera muerto un niño.* Several poems are built around one
central metaphor each; several metaphors appear in more than one
poem, and suggest relationships between poems. More often, however,
Sahagún uses many individual images to convey emotive nuances and
experiences. He often combines metaphors with synecdoches, symbols,
or "visiones"; all of these, however, tend to operate alike. Much like the
metaphors of Sahagún's earlier work (though without becoming part of
single structures), they introduce new planes and new perspectives to
convey subjective meanings with precision.

Some sections of the prose poem "Visión en Almería" offer good
examples:

> Yo guardo de esa infancia un recuerdo duro, macizo
> como una roca insoslayable, antiguo y reciente al mismo
> tiempo. . . .

> La ciudad toda es para mí una habitación de realquilados,
> una escalera oscura y un abrigo negro, con botones enormes
> y brillantes. Es el abrigo que llevaba mi madre al volver
> del trabajo. . . .

> El niño es sólo una mirada limpia y sin culpa, nacida
> para algo tan sencillo como ver. . . .

¿Soy yo ese niño que ha conocido tan pronto la soledad y su
daño? Por encima del tiempo veo su imagen indómita y frágil,
que se pierde en la noche del recuerdo, y reaparece clamando
justicia, y alza los brazos hacia todos. . . . [pp. 107-08]

The first example, a simile, performs a traditional metaphoric function:
it objectifies the permanence, intensity, and inescapability of the
speaker's memories. The linking of memory and rock, based on those
traits, also imparts to the former some of the negativeness and deadness
of inanimate stone. The second example quoted differs from the first in
that the things mentioned are part of the speaker's real memories rather
than metaphors or similes for feelings. Technically speaking it is a
synecdoche: pieces of the city stand for the whole. But it functions as
metaphor, since it links two planes, life in the city and objects with
negative connotations. The link produces in the reader feelings similar
to those engendered by the earlier simile, and in much the same way;
all of the things mentioned objectify the negative feelings produced by
the city. "Habitación de realquilados" captures the transitory quality of
life there, while the darkness of staircase and coat portray its lugubri-
ousness, and the large buttons evoke something distorted, almost eerie.

The third example is somewhat different. Technically a combination of synecdoche and symbol (the child's look stands for the whole
child; the look's candor represents the child's innocence), the image
synthesizes all notions about the child's innocence and sets this child
in contrast to the guilts and decrepitudes of the city. Rather than just
infuse the scene with feeling, as did the previous examples, this one
both evokes in us feelings about the child's innocence and pulls them
together into a symbol which is opposed to the evils of the city.

The last example quoted functions much like the third. Technically
it differs from all the others; neither metaphor nor synecdoche, this
image of the child is a "visión" conjured up by the protagonist, who
makes its imaginary physical traits represent its attitude. (Its raised arms
do not refer to any real actions performed by a child, but simply evoke
—and represent symbolically—the desire for justice and solidarity that
the speaker envisions the child will have after it grows up and sees the
damage done by its unhappy youth.) But in the context of the poem this
image objectifies all the feelings of suffering and rebellion produced in
the child, gives us a visual figure with which to sympathize, and offers
a specific contrast to the murkiness of the city.

Sahagún has created a variety of diverse images, from synecdoche
to symbol and "visión." Yet a metaphorical process underlies them all:
in each case, a new plane is introduced into the description of an exter-

nal reality (childhood memories become rock, the city becomes black things, the child becomes a blameless look, its later attitude is represented by a protesting figure). In each case this new plane objectifies an attitude or feeling and brings it forth within us. Hence it takes us away from the normal, referential way of looking at the external reality in question: the childhood memories do not involve us in the details of the speaker's biography, the city does not become interesting for itself. Instead, the feelings evoked by the second plane make us read reality as a representation of the speaker's negative attitude.[11] Finally everything comes together into an experience of meaninglessness and suffering at a time in the speaker's life, and of the rebellion that these have motivated. The metaphorical process is the means by which this experience is produced and explained.

A similar effect is achieved in "Sol en la plaza," from which the following two passages are taken:

> Estaban sentados en aquel banco, la piel rugosa y ya
> vencida, viejos sarmientos nudosos, jubilados, expuestos ya para
> siempre al sol de mediodía. De toda esa delgadez marchita y
> pétrea, de ese barrunto de tiempos indudablemente peores, más
> oscuros, emergía la luz escasa, de cirio titubeante, de unos ojos
> que se perdían a lo lejos. . . .

> En esos instantes, todo crecía en profundidad para gozo de
> los sentidos: el olor de las flores y el estiércol, el murmullo
> penetrante del agua, e incluso la visión de una mujer joven que
> pasara. Visión que era al mismo tiempo tacto, mirada, olfato,
> sonido.
> Los viejos, en aquellos momentos, permanecían inmóviles,
> pero la conversación se interrumpía. Sus ojos, hermosos y
> tristes como un pozo sin fondo, brillaban más ahora. Yo me
> asomaba de nuevo a ellos y adivinaba . . . la figura irrenunciable
> del amor, de la costumbre, del deseo. [pp. 110-11]

The initial vignette of the old men combines descriptive detail with the metaphor of old, knobby vines to make the men seem spent, worn out. This is stressed even more by describing the men as "delgadez marchita y pétrea," denying them individuality and accenting their inactivity. The very use of images of inanimate or spent natural elements (stone, wilted flowers, old vines) links them with the inevitable process of death. Even the light in their eyes becomes tied to death through the image of candles. (Sahagún uses the word "cirios," evocative of church ceremonies and funerals, rather than "velas.") Metaphorical elements remove this description from its referential meaning and make us read it as an evocation of the deadening effects of age and suffering.

In parallel fashion, the details and images of the second passage portray the renewed vitality that suddenly appears in the scene. The young woman is not a specific figure but a compendium of all sensations: her figure, together with the smells of flowers and the sound of water, makes life irrupt upon the stagnant scene previously described. The shining of the old men's eyes contrasts with the eye/candle image of the first section, highlighting a change. Everything contributes to accent that change and to lead us to the overall meaning of the work, its view of life irrepressibly emerging from and overcoming the effects of time and suffering.

The metaphoric transformations which we have observed in both of these works take the focus away from the referential value of the scenes portrayed and lead us to their subjective meanings. They lie at the heart of these works' poetic nature, separating them from narrative and linking them to Sahagún's verse. Similar transformations occur in many poems in verse. In "Parábola y metamórfosis" (pp. 165-68) Sahagún weaves a whole biography of a modern Spanish nobleman to show the decay and the corrupting effects of his society. After suffering the stifling effects of this society and rebelling briefly, the protagonist comes back to its deadening routines. Several images highlight his path: gold evokes the hollow shine of his youth, a storm his rebellion, lights and incense his return. At the end, the man becomes "un gusano caído tristemente," climaxing the pattern of dehumanization that has been taking place.

In several poems Sahagún uses images that appeared in his earlier books. In "A imagen de la vida" (p. 117) the sea and its waves represent the destructiveness of life; in "Puentes del Elba" rivers evoke the passing of the protagonists' lives (p. 127). In general, however, Sahagún now employs more diverse images and a greater variety of techniques, as we saw in "Visión en Almería." This is especially true in poems with social implications; in "Epitafio sin amor" the effects of a dictatorship are presented through the metaphor of a machine:

>Pero la maquinaria que creó
>no dura. Pieza a pieza, el engranaje
>fue destruido sin piedad.
>Un viento popular barrió las vigas
>carcomidas, el moho, las distancias,
>y en el silencio que quedara en pie
>fue posible por fin la primavera. [p. 171]

By making the dictator's system into a machine, the poem contrasts its lifelessness and impersonality to the life of natural things (wind, spring). This makes its destruction a justifiable process and allows the poem to present what could have been an ideological message as a self-justifying natural scheme.

The metaphors and metaphorical effects present in this book, although they do not form elaborate systems like those of *Como si hubiera muerto un niño,* fulfill the same general function of highlighting meanings and experiences that lie beneath the poems' referential levels, and leading us to various aspects of Sahagún's vision—the tragedies of a loss of childhood and innocence, the negative effects of a corrupt environment, the nostalgic longing for the beloved. Several poems also reveal a consciousness of the poetic process itself. In "La palabra" a child who has been idealistically watching a sea has to confront its disappearance in the night, and has to face his fears of death. In this poem the boy seeks to overcome his fears through language:

> A solas, juez y parte de la historia extinguida,
> buscó en sí mismo la noticia exacta
> de lo desconocido.
> Y nació la palabra. Sólo entonces,
> con negación y sin remordimientos,
> halló una certidumbre duradera. [p. 120]

The child's actions echo the quest of the poet who seeks to embody his vision of the world in language and in that fashion to preserve it. This vignette exemplifies the creative power of poetic language, as well as Sahagún's consciousness of that power.

Memorial de la noche contains a section entitled "En la noche (1973-1975)"; several of its poems make use of metaphor. In "Vegetales" (p. 186), for example, the speaker envisions himself and his beloved as plants to suggest their natural union, the chaos and difficulties of their surroundings, their susceptibility to destruction, and a paradoxical view of destruction as possible rebirth. Metaphor continues to be one way in which Sahagún takes his reader from a referential to a subjective level, and in which he embodies enigmatic meanings in a creative and communicable form. It is also used occasionally in Sahagún's latest book, *Primer y último oficio.* Many poems in this volume consist of melancholy evocations of the past, and the poetic representation of these evocations often becomes a means of both finding and preserving meaning. Vignettes of past places and events are used more frequently than explicit metaphors, but the poetic process remains a part of a more general quest for significance.

In characterizing Sahagún's poetry as a whole, one must note that its themes are few and almost always personal in nature. Evocations of childhood motivate nostalgic visions on the one hand and views of life's bleakness on the other; portrayals of love and the beloved reflect a striving for meaning and union. In *Estar contigo* more frequent references are made to the social dimensions of life, although these are often incorporated in works dealing with love or with the past. All of these subjects could have led to a confessional or anecdotal verse, which would merely report the poet's feelings. But the metaphors and metaphorical processes we have examined take Sahagún's poetry beyond confessionalism and beyond its referential meanings. Using plain language and many conventional metaphors, Sahagún has established easy bonds between implied speaker and reader. By creating unique perspectives and premises, forging compelling fables, and alluding to the very process of poetic creation, he has woven original experiences out of his materials.

9 ELADIO CABAÑERO
Imagery, Style, and Effect

Eladio Cabañero's background differes considerably from those of the other major poets of his generation. Born and raised in the small town of Tomelloso, Cabañero worked as a laborer in his youth and was largely self-educated when he arrived in Madrid in his late twenties. His early poetry is affected by this background in two different ways. On the one hand it contains many references to farm life and village people and scenes; on the other it is marked by the use of carefully controlled forms and patterns, suggesting the poet's conscious efforts to learn from and assimilate previous traditions, and recalling the process of learning by imitation of Miguel Hernández. The evocations of local scenes and vignettes are still present, although less frequent, in Cabañero's later books; the tight forms of the earlier poetry often give way to longer poems written in free verse and in a conversational tone. Thematically, Cabañero's poetry increasingly focuses on social issues, and also on the beloved and the relationship between two lovers.

None of these features, however, really define Cabañero's verse. The use of tight forms in the early works and the subsequent development of other kinds of expression do make clear the poet's concern with language, something which critics have noted in distinguishing Cabañero's poems from earlier and less artistic social verse.[1] But neither the forms used nor the themes treated pin down the value of the work. One way of doing that is to examine closely how individual poems present and transform various scenes and figures. In spite of its varied subjects, Cabañero's poetry has a unique manner of focusing on details, of elaborating them via images and poetic techniques, and of using them to embody more general visions. Frequently Cabañero uses personifications of natural scenes and deindividualizations of human figures to create a vivid yet stylized reality; through this reality, and through selected images (which often acquire symbolic overtones), he leads the reader to larger meanings. In one sense Cabañero's use of image, personification, and deindividualization situates him in the mainstream of all poetry which seeks to capture "concrete universals"; in another, it helps us define the very original and effective way in which his works convey experiences.

Cabañero's first book, *Desde el sol y la anchura,* has been praised for its formal perfection and its descriptive skill, but has also been evaluated as a work of apprenticeship which does not yet reveal the poet's originality nor deal with deeper problems of human life.[2] Yet if we look more closely at the book's descriptions, we discover techniques which will be basic to all of Cabañero's work, as well as ways in which these techniques give meaning to the vignettes portrayed. We can see this in "El segador," which seems simply to evoke a common rural scene and produce sensorial effects:

Empuñando la hoz, porificando
la sangre, enmadejada, endurecida,
a contra fauces gira las dos manos
tronchando cañas y venciendo espigas.

Los ojos dilatados y el resuello
pegándose en la carne y la camisa.
Hay soles convocados sobre junio
en la estrechez del aire. A toda herida
la hoz acosa el surco que acomete
el brazo talador que abate y tira,
impulso a impulso, al segador curvado
contra la tierra seca y desnutrida.
. . . .

Les duele el sol caído a los trigales.
Por el cielo las mieses adivinan
pristinales reposos y palomas
y eucarísticas rosas amarillas.
Amarga el trigo y el sudor. La siega
es la tierra que está recién parida.
. . . .

Sigue segando en pie sobre sus huesos
mientras brilla el paisaje a toda prisma
por la anchura del campo, interminable,
de horizonte continuo, sin orillas.

Quizá una hoja verde, temblorosa,
con su gota de agua cristalina,
llegue desde remotas primaveras,
cruce bajo el rastrojo, a la deriva . . . [pp. 32-33]

The description of the harvester deindividualizes him. By stressing the way in which the man holds his sickle and by describing in detail the movement of his hands, Cabañero makes his actions mechanical; the image of his blood rolled up in a skein focuses on him as if he were an object. (The neologism "porificando" suggests that this blood melts and comes through his pores, contributing to this focus.) The reference to the man's dilated eyes and the image of his breath sticking to him do accent his work and his effort, but only in physical terms. This whole description highlights the harvester as a *type,* and fits the book's purpose of portraying diverse vignettes of peasant life. But it does more: the lack of individuality, the stress on physical details, and the mechanization forcefully embody the limitations of this man's existence and suggest its inadequacy for a full human life. Our negative attitude toward this man's life is supported by the imagery of his reaping as a wounding and by the vignette of the harvester as "curvado" and set against the sterile land.

In contrast to the dehumanized harvester, the landscape is personified, reversing our normal perspective on persons and things. The wheat fields suffer the fallen sun (alluding to the loss of light in the evening, and perhaps to the red light of dusk as bloody and therefore wounding); the grain fields think, envisioning fulfillment, a fulfillment further ennobled by the image of the eucharist (though "eucarísticas" may also go back to its etymology of "giving thanks"); the harvest is the land's giving of birth.[3] These personifications and the suggestions of higher values, of religious achievement, and of life-giving that they possess stand in stark opposition to the harvester's mechanization and lack of individuality. And although some of the personifications link the landscape with suffering and wounding, the final effect is one of transcendence and life-giving, as contrasted to a limiting mechanization.

The ending of the poem sets the opposing visions of harvester and landscape against each other: the former continues his mechanical activity while the latter spreads out in a limitless continuum and evokes the hope of rebirths in springs to come. The reference to the man's bones and the emphatic "sigue segando" underline his limitation; the image of light shining through a prism embodies the vitality of nature. In the last lines, the juxtaposition of the spring leaf and the stubble left by the harvester condenses the overall contrast between them. In one sense this juxtaposition evokes the paradox of nature being both harvested and renewed. But in another it makes us feel the opposition between natural vitality and the harvester's limitation: each is part of a continuum, but while that of nature promises rebirth and renewal, that of the man consists of mechanical repetition.

We should be careful not to attribute an overt social message to this poem, tempting though that may seem: the harvester is nowhere defined as an exploited being, and his very lack of individualization prevents us from seeing him as a particular victim. Yet the contrast between him and the landscape creates a general sense of the limiting pattern of his life, which may well be the underlying perception we derive from the poem.

The way in which this sense is conveyed to us is most important in characterizing Cabañero's poetry. Very specific details (the way in which the man holds the scythe and uses his hands) are coupled with precise visual images (cutting as wounding, blood as a skein) to create an effect. The depersonification of the harvester as well as the vivification of nature are constructed out of such details and images, giving the poem great precision. Yet all the precise details and images are also set into a pattern of oppositions that points to a larger vision.

A similar procedure is used in "Carrero de la Mancha," though here man and nature blend rather than contrast:

> El sudor que le surca los tendones;
> los callos como rocas, casi heridas;
> el traje es un barbecho de jirones;
> los dientes poderosos, sin saliva,
> amarillos y duros. Es alto y tira
> de sus huesos al aire y a los soles.
>
> La tierra se le sube a piel y a poro,
> no sabe de leer ni necesita
> otro país que no tenga este cielo;
> le han dicho que al morir se rescucita. [p. 31]

Again the emphasis falls on a few physical details describing the cart driver; two of them, (his calluses and his clothes) are linked to objects in his landscape (rocks, fallow fields). This makes the man both a physical "type" and a part of his surroundings, and makes his toughness and his elemental nature a reflection of the innate starkness of this land. The allusion to his illiteracy does not seem in this context a negative judgment, but merely one more index of his function and his limits. The allusion to his belief in resurrection, never picked up again in this poem, may suggest a faint desire for transcendence, or more likely a belief in some form of continuity.

This picture of the cart driver as fitted into his world is developed throughout the poem and culminates in a final portrayal of the Castilian as both defined and limited by his world:

> Timoneros, carreros de la Mancha,
> estamos solos en la geografía,
> aquí acaba la luz. Abandonados
> en el centro de España nos limitan
> los vientos más fronteros. Los carreros
> acechan las llanuras infinitas. [p. 32]

Although there is a clear ambiguity in this presentation (the cartdrivers are both fitted into their world and lost in its barrenness), the speaker identifies himself with them ("*nos* limitan") and leaves us with a sense of order. This makes the poem's meaning different from that of "El segador," in which the contrast of man and nature pointed to the limitations of the former. But its way of using descriptive detail and of depersonifying the protagonist in order to produce a wider vision is much the same.

This is also true of "Campesino trágico" (pp. 37-38), in which the peasant is deindividualized to portray his immersion in his setting and its limitations. Here the personification of nature and a series of images of suffering emphasize this limitation; much like "El segador," the work leaves us with a feeling of the confines of Spanish peasant life.

In a few poems of *Desde el sol y la anchura*, Cabañero uses images and personifications for purely aesthetic effects. "Soneto del racimo recién cortado," for example, fancifully transforms a bunch of grapes into a living being:

> Bien colmado y lujoso, reengarzado
> en su collar de perlas, se figura
> tener cuello y garganta, entre verdura,
> del sarmiento jugoso columpiado.
>
> Bien colmado, racimo, bien colmado,
> luces tu escaparate, tu espesura
> de pámpanos triunfales . . .
> . . . .
> Y en tu herida, de bruces, te has quedado
> sin venas y sin brisa, sin altura:
> la navaja al cercén te ha derribado. [p. 51]

The personification, based on the comparison between grapes and pearls, simply offers us a new and unexpected perspective, which the poet then develops—at the end, the cutting of the grapes becomes an assassination. But there is no serious tragedy here, no wider vision of human existence. Cabañero has simply exercised his gift for language to forge an unusual perspective of a common object.

Throughout this book Cabañero skillfully develops and elaborates detailed descriptions to produce poetic meaning. Metaphorical relationships, personifications, and depersonifications create novel perspectives. In the most significant poems of the book, however, they also embody wider views of the inhabitants of Castile—and, by extension, of other human beings. Most often their meanings center on the rhythms, values, and limitations of their existence, and on their relationships with their landscape; at times they touch on the social concerns that will later become central to Cabañero's poetry, and at others they relate to the poet's search for order and fulfillment in everyday existence. The last poem of *Desde el sol y la anchura,* titled "Ruego al Señor desde la tierra," stresses that search: "Siémbranos, lluévenos, siega y destierra / esta sed que nos quema y nos moltura" (p. 72).

Though published only two years after *Desde el sol, Una señal de amor* marks a considerable shift in Cabañero's poetry. The book contains no sonnets; most of its poems adopt a much more conversational style than the ones in *Desde el sol.* Although we will find in it images, personifications, and depersonifications akin to the ones we have seen so far, these become parts of more extensive patterns of imagery, which often acquire symbolic meaning. These patterns connect the immediate reality evoked to larger issues. Thematically, *Una señal de amor* focuses on human relationships and on feelings of love (toward a beloved, toward fellow human beings); these themes extend out of the concern for man's situation as it appeared in *Desde el sol,* but take it further and deal more explicitly with his situation in society.[4]

The first poem, untitled, illustrates several characteristics of the book. It begins with a series of similes describing the speaker:

> Como la hoz y el trigo estoy dispuesto;
> veo el amor que viene
> y a la primera señal que haga
> como un barbecho me abro.
>
> Siempre diré que sí, tiraré al arma
> de hombre perseguido aunque me venzan.
> . . . .
>
> Y ahora, amigos,
> estos años, que voy a menos
> como esas tiendecitas que no venden de nada,

> veo una flor caída en todas partes,
> no sé de qué color es la justicia: [p. 77]

By comparing himself to several items connected with the harvest, the speaker keeps the focus away from his individuality and places it on his role as a natural receptor, open to "el amor." Subsequent images define further his role and the characteristics of this "amor": the simile of the small store conveys his lack of material success, the fallen flower his awareness of losses surrounding him. In later sections of this poem the speaker makes clear his desire to love those around him, and uses a gong to portray his desire to convey that love in his poetry (p. 78). All these images are less grounded in visual detail than those we saw in *Desde el sol;* they quickly take us beyond any literal scene to a symbolic pattern in which the speaker is a seeker for love and harmony in a turbulent world.

A new series of images describes the state of that world later in the poem:

> voy debajo del cielo lentamente
> en busca de las hierbas más tranquilas . . .
> Pero siempre, implacable,
> un toro apunta, vuela un cuervo, lucho
> contra las piedras,
> se me derrama el puño y no descanso. [p. 78]

The speaker's walking in search of a tranquil setting fits into a symbolic quest for love and order. The following images, in this context, evoke the destructive forces with which he must contend. The bull and the crow are not explainable anecdotally: they constitute "visionary metaphors," in terms of Carlos Bousoño's definition, and are objective equivalents to the feelings of danger, struggle, and menace which the world holds for the speaker.[5]

Seen as a whole, this poem is less objective than "El segador." It is grounded in the speaker's feelings rather than in a vignette; the images used not only deindividualize the speaker but point explicitly to his symbolic search (where in "El segador" the wider meaning emerged indirectly); their variety and the presence of visionary metaphors make clear that the poem's unity lies in its overall theme and not in one specific visual scene. All this suggests that Cabañero has not only left behind the tight forms of his first book, but also gone beyond its more descriptive focus. Yet he continues to use detailed visual images and transformations to create symbolic patterns and embody wider visions.

One of the most impressive poems in this book is titled "Fotografía del pocero":

> La foto es en un pozo,
> la soledad del día
> distribuido por los campos,
> durando estaría arriba en el paisaje.
>
> En conjunto está sucio y nos da pena.
> Atareado en sus jornales,
> con greda hasta los ojos, tanteando
> la sombra cardinal, golpea y tunde
> el corazón de los chinarros.
>
> En realidad está triste.
> Depende de su nombre y apellidos,
> del pan poco y su aliento,
> quizá también de Dios y de los músculos;
> cuando llegue la noche
> dependerá del sueño . . .
>
> Casi no importa.
> Cuadra con la desgracia solamente.
> Si así se puede hablar, hecho una lástima,
> trabaja allá perdido,
> con el cabello a punto de ser cieno,
> con los huesos hundidos, con las uñas
> agarradas el fondo.
>
> Así, bajo las calles,
> en las cloacas turbias, en las minas.
> Después de haberle visto
> es un martillo que golpea siempre
> contra el sueño de todo el que descansa. [pp. 110-111]

By focusing on a photograph of a well-digger rather than just describing the man directly, the poem already signals a stepping back from literal reality. The impression of stylization is confirmed by the images of day as spread through the fields and of solitude as pervading the landscape. Each of these concretizes something intangible (a unit of time, a feeling), but at the same time makes us aware that the scene is being transformed by the speaker. The impression of a reality simultaneously made concrete and stylized prepares us for the subsequent description of the well-digger, who too will be made vivid on the one hand and turned into a wider sign on the other.

Looking over the portrayal of this man in stanzas 2-4, we notice the presence of descriptive details; the well-digger has clay up to his eyes, he savagely attacks the stones, his hair seems to turn into mud, his fingernails scratch the bottom of the well. Yet we are immediately invited to give these details symbolic value, to make them signs of the limitations and the trap which the man's life represents. Such a reading is in my opinion not arbitrary but engendered by the text. Having been alerted to the transformation of the reality described in stanza 1, we quickly notice words which give the well-digger's situation a representative rather than a literal meaning. "Tanteando / la sombra cardinal" suggests a basic groping for meaning; the man's dependence on his name, on sleep, on basic fare (bread) makes him an embodiment of the striving for survival in elemental fashion. His situation—digging amidst dirt in a well—has archetypal echoes, since the underground carries negative (perhaps infernal) connotations, and turning into dirt also suggests negativity, maybe death. In addition, all of the details make the well-digger vivid as a type rather than an individual: thus they intensify the impact of the scene and simultaneously support its symbolic value.

The well-digger's function as type and symbol is underlined in the last stanza. The speaker again focuses on the man's underground location: the reference to "cloacas" accents its negative value and its earlier archetypal connotations. By then making the man's image a hammer interrupting one's sleep, he defines him as a representative social victim weighing on our consciences.

"Fotografía del pocero" contains images and descriptive details as specific and precise as those we saw in *Desde el sol.* Yet Cabañero now focuses on fewer such elements, and does not construct patterns of humanization and depersonification out of them. Instead, he works them into archetypal schemes and gives them symbolic value. This produces a poem less elaborate and seemingly more direct than "El segador" or "Carrero de la Mancha," but one that is even more effective in making a larger theme emerge from concrete images.

A yet more evident symbolic scheme portrays another social theme in "El andamio" (pp. 108-10), in which the action of building the scaffold embodies men's efforts to collaborate and better their situation. The symbolism is not defined conceptually but emerges from the details of the scene and from occasional references to the contemporary world. On the most immediate level the poem contains descriptions of the way in which the ropes should be tied, of the need to make strong knots, of a previous episode in which a scaffold fell down and killed a man. Yet the references to our world, the continued allusions to the need for solidarity, and some very basic juxtapositions (between working to build the scaffold and idly watching a bird or a girl, for example) lead the reader to the work's social theme.[6] Like the other poems from *Una señal de amor,* this one is successful in using descriptive detail to engender a wider social meaning.

Recordatorio, published in 1961, reveals a similar use of imagery and description. As the title indicates, it is based on a series of past memories and evocations, many of them presented in great detail. Cabañero makes them very specific and yet never merely anecdotal. Florencio Martínez Ruiz has suggested that the colloquial elements and expressions in the book are cleansed of any possible vulgarity, and are given "con toda la viveza de la palabra elemental."[7] This is done not by eliminating realistic detail but by making the individual elements point deeper. Cabañero again uses archetypal resonances, personifications, and images to infuse meaning into his text, and offers us poems at once specific and significative.

This is apparent in the book's first poem, titled "Castilla 1960":

> Poco era el silencio. Aún bastaba
> distraer los oídos, ser la vida,
> la carretera hacia Madrid, viajeros
> en aquel autobús . . . Se oía la radio:
> una jota de ha tiempo, castellana,
> se escuchaba ancestral, tónica. Un treno
> envolvente, con sueño, con sonido.
> Regresaba una época entre gentes
> de labor y de fiesta y de combate,
> esclava y medieval, de en par al miedo.
> La encina inextinguible, allá en las lomas
> del contraluz poniente de la tarde,
> y al compás de esa jota, terminada
> en un lamento corto, un arañazo,
> un tapiado quejido, la cantata
> de alguna voz pasada que aún moría.
> Había silencio apenas. Las gargantas
> enjutas de los montes transponían
> —oh santidad impintable del crepúsculo—
> torrenteras románicas, arrugas
> del rostro del paisaje en el silencio,
> pastada geología de la muerte. [pp. 121-22]

The people in this scene are backgrounded and seen collectively rather than individually. Described as "gentes / de labor y de fiesta y de combate," they become part of the setting; called medieval, they fit very well with the feelings of the Spain of old that are brought in by the music. This music in turn is vivified and becomes central to the scene. (We notice that it becomes a moan and a lament, offers dreams, and recalls the song of some voice of the past.) This inversion of the normal roles of people and of music (somewhat reminiscent of the personifications and deindividualizations of "El segador,") is here used to reduce the distance between them, to bring them together into a single evocation of the traditions of the Spain of old, still in evidence in the present. In the second stanza the landscape is presented and personified: it has a face, and the mountains have throats. This intensifies the impression of an evocation which integrates land, music, history, and people into a single subjective reality of Spain.

The speaker's attitude to this world is ambivalent: he is captivated by the echoes of the past on the one hand, yet sees the scene as "pastada geología de la muerte" on the other. The ambivalence is reflected in his simultaneous vivification of the landscape and its characterization as an image of death. As the poem develops, he is tempted to focus even more on this past: "Bastaría callar, volver la frente / a algún borroso icono, a la escultura / . . . / Bastaría cerrar los ojos sólo" (p. 122). Up to this point in the poem, the vivifications and collectivizations have contributed to forge a vision of an archaic music, land, and people, at once inviting and frightening in their pastness.

In the last stanza the music is intensified and mixes with the landscape and the speaker's imaginings of the past:

> La jota en funerales oleadas
> lo hería todo. Combatían en las sombras
> fantasmas a caballo, lanzas, yelmos,
> espadones terribles, observados
> por la presencia sola de los valles.
> Los ríos apurados, mil castillos
> sin muros, en huida; . . . [p. 122]

The vivification of the music and of the rivers and castles (their movement based, of course, on the impressions they create as one passes them on a bus) contributes to the sense of a single, overwhelming sensorial experience. The speaker becomes totally immersed in it until he suddenly takes stock of himself and focuses on the present:

> . . . Mas nosotros
> íbamos a Madrid por este año
> y estos trigos nacientes—oh esperanza
> del hombre en paz y a salvo—hacia un tiempo
> de libertad, sin miedos. Todos juntos

hacia el amor. Ahora, en este tiempo
que no vuelve atrás nunca, mas nosotros
pidiendo, deseando que así sea. [p. 122]

The tone of the poem has changed completely; the personified fantasies
linked with the past give way to a clear, rational view of present goals.
The only visual image, the wheat, stands as an explicit symbol of hope.
The profusion of sensations and the long rhythms of the previous
sections (reinforced by "encabalgamientos suaves") give way to a discursive presentation, punctuated by caesuras and "encabalgamientos
abruptos" that interrupt the flow of the lines.[8] All of this marks the
speaker's shift to a more pragmatic attitude, his decision to leave past
dreams behind and deal with present goals. He does so, of course, with
reluctance, still wishing that the past might return; yet he knows that
it will not do so, and prepares to deal with the real future.

Seen as a whole, this poem is a dramatization of the speaker's
nostalgic evocation of Spain as past, of his awareness that evidence of
it still remains in the land, the people, and the music, and of his reluctant
resolve to leave all that behind and face the present—the world of the
city of Madrid, as contrasted to the men, music, and lands of rural
Castile. Indirectly the poem underlines a social theme, the necessity of
working in the present for the common good rather than reliving the
past, however attractive that might seem. The poem's value and impact,
however, depend to a great degree on the ways in which images, personifications, and deindividualizations create a single experience of the
past, immerse us in it, and then dramatically lead us away.

In other poems of the book, images and scenes of country life are
used to construct symbolic schemes which recall "Fotografía del
pocero" or "El andamio." In "Trigo nuevo del amor," for example, the
growth of wheat becomes a symbol and a model for the striving for
peace and harmony among men. Specific images of the wheat's growth
and harvest both give immediacy to the poem and point to its symbolic
level. At the end, the patterns of life of wheat and man are explicitly
fused, and the harvest of the former becomes the fulfillment of the
latter's desire to give himself and to love others: "Cómo es corta esta
vida para amarnos / unos a otros, como nos pedía / el haz primero que
vino a sembrarnos / en fondo y forma de cosecha un día." (p. 169).

In "El disfraz," Cabañero portrays modern man as a masked participant in a carnival, whose disguises conceal his essence and make him
live in a world of dishonesty and deceit. Various detailed images illustrate the falsehoods of his life; specific references to his existence as a
carnival underline its hollowness and its lack of purpose:

Siga el juego.
Salgamos a la calle todos juntos
al baile, al carnaval, a la verbena,
con el traje mejor, con la cara mejor,
con el disfraz mejor.
. . . .
Oh norma acostumbrada, larga risa
extendida hacia el mundo y sus derechos;
hombres mal destinados a beberse
este mal vino, digo este brebaje
del parecernos bien todas las cosas; [p. 149]

As in so many of Cabañero's poems, the detailed images ground the poem in concrete reality while configuring a larger symbolic scheme.

In several poems of *Recordatorio,* a few visual images highlight the theme. In "Primer recordatorio," for example, remembrances are portrayed as a beehive; later on, the speaker who recalls his past sees himself as if he were eating the prey collected in a painful hunt (pp. 123-25). Both images convert an abstract and complicated activity (the difficult, painful, and yet necessary recall of the past) into simpler, concrete acts. They fulfill a symbolic as well as a descriptive function and account for the poem's effectiveness in conveying its theme. The image of eating one's memories serves a similar purpose in "Para mis amigos" (p. 137).

The detailed recollections of the past give *Recordatorio* much of its immediacy and let Cabañero embody his social themes in dramatic patterns like the one we saw in "Castilla 1960." Aside from this, the book reveals the same use of images and personifications for the embodiment of wider themes which we have observed throughout Cabañero's poetry, and the construction of symbolic patterns out of selected images and scenes which became important in his work beginning with *Una señal de amor.*

The theme of love dominates *Marisa Sabia y otros poemas* (1963); again and again the speaker focuses on the beloved as reason and guide to his life. Many poems of this book, like those in *Recordatorio,* portray detailed objects and events; but these are imagined rather than recalled, and refer to future plans or to fantasies which help the speaker define his love. The book therefore acquires a different dimension, in which imagining, inventing, and poetizing become a form of living and loving. Certain oft-repeated images support this dimension: the speaker sees himself as filming his visions, and refers to ways in which he wants to recreate his actions.[9] The renewed use of the sonnet form may also reflect Cabañero's increased consciousness of the poem as creative act.

This consciousness is apparent in the title poem, which describes
the discovery of Marisa as a motivating factor in the speaker's existence
and activities:

> A cántaros se han hecho los mares para un niño:
> con los besos no dados, el amor verdadero.
> Hoy sé que por ti he sido capaz, Marisa Sabia,
> de levantar a pulso, espuerta a espuerta,
> un cerro o una torre,
> un chorro de silencio incontenible
> hasta subir al infinito y verte.
>
> Te he visto hacia el amor, la fe y la dicha.
> Y encontrarte, Marisa, el sólo verte,
> ha sido el pan y el premio que ya no me esperaba
> después de tantos años de amor falso,
> sueño a crédito y ruina.
>
> En la vivida feria tengo visto
> brazos, piernas, caderas, pechos y ojos
> más chicos y mayores que los tuyos. ¿Qué importa?
> Acaso tan difíciles, otros más cariñosos.
> Algunos—¿cuáles de ellos?—he logrado tenerlos,
> muy fácil: por dinero a por dolor.
> Tú me has costado más que todo junto,
> que hasta ti he consumido los días de mi vida,
> mi obrero corazón, las dioptrías restantes.
>
> Cuento en versos las horas desde que te conozco,
> y hoy, al pensar en ti, pregunto: ¿cómo eres?
> Hablo sin hacer ruido: ¿dónde estabas?
> O estás un poco enferma,
> o tienes un examen, o te callas, o fumas
> viendo tendida el río del tiempo consumirse.
> Yo sigo todo un curso de fe. Tú miras, piensas;
> te marchas a tu pueblo; vuelves, dices
> con tu voz que se escucha venir convalesciente,
> con tu raza y tu línea de judía castellana,
> igual que los frutales apuntando,
> las estatuas más bellas
> y el color sefardí de tu garganta hermosa.
>
> Para poder quererte y no morirme
> creí en sueños, atrás, hacia adelante,
> tomé oficios hermosos. ¿Cuánto hace
> que aré por ti y segué, corté racimos de uva,
> teché tu cuarto entonces, abrí balconerías
> directamente dando a la luz de tus ojos?

Desde que el mundo fue corazonándome
filmé a oscuras los versos que esta noche te escribo;
para poder quererte como ahora,
tomé trenes en marcha cada día;
viví por ti, gané el jornal exacto
para el café y los libros . . . [pp. 195-96]

Like the actions described in Cabañero's earlier poems, those here presented carry symbolic meanings and give concrete embodiment to subjective attitudes. The speaker's dedication to Marisa is portrayed by his laborious building of a hill by basketfulls; his willingness to devote all efforts on her behalf is represented by his having performed a variety of physical labors. But in this poem, unlike "Fotografía del pocero," all the actions are imagined and metaphorical. The poem's symbolic meaning emerges not from a scene observed and described but from vignettes specifically invented to express the speaker's attitude. The images used in the poem function in the same fashion: bread and a prize express the value Marisa holds for him. All of this not only removes the poem from literal reality but also makes us aware of the poetic process going on within it: its speaker is explicitly drawn as a poet who makes up images and imaginary activities to represent his love.

Like many of Cabañero's poems, this one uses depersonifications and deindividualizations. By reducing the other women he has loved to fragments of their bodies ("brazos, piernas, caderas, pechos y ojos"), the speaker dramatizes their insignificance and contrasts their purely physical effect to Marisa's poetic and imaginative one. Later on, he deindividualizes Marisa herself in a very different way: comparing her to fruit trees and statues, he links her with natural and artistic fulfillment. In the light of the speaker's explicit role as creator, these devices acquire even greater importance: they exemplify how images and poetic devices *make* meaning, how they define Marisa as an ideal and other female figures as valueless.

The speaker also makes explicit references to his creative activity. In stanza 4 he states that he measures in poetry the time he has known the beloved. While this is a way of stressing his love, it also highlights his poetic role. When in the next stanza he alludes to the writing of this very poem and sees himself as having filmed it in advance, he again underlines this role. In the light of it, the desire that he expresses at the end of the poem—that he may be inspired by Marisa to live more fully —reflects his dedication not only to the beloved herself but also to the poetic vision and creativity which she has motivated.

The link between the beloved and poetic creation is also evident in "Nocturno vivo":

Mientras se pone su antifaz el sueño,
en un hortal, coloreadas sombras
encharcan las regueras, entre calles
de yerbolito intermitente y fronda
de aire en vetas parado, las cigarras,
cuyos ruidos al fondo del agosto
calan el pecho y su temperatura,
inventan un país dodecafónico
donde tu cuerpo roza el agua, el leve
invencionero mar del amor solo.

Querida mía, pequeña Sabia, novia
nacida no en Castilla ni otro reino,
sino del alma universal llegada
justo a la vida, al tiempo de quererla;
niña mayor, porosa piel tan clara,
viento por la cintura, fe en los ojos
en el cine de ayer, querida mía,
coral del Duero, femenina égloga.

Estos días que ausente estás, de noche,
por entre el sueño llegarán tus manos,
alcanzarán mi frente con los dedos
que has posado en las fotos que me diste,
dedos que filmo y pulsan en la noche
hasta hacerme llorar, querida mía . . .

Tengo una vida incontenible al borde
de tus brazos, que salvan carreteras,
la guerra aquella y tanta paz cansándonos,
brazos por mayo verde y romancero,
entre las peregrinas mariposas
desarropadas en los viejos días
de la infancia, y tu rostro en travesía,
. . . .
es ya la hora pura de querernos
ellos, los dos, nosotros, todo el mundo. [p.201-02]

The first stanza describes a garden scene, but one that has been poetically transformed. The reference to a personified dream that puts on its
mask points to this transformation; the description itself stresses subjective effects produced by the scene, and gives way to the image of the
locusts' song as motivating a fantastic atmosphere ("dodecafónico" may
stress its irreality by referring to contemporary music). By then placing
the beloved in this setting and linking the scene to love, the poem makes

us feel that his beloved is the motivating force of the speaker's poetic portrayal of this scene.

This leads right into the description of Marisa in the second stanza, in which she is removed from the literal circumstances of her life and birth, and made into an idealized source of love. By metaphorizing her as coral and as an eclogue, the speaker links her to natural and poetic beauty; by relating her to a movie, he also ties her to a more modern source of inspiration. All of these deindividualizing images stress her value as a muse. In the light of them, the speaker's vision of the absent Marisa as coming to him in dreams makes perfect sense: since she is primarily an ideal and a poetic inspiration, her image and meaning can transcend the literal distance between them and continue to offer him meaning. The last lines of the poem extend this meaning further and suggest a social theme: the love she motivates brings forth an awareness of the need for general love among men.

In both of these poems from *Marisa Sabia,* Cabañero continues using imagery, personfication, and deindividualization to lead his reader to a wider vision; in both he highlights key images which acquire symbolic resonances. But the new emphasis on the theme of love (which at times encompasses the social), and above all the stress on the creative act itself, bring a new dimension to this book.

Frequently a few key images stand out in a poem from *Marisa Sabia,* and govern its meaning. In "Primeras vacaciones," for example, the speaker first describes himself as formless water seeking its form in the ways of loving Marisa, and later as a creature desperately scratching "la amaneada bestia gris del tiempo" with his fingernails (p. 198). Both of these images embody the speaker's desire to give expression and permanence to his feelings. In that sense they function very much like the symbolic images of *Recordatorio,* objectifying the poem's theme. In this particular text they lead us to view loving and writing poetry about love as a creative task, a battle against nothingness: "Amar es inventar, borrar un rostro / contra un espejo, blanquear la nada" (p. 198). At the end of this poem, the protagonist envisions himself collecting things that belong to his beloved and holding and transforming the landscape in his efforts to win this battle. In another poem of the book, "La diosa" (pp. 204-05), Cabañero uses the image of filming the memories of the loved one to portray the speaker's efforts to capture and preserve her and her love.

Despite its thematic and stylistic variety, Eladio Cabañero's poetry consistently exhibits an extremely precise use of description, imagery, personification and depersonification. By means of these, Cabañero can treat subjects as traditional as transcendent love or as overdone (in the Spain of the 1950s) as social problems, tangibly and meaningfully. This in turn sets him apart from many other Spanish social writers and ties him to the artistic consciousness and achievements of the other salient poets of his generation.

10 ANGEL CRESPO and MANUEL MANTERO

The two poets I will study in this chapter are not often considered members of the group I have been studying in this book. Neither Angel Crespo nor Manuel Mantero is included in the anthologies of Ribes and Batlló, or discussed in José Olivio Jiménez's *Diez años de poesía española.* Some of this may be explained by the fact that Mantero never associated with the other poets and has spent twelve years teaching in the United States, while Crespo published many of his books prior to 1960 and has been living in Puerto Rico for many years. Both of these authors have nevertheless written excellent poetry, similar in many ways to that of the other poets here studied, and important in assessing the production of this generation. Again and again both Crespo and Mantero present ordinary objects in everyday terms and yet evoke significant visions. Their ways of transforming common materials into valuable poetic creations illustrate and contribute to one of the main achievements of their generation.

Angel Crespo was born in 1926 and published his first five books of poetry between 1950 and 1957; he also participated in the *Postismo* movement and directed two poetry magazines of the early 1950s, *El Pájaro de Paja* and *Deucalión.* This has led Carlos de la Rica to consider him, together with Federico Muelas and Gabino-Alejandro Carriedo, as a member of a "Generation of 1951," characterized by a poetic use of humor and opposition to the rhetoric of the 1940s.[1] Correct though this assessment may be, it excessively limits Crespo's poetry, which has longer-lasting values. Throughout Crespo's poetic trajectory, we can see his constant striving to discover and create significant meanings amidst the everyday. Sometimes playfully, by distorting the appearance of things, and at other times in a more serious vein, Crespo keeps producing original works. He also makes use of references to literature and art, revealing his interest in the creative process, in poetry, and in the visual arts. These references have become increasingly important in his most recent work.

Since I will not concern myself with the chronological development of Crespo's poetry, I will look at works from *En medio del camino,* a collection in which Crespo has edited and rearranged almost all of the poems he published between 1949 and 1970, and which gives a good idea of the range and depth of his work. The first part of that volume, which contains poems written between 1949 and 1955, includes one titled "Los pequeños objetos":

> Los pequeños detalles de la casa:
> el hilo en el tapete abandonado,
> la cerilla en el suelo,
> la ceniza,
> que pone en la baldosa su frágil contextura,
> la uñita del pequeño recortada
> al lado del zapato,
> ponen gusto en los ojos que, sin dar importancia,
> coleccionan imágenes de objetos que no sirven.
>
> Se ama más a la madre por el hilo,
> se acuerda uno del padre
> por la cerilla y la ceniza,
> y del niño por la uña y el zapato.
>
> Los pequeños objetos que se barren,
> que ya nadie recoge,
> sumamente importantes, nos recuerdan
> los pequeños disgustos de la vida
> y los pobres placeres, tan pequeños. [p. 20]

The effect of this work is based on a paradox: the most insignificant objects turn out to be very important in recalling and preserving emotive meanings. Crespo stresses this paradox by the way in which he develops the poem. The slow, detailed description of the objects in the first stanza focuses our attention on them, while making us wonder why they are so important, why it is necessary to visualize a toenail lying on the floor next to a shoe. The last lines of the stanza offer a partial answer in the speaker's pleasure at collecting useless objects; his interest in these minutiae is due to his antipragmatic attitude. But we still do not know how these things are valuable to him, and still find his attitude somewhat incomprehensible. (We do notice the speaker's passivity: he portrays himself as a pair of eyes contemplating, not as a doer.)

The explanation emerges in the next stanza: these objects recall key persons in the speaker's life. This explains and emphasizes the speaker's subjective and antipragmatic attitude, making us see him as someone who rejects materially valuable things in favor of those linked to emotional meanings. It also suggests that concrete reality acquires unexpected significance when seen in subjective terms. This idea becomes more explicit in the last stanza, as the speaker asserts the importance of small things and events, and ties together his central paradox in the juxtaposition of "pequeños objetos" and "sumamente importantes."

The way in which this poem has been set up and developed is crucial to its meaning. Had it started with a direct statement about the importance of small objects, or even with its last stanza, it would have seemed both forced and didactic—the assertion of an odd attitude on the part of an idiosyncratic speaker. By immersing us instead in the details of the first stanza, the poem both involves us in the speaker's perspective and builds our curiosity regarding its central paradox. The explanation offered in the last stanza becomes a justification and a resolution of an enigma instead of a didactic assertion. By his selection of detail, his pattern of development, his sense of pacing, and the use of a nonassertive speaker who involves the reader in his perspective, Crespo has effectively conveyed a vision of the poetic significance of the everyday.[2]

A similar process develops in "Las cosas," which also appears in the first part of *En medio del camino.* The poem begins with a plain description of a rural scene, only to surprise us with a very unusual shift in perspective:

> Por los caminos encontramos bueyes.
> Vamos contando testas de animales cornudos.
> En los caminos encontramos árboles.
> Vamos contando ramas de vegetales altos.
> Vamos por los caminos contando hierbas.
> Pero también los bueyes cuentan presencias de hombres.
> Y los árboles cuentan nervudos brazos de hombre.
> Y las hierbas nos cuentan las pestañas.
>
> Todas las cosas tienen
> ojos para mirarnos,
> lengua para decirnos,
> dientes para mordernos.
> Vamos andando igual que si nadie nos viese,
> pero las cosas nos están mirando. [p. 23]

The first five lines focus on the literal scene in a totally uncreative fashion: the direct style, the lack of run-on lines, the repetition of words and syntactic constructions heighten the prosaic effect. This makes the statements of lines 6-8 very jarring: pragmatic reality has been left behind and a whole new vision of the world emerges. This vision seems even more puzzling because it is presented in the same declarative style as the first lines; style and perspective simply do not match.

The second stanza picks up the novel idea that reality contemplates us and turns it into a general philosophic statement, the form of which, as Pilar Gómez Bedate has pointed out, recalls fourteenth-century didactic verse.[3] In the context of this poem's development (and of Crespo's poetry as a whole), this statement that reality contemplates us acquires wider meaning: it suggests that in the world around us there are values and perspectives that transcend our literal view. The way in which Crespo first immerses us in the most pedestrian of realities and then shocks us with an unusual attitude is a demonstration of this theme, since it makes us first fall into a pragmatic perspective and then be shaken out of it. "Las cosas" is an excellent example of Crespo's ability to present an everyday reality so as to trap the reader into a certain viewpoint, and then to dramatically undercut that viewpoint, lead him to a more poetic vision, and present his theme of the imaginative values hidden in the everyday.

The use of anecdotal reality to convey larger meanings is also evident in the second part of *En medio del camino,* composed of poems written between 1954 and 1959. Here, however, common scenes and things are presented from the very beginning through the eyes of a speaker who alters and interprets them. "La vuelta" furnishes a good example:

> Por el camino se me van cayendo
> frutas podridas de la mano
> y voy dejando manchas de tristeza en el polvo
> dondequiera que piso;
> un pájaro amanece ante mis ojos
> y en seguida anochece entre sus alas;
> la asamblea de hormigas se disuelve
> cuando en mí la tormenta se aproxima;
> el sol calienta al mar en unas lágrimas
> que en el camino enciende mi presencia;
> la desnudez del campo va vistiéndose
> según van mis miradas acosándole
> y el viento hace estallar
> una guerra civil entre las hierbas. [p. 75]

All the things evoked embody the speaker's negative attitude toward his life and his surroundings. The rotten fruit that he drops and the spots that he leaves objectify his feelings about the meaninglessness of his life; the abrupt changes in the figurative landscape ("un pájaro amanece . . . / y en seguida anochece"), as well as the constant shifting from image to image, evoke the discord present in him and in his surroundings. Concrete reality is used to immerse the reader in a negative vision of life's process. (The sense of process, as Metzler has noted, is intensified by mixing verbs in the present and the present progressive.[4])

This whole vision of the speaker's present state and surroundings later gives way to a very positive evocation of his past:

Vengo desnudo de la hermosa clámide
que solía vestirme cuando entonces:
clámide con las voces de los pájaros,
el graznido del cuervo,
la carrera veloz de la raposa,
del arroyo que un día se llevaba mis pasos
y de olores de jara y de romero,
hace tanto tejida. [p. 75]

The cloak, as well as the images of birds and animals woven on it, embodies the past feelings of harmony and contentment, dramatizing the contrast between lost happiness and present discontent.

Physical details here serve, as they do in the poems studied earlier, to involve the reader in the speaker's view of the conflict between beauty and disorder. Unlike those poems, "La vuelta" subordinates these details to the speaker's perspective and also endows them with an almost symbolic function, making them configure the opposition between two realities and two states of mind. But it still illustrates Crespo's constant skill in using common elements to make his reader experience significant visions. This is even more apparent when we consider the poem's ending, in which the speaker's recall of past order leads him to overcome his discontent:

Pero yo te conozco, campo mío,
yo recuerdo haber puesto entre tus brazos
aquel cuerpo caliente que tenía,
y haber dejado sueño entre los surcos
que abrían los caballos de otros tiempos.
Yo te conozco y noto que tus senos
empiezan a ascender hacia mis labios. [p. 76]

The vignette of the speaker's fitting his body in with a personified nature again underlines his orderly past and leads him to reestablish his sense of harmony as he personifies nature and feels his union with it. The blend of visual, sensual, and visionary images of this last part brings to a close the poem's dramatic development, making vivid the answer which the speaker has found to his initial discontent. As we look back at the whole poem we can see that concrete details, manipulated by the speaker's perspective, have combined with symbolic suggestions and with a dramatic progression to convey the conflict between two visions of life and its resolution.

A similar elaboration of natural details occurs in "La lluvia":

> Cuando la tierra suda hacia su centro
> y abren la boca las raíces
> y, a golpe vegetal de diente y lengua,
> trituran gotas de agua
> que han de ascender cantando hacia lo verde;
> cuando la lluvia, cuando por la noche
> —cuando es de día en muchas ocasiones—,
> cuando un país vive de guerras
> y de comercios espantosos,
> y está lloviendo y, sin embargo,
> hay personas que vagan por las calles
> y corren por los campos y se esconden;
> . . . .
> una palabra encima de la mesa
> cambia de tono, se diluye,
> o se convierte en cínife y escapa. [p. 58]

A constant process of personification underlies the initial description, which progressively turns rainwater into earth's inward sweat, into food for mouths (roots) of plants, into food which these plants turn to leaves. Contrived as these images may seem, they are all based on the details of the literal process by which rainwater seeps into the earth and is absorbed by plants. This description is an excellent example of how Crespo uses the details of physical reality as a basis for his poems.

The images and personifications themselves turn literal reality into an eerie scene, a Bosch-like picture of humanized earth and roots absorbing and chewing. This scene reflects the perspective and state of mind of the speaker, defining him as a pessimist who sees this natural process in almost grotesque fashion. The fact that this whole description is composed of a series of phrases beginning with "cuando" focuses us even more on the scene and moment being evoked, and intensifies the eerie feeling. It also creates a tone of restlessness and anxiety, since these phrases succeed each other without reaching resolution. (In grammatical terms, they all form a chain of subordinate clauses that does not end until much later in the poem, with the main clause "una palabra encima de la mesa / cambia de tono.") Having set his poem in a detailed scene of nature, Crespo has used this scene to embody a highly subjective, anguished vision. The references to a country that lives off wars, to "comercios espantosos," and perhaps even to the people wandering through the streets link it to the social realities of Spain and of our time. But the poem's main thrust is on the subjective mood itself and on its embodiment through physical details.

The last three lines I have quoted complete the poem's first sentence and introduce a new idea, which becomes a main theme of this poem. In some fashion, the scene previously evoked and its subjective implications cause the dilution and loss of words—and, by implication, of poetic expression. Having words turn into mosquitoes adds a humorous note but does not eliminate the feeling that the negative mood which has been evoked somehow destroys verbal expression and creativity. This impression is confirmed in the poem's ending, which shows strong men hiding from the rain and weak ones gnawed ("roído") by hopes and disappointments. The negative feelings and memories conjured by this scene emerge, in the final analysis, as something which inhibits expression and creativity.

Looking back over the poem, we can see that the distorted view of a detailed natural process has situated us within an anguished mood, and has made this mood and the negative memories which it has evoked in the speaker the reason for a loss of confidence and expression. Crespo has again made use of descriptive detail—albeit highly distorted detail—to involve his reader in a subjective experience underlying his theme.

Part three of *En medio del camino* contains mostly works devoted to poets and painters, written between 1958 and 1964. It reveals Crespo's growing concern with the creative process and his belief in the need for poetry as well as painting to discover forms through which to express creatively significant visions of his time. (As Metzler has pointed out, Crespo focuses on artists who dealt with universal questions in original fashion.[5]) In this sense, it relates Crespo to the other members of his generation, although it does not contain poems which evoke common scenes and events.

The fourth part of the volume, on the other hand, includes many such poems. Also composed of works written between 1958 and 1964, it does not reveal the imaginative recreation of the everyday through imagery that we saw in part two; rather than transforming reality in a search for meanings, their speaker presents an object or scene and suggests wider implications. Frequently the contemplation of an element leads to a symbolic pattern or to some underlying vision of life or society.

"La cabra" offers a good example:

> La vieja cabra que el cuchillo
> respetó. Se movía
> como la hierba cuando crece.
> De pronto, sus orejas
> ya estaban lacias, o su belfo
> entreabierto, o estaba
> el animal junto a la puerta
> del horno. El animal
> —o más bien bicho, fardo
> de piel y huesos, con las ubres
> como viejas talegas que guardaron
> cobre y, a veces, plata—,
> el bicho melancólico
> que se dormía al sol tocando tierra
> con los hermosos cuernos.
> Porque los cuernos eran su sonrisa,
> su afirmación, su gesto de haber sido:
> brillantes de mañana, por la siesta
> mates de polvo y tedio, por la noche
> oscuros de abandono, y humeantes
> de bruma con la aurora. [p. 165]

By forming his poem out of a series of phrases and sentence fragments, Crespo gives it the sense of a spontaneous description, a vignette thrown at us rather than a story developed in time. He also draws attention to various descriptive details (ears, lip, udder), modifying some of them metaphorically (the udder is a moneybag). All this creates a strong sense of immediacy and makes us visualize the goat in physical and almost crude terms. Yet this goat simultaneously acquires symbolic resonances: by having it move "like grass when it grows," Crespo ties it to the natural process; by saying that the knife respected it he identifies it as a survivor of some sacrificial act. And the description of its horns at the end of this section turns the goat even more into a sign of natural endurance and survival in the face of life's stages and vicissitudes.

The rest of the poem develops this vision of the goat, making it the representative of a basic vitality which affirms itself against destructive

forces: in a final ironic twist the animal asserts this vitality even at the
moment of its death by goring "el contemplador desprevenido" (p. 166),
using its symbolic horns to keep fighting for survival. Yet the effectiveness of the poem's symbolism depends in large part on the specificity
and objectivity of the description of the goat. By using a visual close-up
of that goat, Crespo draws his rather ethereal wider theme from immediate reality.

In the prose poem "Amanecer," a detailed description again conveys
a wider pattern:

> Las piedras de la calle, lavadas por la escarcha, crecen y se
> avecinan; como losas, hacen a mi paso ruido de rompeolas.
>
> Las paredes encaladas ascienden vertiginosamente contra
> la naciente luz y se curvan, a modo de viseras, sobre las calles,
> proyectando su sombra fluyente en la paja derramada por las
> aceras de cemento.
>
> Al llegar a la plaza, la iglesia se muestra con su enorme y
> destartalado cajón en el que no cabe la imagen de la patrona.
> La santa, como imposible diosa rural, asoma por el tejado y
> se confunde con la torre.
>
> Y un buey que muge, un can que ladra, un vecino que tose,
> me ponen en fuga, apedreándome con su guerra. [p. 195]

The speaker begins by highlighting and magnifying a common object
and immersing us in the specificity of a common act, that of walking
down a cobblestoned street. Yet by seeing the stones as washed by the
frost, he evokes a sense of purity, supported perhaps by the image of
steps sounding like the splashing of water over a dam. Both the impression of immediacy and the hint of freshness and purity are reinforced
in the second stanza: the description of walls ascending and the detailed
picture of the shadows falling on straw-covered sidewalks accent the
former, while the sense of motion and geometry as well as the adverb
"vertiginosamente" suggests the latter.

The next stanza again creates an impression of immediacy by its
description of the church as a messy bin or drawer and by the fantastic
but visual image of the saint's statue protruding through the roof of this
too-small church. But a double change has occurred: physical objects are
now not only described but also distorted, and the impression created
by them is one of chaos rather than purity. This produces a dramatic
shift to a negative vision which carries over into the last stanza, with

its prosaic evocation of vulgar realities and the image of this whole vulgar reality as chasing the speaker away.

Physical details have been evoked and magnified in "Amanecer" to juxtapose contrasting impressions of cleanliness and disorder, of beauty and ugliness.[6] While not as evidently symbolic as "La cabra," this poem nevertheless uses descriptive detail to embody poetically the conflicting subjective impressions which the reality of dawn in a village can produce.

If we compare the different poems of Crespo that I have examined, we will note an increasing complexity in the use of descriptive detail, and an increasing tendency to find symbolic implications in the everyday. But underlying such shifts is the poet's constant ability to immerse his reader in the details of ordinary reality, to control these details through language and form, and to use them to guide and alter the reader's perspective. In this fashion his poems produce dramatic, gradually unfolding experiences of significant themes.

Manuel Mantero's poetry seems more heterogeneous and uneven than that of Crespo, and exibits a great variety of tones and attitudes. Many of Mantero's poems are especially effective in giving new life to worn themes and situations—usually by casting them in colloquial language, by presenting them through unexpectedly contemporary settings, or by embodying them in modern objects. Even though much of Mantero's poetry deals with matters such as nostalgia for a past love, the fate of man and the apprehension of death, and the search for truth and poetic value, its images and perspectives let it portray such subjects in original ways.

This is apparent in "Una pelota de tenis," which forms part of Mantero's first book of poetry, *Mínimas del ciprés y los labios,* first published in 1958:

> De mis objetos viejos
> eres el que más amo,
> pues tú te doblegaste
> al tacto de unos dedos que siempre quise míos
> y nunca pude acariciar minúsculos
> Condenada a quietud histórica
> por mi juventud de hoy,
> me regalas aquel veloz encanto
> de serlo todo o nada frente a ella,
> raqueta y red apenas, cielo liso,

cuando el placer más limpio ilustraba los ojos
(ágiles piernas y faldilla blanca, mi corza)
y la angustia se hacía de la flor venidera. [p. 34]

The recall of a beloved through some object that belonged to her is a poetic commonplace, especially familiar to anyone acquainted with Renaissance verse. Making the object a tennis ball, however, brings in a fresh perspective, alerting us to the new way of treating a traditional subject. By addressing the ball itself, just as Garcilaso and others addressed the beloved's mementos, the speaker intensifies both the parallel and the contrast with conventional poems on the subject. All these coincidences and the use of a tennis ball undercut as well as elaborate the convention so much that the poem becomes humorous.

But the image needs also to be taken seriously. Mantero exploits it to the fullest by focusing on the physical contact between the woman and the tennis ball, and makes the ball's bending in her hand a touch and a yielding. This anchors the poem in a specific scene and act, and turns the commonplace of a beloved's "prenda" into a new and vivid evocation of a time and a person from the speaker's past. It also sets up an ironic contrast between the ball's "experience" in feeling the woman's hand and the speaker's lack of that experience, which highlights his melancholy and intensifies the sense of unfulfillment. All in all, the use of details in presenting the ball's "history" pins down and magnifies the poem's effect. This effect is further intensified by other details in the second part of the text: the evocation of the woman tennis player's vignette as "ágiles piernas y faldilla blance," the references to the racket, net, and sky, and the image of woman as deer, all conjure up the memory of a specific event. They also underline the theme of a past gone by and the speaker's nostalgia in the face of that past.

Throughout the poem, visual and anecdotal details of the tennis match and ball have been used to give a new dimension to an age-old theme. Both by modernizing a convention and by anchoring the poem in a specific reality, seen through close-ups, Mantero makes the evocation of a past time and love into a significant experience. The poem does suggest wider symbolic overtones to the event described: the speaker makes the tennis game into an attempt to be "all or nothing" to the woman, hence into a kind of battle for her love. But the poem's originality resides less in such overtones or in the theme of the lover's lament than in the impact produced by the image of the tennis ball and the concrete evocations of the scene.

In "Callao-Argüelles" from *Tiempo del hombre* (1960), an ordinary scene of contemporary life acquires symbolic overtones. The poem's

value, however, resides in its use of detail to give immediacy to its
theme:

> Me traga antes de tiempo
> la tierra. Caras pálidas tropiezan
> con mis ojos, cinturas de mujer
> se inhiben en la lid sin aventura.
> Huele a Egipto mortal, a luz de siglos.
> Ya no hay remedio ni salida.
> "Metro" del hombre, manadero
> de hastío, vida que nos lleva
> a la estación de Dios y nos desagua.
> Manos asidas a la prisa, gestos vagos
> de almas furiosas en su invernadero.
> Debajo de la tierra vamos todos
> como raíces desbocadas. Alguien
> silba entre dientes, alguien lee el periódico.
> No somos hombres, somos sombras,
> pesadillas camino de un osario
> bañado por la luna de diciembre.
> Busco el barro que el dedo pide
> para hacer una infancia junto a un pozo,
> como en el tiempo aquel, cuando el verano.
> (Barro de hombre me entregan, malo y duro,
> y me lo ponen contra las costillas.)
>
> Llegamos. Hombres, ratas,
> salimos, bruto río que asesina,
> salimos a lo claro como si alguien
> nos diera un escobazo y nos echara
> a envenenar de nuevo la hermosura. [p. 53]

The title alludes to one of the most congested subway lines of Madrid.
Mantero builds his poem on the fairly obvious correspondence between
a subway system and a tomb, making this correspondence clear from the
outset by the references to a premature burial and an Egyptian burial
place. It is the specific details, however, that give force to the correspondence and further the vision of the dreariness of daily life. The vignettes
of bored travelers and vague gestures, the image of a fountain of bore-
dom and of people as roots, and the reelaboration of the traditional
image of man as dust (here he is "barro"), all point to that theme. Calling
the people "sombras" and "pesadillas" evokes a Hades or hell. What
Mantero offers us is not so much a neat symbolic scheme as a sensorial
evocation of modern meaninglessness, reinforced by the double parallel

between subway and tomb and subway and hell. In the last stanza the picture of men and rats (and men as rats) emerging from the system, chased by some force into contaminating a natural world, brings to a climax this evocation and the pessimistic view of life that underlies it.

On first impression, "Callao-Argüelles" differs substantially from "Una pelota de tenis": it deals with a social rather than a personal theme, it uses a scene and a series of images rather than a central image, it employs a symbolic pattern not present in the other poem. But both works sketch with precision insignificant objects of modern life; both blend sensorial evocations with traditional patterns (the "prenda" of the beloved, the underground as death and hell) to give forceful expression to larger themes.

Similar effects are achieved in "Salida del cine," in which a crowd of people leaving a movie house on Madrid's "Gran Vía" is also presented as the emergence of people from a kind of tomb. The poem recalls the symbolic overtones and the social theme of "Callao-Argüelles" and also makes use of specific images which create a mood of meaninglessness and alienation:

> . . . Pudre
>
> la carne más a oscuras
> su soledad de tumba.
>
> De siete a nueve salen
> eléctricos cadáveres
>
> buscando a Dios con lágrimas.
> . . . .
>
> Madrid, cine, Gran Vía,
> de siete a nueve. Huída.
>
> Pronto faltará tierra
> para tanta alma muerta. [p. 65]

By making the viewers inhabitants of a tomb and the characters on screen "electric cadavers" or ghosts, Mantero turns the whole scene into a world of the dead, leading the reader to a final symbolic picture of Madrid as a cemetery holding people who are emotionally dead and can only exist in the escapist reality of movie houses.

Misa solemne (1966), probably Mantero's best-known book of poetry, uses the framework of the Mass and allusions to its various parts to deal with the problems of man's existence in the modern world. As Mantero himself has noted, the religious ceremony and religious references constitute the form and vehicle of the book rather than its theme;

but they serve very effectively to place modern issues in a wider context.[7] Again, detailed evocations of daily reality combine with religious evocations to create poems of great originality. In the section titled "Evangelio," Mantero places Christ in a series of contemporary Spanish situations and occupations. If the Gospel during the Mass portrays moments of Christ's life in order to teach key principles of Christianity, Mantero's modern "Gospel scenes" dramatize the experiences that a man of Christian vision might have in our world. In one section (pp. 148-50), Christ is a poor man who goes with his friends to claim a harvest that is due him by law, and is met by a wealthy owner who beats him and runs him off. In another, Christ becomes a bus driver who offers sympathy and understanding to his passengers:

> En aquel tiempo, Cristo era
> conductor de autobús.
> Miraba
> las calles de la gran ciudad con fe,
> como algo suyo, familiar
> de tanto usarlo. En sueños
> podía describir exactamente
> el contorno urbano:
> jardines, plazas,
> comercios,
> quioscos de flores,
>
> . . . .
> Tenía sus amigos,
> según las horas:
> a las diez se montaba
> la anciana que iba al cementerio,
> cana, enlutada; al descender,
> lo saludaba con un gesto exótico
>
> . . . .
> A las dos, regresaban
> de la universidad aquellos novios:
> él
> de barba negra y labios apetentes,
> y ella
> menuda,
> serena de filosofía y ojos
> pendientes del arrimo en los vaivenes
> que el generoso conductor forzaba,
> pensando al verlos
> así apretados que
> cada vez que ama el hombre,
> lo eterno se provoca y se comprueba.

. . . .
Cristo era
conductor de autobús.
Al fin de la jornada,
en su casa, aliviado,
se miraba las manos sorprendido
de que ellas tanto dispusieran,
pensaba en la fragilidad del cargamento
que le era encomendado,
y se dormía
para soñar con calles y jardines,
con fuentes, automóviles, estatuas,
y la masa mortal de los humanos [pp. 150-51]

By naming the most familiar places and objects of a modern city
("jardines, plazas, / comercios," "fuentes, automóviles, estatuas") at
the beginning and end of the section, and by having Christ view them
lovingly, Mantero frames this section within an unusually positive vision of our surroundings. This vision extends to the city "types" portrayed: through perceptively observed details the poem makes us see
them as refreshing examples of human gestures, impulses, and concerns.
As a result, the poem offers us a new vision of both Christ and a modern
city. The latter acquires unexpected value once it is contemplated from
this unexpected perspective; Christ, in turn, emerges as much more than
the conventional preacher of long ago or the figurehead of an institu-
tionalized church, and his message of love is related to the circumstances
of our everyday lives.

Some poems from *Misa solemne* are more evidently symbolic; in "El
estiércol" (from the section "Ofertorio"), manure comes to stand for the
process of renovation in life. Mantero gives value to this rather obvious
symbol, however, by situating it within a very detailed evocation of life
in the countryside during the speaker's youth. The theme of renovation
emerges naturally from this evocation: the children's excitement in the
face of various natural scenes leads smoothly to the view of fertilization
as renewal. Like many other poems of this book, this one uses descriptive detail to give novel expression to an old abstract theme.

In *Poemas exclusivos (1967-1971)*, first published as the last part of
Poesía (1958-1971), Mantero frequently makes unexpected use of modern objects. By treating the typewriter as the essential vehicle of his
creativity in "Homenaje a mi máquina de escribir," the speaker simultaneously portrays the excitement of the creative task and adopts a whim-
sical view of his role as poet. This allows the poem to praise poetic
endeavor without succumbing to sentimentality, and to balance a seri-

ous idealism with an ironic awareness of human limitations. At one point the speaker conjures a serious, almost overly idealistic defense of the typewriter as a means of poetic expression:

> Sin ti, mi sangre se coagularía
> y sería mi voz un silencio zahareño
> de estepa dentro de otra estepa.
> En tus teclas redondas como mundos
> cabe el mío creado por mis manos [p. 289]

Were the poem to continue entirely in this vein, we might well deem it excessively idealistic, and its speaker somewhat pompous in his defense of the importance of his craft. Hence we find welcome relief when this speaker can talk of his own selfish needs and mock his small pleasures in typing and using words that contain the letter *ñ:*

> Por ti
> yo puedo apuñalar o agradecer,
> desarrugar el ceño del arcángel,
> sonreír a la idea ya fijada
> y enviar un poema a un antólogo.
> . . . .
> Soy tu poder y el mío tú,
> . . . .
> como una espada contra un bosque en llamas,
> mi corazón nunca cansado
> con el que ahora escribo más la *ñ* exótica
> de mis palabras importantes,
> año, guadaña, viña, sueño, España, mañana . . . [pp. 289-90]

The rather grandiose image of fighting a burning forest is undercut by the final vignette, making us see the speaker / poet as simultaneously serious and filled with human foibles. All in all, the poem is a perfect example of how contemporary details can convey larger visions in such ways as to avoid triteness or hollow solemnity. Together with the other works of Mantero which I have mentioned, it illustrates this poet's remarkable skill in giving new life to old themes by the use of modern allusions.

Many of Mantero's poems, even more than Crespo's, seem on first impression to consist of realistic evocations of the everyday, and to recall the social and descriptive verse so prevalent in Spain in the early 1950s. But, as we have seen, the details of contemporary life are controlled by the poet to seize larger issues in original ways. By combining references to these details with well-known literary resonances and by constant perspective play, Mantero leads his readers to develop new visions of both traditional themes and everyday reality. Though his poetry has fewer surprises and shifts than that of Crespo, it is akin to Crespo's in the way it deepens and poeticizes its materials by allusion and perspective play. In this fashion it exemplifies the ability of the Generation of 1956-1971 to turn common language into uncommon art.

Afterword

A careful study of Spanish poetry of the Generation of 1956–1971 makes evident its innovativeness and importance. Although they base their works on the ordinary reality surrounding them and write in everyday language, the members of this generation create poems of great originality by skillful use of their materials. The combination of diverse language codes in the work of Rodríguez, the blending of colloquial expressions and intertextual effects by Fuertes, and the detailed descriptions and transformations of Cabañero illustrate their transcendence of the pedestrian realism of many earlier post-Civil War writers. The poets I have studied also reveal a concern with wider themes, especially the passage of time, the mystery of existence, the relationships between the specific and the universal, and poetic creativity itself. Their novel handling of such themes should be clear in the preceding studies: these confirm, to my mind, the generation's role in renewing Spanish poetry and directing it to more significant goals. They also suggest closer bonds between these poets and the Generation of 1927, and show the inaccuracy of prior critical views which saw the whole post-Civil War period as a definitive break with the earlier tradition of universal and creative poetry.

My studies suggest some further generalizations. Again and again we have seen these poets dealing with their themes so as to engender within the reader gradually changing discoveries and experiences. To some extent, of course, all good philosophic poetry offers slowly unfolding experiences rather than set messages. But the poets of this generation carry this goal further and make the very process of reading a key part of the subjects they are conveying. The chapters on Brines, González, and Valente have made clear that the visions of their poems come into being within the reader in several stages, as the latter follows clues in the text, rereads, and modifies his or her reactions. The intertextualities used by Fuertes and the traditional metaphors and conventions reworked by Sahagún, as well as many transformations of reality by Gil de Biedma, provide examples of textual manipulation that triggers meanings latent within us. The metapoetic and intertextual features of much of the poetry of this generation intensifies our sense of the poem as process. Rather than merely describing this poetry as philosophic, we will do better to speak of it as a progressive and unfolding confrontation with life's basic themes on the part of both poet and reader. This way of viewing it will also help us to relate it to the more evidently open-ended texts of some younger poets.

All of this suggests needed revisions in some commonly held notions of contemporary Spanish literary history. In their view of poetry as a unique way of both knowing and making, and in the exemplification of that view in their work, the poets of the Generation of 1956–1971 resume and develop a tradition that had its origins in symbolism and found full expression in the 1920s and 1930s but was interrupted, for historical reasons, during and immediately after the Civil War. The stress on the act of writing as an act of discovery that we find in the works of Valente, Rodríguez, and others, and the way in which the poems of these authors become processes of discovery for the reader, take traditional notions of the creativity and significance of poetic meaning further than they were taken in the 1920s, and lay the ground for the even more allusive and more aestheticist writings of the late 1970s.

The works I have studied also make us reflect on the very nature of poetry. The way in which they constitute acts of discovery leads us to think of poetry not merely as texts to be decoded but as a means of the continued exploration of language and of reality through language. It highlights the importance of intertextual relationships and suggests that diverse poems by diverse poets combine into larger units in this process of exploration. By means of this process, the poetry of the Generation of 1956–1971 makes us expand our vision of the roles that poet, poem, and reader can play in defining, extending, and remaking the world we experience.

Selected Bibliography

To save space and minimize duplication, I have limited this bibliography to selected general studies and anthologies (most of which include critical commentary), to the books of poetry written by the authors studied, and to significant critical studies of their work. I have omitted reviews except for a few very important ones. Works of literary theory cited in the text can be found in the notes and the index. Facts of publication for works listed in section I are not repeated in section II. The asterisk (*) indicates the edition from which I quote in the text of this book.

I. SELECTED ANTHOLOGIES AND GENERAL STUDIES

Aleixandre, Vincente. *Algunos caracteres de la nueva poesía espñola.* Madrid: Instituto de España, 1955.

Antología consultada de la joven poesía española. Valencia: Distribuciones Mares, 1952.

Badosa, Enrique. "Primero hablemos de Júpiter (la poesía como medio de conocimiento)." *Papeles de Son Armadans* 10 (1958), no. 28: 32-46; no. 29. 135-59.

Bary, David. "Sobre el nombrar poético en la poesía española contemporánea." *Papeles de Son Armadans* 44 (1967): 161-89.

Barral, Carlos. "Poesía no es communicación." *Laye,* no. 23 (1953): 23-26.

Batlló, José. "An Introduction to Spanish Poetry." *Mundus Artium* 2, no. 2 (1969): 66-71.

———, ed. *Antología de la nueva poesía española.* Madrid: El Bardo, 1968. [Contains study and statements by the poets.]

Bousoño, Carlos. "Poesía contemporánea y poesía postcontemporánea." [1961, 1964] In *Teoría de la expresión poética,* 4th ed., pp. 533-76. Madrid: Ed. Gredos, 1966.

Campbell, Federico. *Infame turba.* Barcelona: Ed. Lumen, 1971. [Interviews with various writers.]

Cano, José Luis. *Poesía española contemporánea: las generaciones de posguerra.* Madrid: Guadarrama, 1974.

Carnero, Guillermo. *El grupo "Cántico" de Córdoba.* Madrid: Ed. Nacional, 1976.

Castellet, José María, ed. *Nueve novísimos poetas españoles.* Barcelona: Barral, 1970. [Anthology preceded by a study.]

———. *Veinte años de poesía española, 1939-1959.* Barcelona: Ed. Seix Barral, 1960. [Study and anthology.]

Ciplijauskaité, Biruté. *El poeta y la poesía.* Madrid: Insula, 1966. [See especially pp. 383-484.]

Concha, Victor G. de la. *La poesía española de posguerra: teoría e historia de sus movimientos.* Madrid: Ed. Prensa Española, 1973.

Correa, Gustavo. *Poesía española del siglo veinte, antología.* New York: Appleton-Century-Crofts, 1972. [Anthology and study.]

———, ed. *Antología de la poesía española (1900-1980),* 2 vols. Madrid: Editorial Gredos, 1980. [Study, athology, bibliography.]

de la Rica, Carlos. "Vanguardia de los años cincuenta (desde el ismo a la generación)." *Papeles de Son Armadans* 37 (1965): no. 109: i-xvi; no. 110: xxv-xlviii; no. 112: iii-xv.

Díaz, Janet W. "Main Currents in 20th Century Spanish Poetry." *Romance Notes* 9 (1968): 194-200.

Fox, E. Inman. "La poesía social y la tradición simbolista." *La Torre* 17, no. 64 (1969): 47–62.

Gil de Biedma, Jaime. "Poesía y communicación." *Cuadernos Hispanoamericanos,* no. 67 (1955): 96-101.

Gimferrer, Pere. "Notas parciales sobre poesía española de posguerra." In Salvador Clotas and Gimferrer, *Treinta años de literatura,* pp. 91-108. Barcelona: Ed. Kairós, 1971.

González Martín, J.-P. *Poesía hispánica 1939-1969 (estudio y antología).* Barcelona: El Bardo, 1970.

González Muela, Joaquín. *La nueva poesía española.* Madrid: Ed. Alcalá, 1973. [Commentaries with extensive quotations.]

Grande, Félix. *Apuntes sobre poesía española de posguerra.* Madrid: Taurus, 1970.

Hernández, Antonio, ed. *Una promoción desheredada: la poética del 50.* Madrid: Zero-Zyx, 1978. [Study and anthology.]

Ilie, Paul. "The Disguises of Protest: Contemporary Spanish Poetry." *Michigan Quarterly Review* 10 (1971): 38-48.

Jiménez, José Olivio. *Cinco poetas del tiempo.* 2nd ed. Madrid: Insula, 1972.

———. *Diez años de poesía española (1960-1970).* Madrid: Insula, 1972.

———. "Medio siglo de poesía española (1917-1967)." *Hispania* 50 (1967): 931–46.

———. "Poética y poesía de la joven generación española." *Hispania* 49 (1966): 195–205.

Lechner, [Johannes]. El *compromiso de la poesía española del siglo XX.* 2d part. Leiden: Universitaire Pers, 1975.

Ley, Charles D. *Spanish Poetry since 1939.* Washington: Catholic Univ. of America Press, 1962.

Mantero, Manuel. "Spanish Poetry in the Twentieth Century." *Topic,* no. 15 (1968): 39–48.

———, ed. *Poesía española contemporánea. Estudio y antología (1939–1965).* Barcelona: Plaza & Janés, 1966.

Marín, Diego. "La naturaleza en la poesía actual española." *Cuadernos Hispanoamericanos,* no. 314-15 (1976): 249-82.

Marra-López, José R. "Una nueva generación poética." *Insula,* no. 221 (1965): 5.

Martínez Ruiz, Florencio, ed. *La nueva poesía española: antología crítica: segunda generación de postguerra, 1955-1970.* Madrid: Biblioteca Nueva, 1971.

Martín Pardo, Enrique, ed. *Nueva poesía española.* Madrid: Scorpio, 1970. [Anthology.]

Millán, Rafael, ed. *Veinte poetas españoles.* Madrid: Agora, 1955. [Anthology.]

Ory, Carlos Edmundo de. "Manifiesto del postismo." In Ory, *Poesía 1945-1969,* ed. Félix Grande, pp. 279-87. Barcelona: EDHASA, 1970. [See also the history of the movement in the same volume.]

Quiñones, Fernando. *Últimos rumbos de la poesía española.* Buenos Aires: Ed. Columba, 1966. [Anthology, with introduction.]

Ribes, Francisco, ed. *Poesía última: selección.* Madrid: Taurus, 1963. [Reprinted 1969, 1975. Study, anthology, and statements by the poets.]

Rubio, Fanny. "La poesía española en el marco cultural de los primeros años de posguerra." *Cuadernos Hispanoamericanos,* no. 276 (1973): 441-67.

St. Martin, Hardie, ed. *Roots and Wings: Poetry from Spain, 1900-1975.* New York: Harper & Row, 1976. [Bilingual anthology, with brief but telling comments.]

Siebenmann, Gustav. *Los estilos poéticos en España desde 1900,* pp. 452-90. Madrid: Ed. Gredos, 1972.

Silver, Philip. "New Spanish Poetry: The Rodríguez-Brines Generation." *Books Abroad* 42 (1968): 211-14.

Torre, Guillermo de. "Contemporary Spanish Poetry." *Texas Quarterly* 4 (1961): 55-78.

Valente, José Angel. *Las palabras de la tribu.* Madrid: Siglo XXI de España Ed., 1971.

II. WORKS BY AND ABOUT THE POETS

FRANCISCO BRINES

A. BOOKS OF POETRY

Las brasas. Madrid: Ed. Rialp, 1960. 2d ed., 1971.

El Santo Inocente. Madrid: Poesía Para Todos, 1965.

Palabras a la oscuridad. Madrid: Insula, 1966.

Aún no. Barcelona: Ocnos, 1971.

* *Poesía 1960-1971: ensayo de una despedida.* Barcelona: Plaza & Janés, 1974.

* *Insistencias en Luzbel.* Madrid: Visor, 1977.

B. SELECTED CRITICAL STUDIES

Amusco, Alejandro. "Algunos aspectos de la obra poética de Francisco Brines."
   Cuadernos Hispanoamericanos, no. 346 (1979): 52-74.
―――. "Francisco Brines: estética de la nada y del sufrimiento." *Insula,* no. 376
   (1978): 1, 12.
Buosoño, Carlos. "Prólogo." In Brines, *Poesía 1960-1971,* pp. 11-94.
Bradford, Carole. "Francisco Brines and Claudio Rodriguez: Two Recent Ap-
   proaches to Poetic Creation." *Crítica Hispánica* 2 (1980): 29-40.
―――. "The Dialectic of Nothingness in the Poetry of Francisco Brines." *Taller
   Literario* 1, no. 2 (1980): 1-12.
Jiménez, José Olivio. *Cinco poetas del tiempo,* 2d. ed., pp. 417-75.
―――. *Diez años de poesía española,* pp. 175-204, 345-49.
Nuñez, Antonio. "Encuentro con Francisco Brines." *Insula,* no. 242 (1967): 4.
Sanz Echeverría, Alfonso. "La insistencia de Francisco Brines." *Jugar Con Fuego*
   [Avilés, Asturias] 3-4 (1977): 33-49.
Simón, César. "Algunos aspectos linguísticos en la sátira de Francisco Brines."
   Cuadernos de Filología, June 1971, pp. 63-70.
Stycos, María Nowakowska. "¿Poemas o silencio? O la pregunta fundamental
   de la poesía de Francisco Brines." [Unpublished.]
Villena, Luis Antonio de. "De luz, de tiempo, de palabra, de hombres: sobre la
   poesía de Francisco Brines." *Insula,* no. 338 (1975): 4-5.
―――. "Sobre 'Insistencias en Luzbel' y la poesía de Francisco Brines." *Papeles
   de Son Armandans* 89 (1978): 213-22.

ELADIO CABAÑERO

A. BOOKS OF POETRY

Desde el sol y la anchura. Tomelloso: Ayuntamiento de Tomelloso, 1956.
Una señal de amor. Madrid: Adonais, 1958,
Recordatorio. Madrid: Palabra y Tiempo, 1961.
Marisa Sabia y otros poemas. Madrid, 1963.
Poesía (1956-1970). Barcelona Plaza & Janés, 1970. [Collected poetry.]

B. SELECTED CRITICAL STUDIES

Manrique de Lara, José Gerardo. "La voz personal y simplista de Eladio
   Cabañero." In *Poetas sociales españoles* pp. 147-52. Madrid: EPESA, 1974.
Mantero, Manuel. *Poesía española contemporánea,* pp. 191-94.
Martínez Ruiz, Florencio. "Prólogo: La poesía de Eladio Cabañero." In
   Cabañero, *Poesía 1956-1970,* pp. 9-23.
Ríos Ruiz, Manuel. "La poesía de Eladio Cabañero." *Cuadernos His-
   panoamericanos,* no. 262 (1972): 151-67.

ANGEL CRESPO

A. BOOKS OF POETRY

Una lengua emerge. Ciudad Real: Instituto de Estudios Manchegos, 1950.

Quedan señales. Madrid: Col Neblí, 1952.
La pintura. Madrid: Agora, 1955.
Todo está vivo. Madrid: Agora, 1956.
La cesta y el río. Madrid: Col. Lazarillo, 1957.
Junio feliz. Madrid: Adonais, 1959.
Júpiter. Madrid: Librería Abril, 1959.
Oda a Nanda Papiri. Cuenca: Col. La Piedra que Habla, 1959.
Antología poética. Valencia: Ed. de la Revista Verbo, 1960. [Selected poems.]
Puerta clavada. Montevideo: Ed. Caballo de Mar, 1961.
Suma y sigue. Barcelona: Col. Colliure, 1962.
Cartas desde un pozo. Santander: La Isla de los Ratones, 1964.
Poesie. Ed. Mario Di Pinto. Roma: Salvatore Sciascia, 1964. [Anthology with translations into Italian.]
No sé cómo decirlo. Cuenca: El Toro de Barro, 1965.
Docena florentina. Madrid: Poesía Para Todos, 1966.
* *En medio del camino: Poesía, 1949-1970.* Barcelona: Seix Barral, 1971. [Collected works to date, in reorganized form.]
Claro: oscuro (1971-1975). Zaragoza: Col. Puyal, 1978.
Colección de climas. Sevilla: Aldebarán, 1978.
Donde no corre el aire. Sevilla: Barro, 1981.

B. SELECTED CRITICAL STUDIES
Albi, José. "Introducción a la poesía de Angel Crespo." In Crespo, *Antología poética*, pp. 9-83.
de la Rica, Carlos. "Vanguardia de los años cincuenta (desde el ismo a la generación." *Papeles de Son Armadans* 37 (1965), no. 109: i-xvi; no. 110: xxv-x1viii; no. 112: iii-xv.
Di Pinto, Mario. Preface. In Crespo, *Poesie* pp. 5-31.
Gómez Bedate, Pilar. "La contestación de la realidad en la poesía de Angel Crespo." *Revista de Letras,* no. 4 (1969): 605-45.
Metzler, Linda. "The Poetry of Angel Crespo." Ph.D. diss., Univ. of Kansas, 1978.

GLORIA FUERTES
A. BOOKS OF POETRY (excluding those directed at children)
Isla ignorada. Madrid: Musa Nueva, 1950.
Antología y poemas del suburbio. Caracas: Lírica Hispana, 1954.
Aconsejo beber hilo. Madrid: Arquero, 1954.
Todo asusta. Caracas: Lírica Hispana, 1958.
. . . Que estás en la tierra. Barcelona: Literaturasa, 1962.
Ni tiro, ni veneno, ni navaja. Barcelona: El Bardo, 1965.
Poeta de guardia. Barcelona: El Bardo, 1968.
Cómo atar los bigotes al tigre. Barcelona: El Bardo, 1969.
Antología poética (1950-1969). Barcelona: Plaza & Janés, 1970.
Sola en la sala. Zaragoza: Javalambre, 1973.

Cuando amas aprendes geografía. Málaga: Curso Superior de Filología, 1973.
* *Obras incompletas.* Madrid: Cátedra, 1975. [Complete works to date. I used the third edition, published by Cátedra in 1977.]
Historia de Gloria (amor, humor y desamor). Madrid: Cátedra, 1980.

B. SELECTED CRITICAL STUDIES

Bellver, Catherine G. "Gloria Fuertes, Poet of Social Consciousness." *Letras Femeninas* 4, no. 1 (1978): 29-38.
Cano, José Luis. *Poesía española contemporánea,* pp. 174-80.
González Muela, Joaquín. "Gloria Fuertes, 'Poeta de guardia.' " *La nueva poesía española,* pp. 13-29.
Mandlove, Nancy B. "Text and Context: The Letter-Poems of Gloria Fuertes." [Unpublished.]
Miró, Emilio. "[Gloria Fuertes] Poesía." *Insula,* no. 288 (1970): 7.
Persin, Margaret H. "Humor as Semiosis in the Poetry of Gloria Fuertes." *Revista Hispánica Moderna,* in press.
Rogers, Timothy J. "The Comic Spirit in the Poetry of Gloria Fuertes." *Perspectives on Contemporary Literature,* in press.
Ynduráin, Francisco. "Prólogo." In Fuertes, *Antología poética 1950-1969,* pp. 9-45.

JAIME GIL DE BIEDMA

A. BOOKS OF POETRY

Según sentencia del tiempo. Barcelona, 1953.
En favor de Venus. Barcelona: Literaturasa, 1965. [Anthology of love poems by Gil de Biedma.]
Compañeros de viaje. Barcelona: Joaquín Horta, 1959.
Moralidades, 1959-1964. Mexico City: Joaquín Mortiz, 1966.
Poemas póstumos. Madrid: Poesía Para Todos, 1968. 2d ed. 1970.
Colección particular. Barcelona: Seix Barral, 1969.
* *Las personas del verbo.* Barcelona: Barral Ed. 1975. [Complete works to date.]

B. SELECTED CRITICAL STUDIES

Carnero, Guillermo. "Jaime Gil de Biedma o la superación del realismo." *Insula,* no. 351 (1976): 1, 3.
Gimferrer, Pere. "La poesía de Jaime Gil de Biedma." *Cuadernos Hispanoamericanos,* no. 202 (1966): 240-45.
González Muela, Joaquín. "Imágenes de Gil de Biedma." *La nueva poesía espanóla,* pp. 81-108.
Jiménez, José Olivio. *Diez años de poesía española,* pp. 205-21.
Mangini González, Shirley. *Jaime Gil de Biedma.* Madrid: Júcar, 1980.
Rodríguez Padrón, Juan. "Jaime Gil de Biedma desde sus 'Poemas póstumos.' " *Cuadernos Hispanoamericanos,* no. 237 (1969): 788-95.

ANGEL GONZALEZ

A. BOOKS OF POETRY

Aspero mundo. Madrid: Ed. Rialp, 1956.
Sin esperanza con convencimiento. Barcelona: Literaturasa, 1961.
Grado elemental. Paris: Ruedo Ibérico, 1962.
Palabra sobre palabra. Madrid: Poesía Para Todos, 1965.
Tratado de urbanismo. Barcelona: El Bardo, 1967. 2d ed., 1976.
Palabra sobre palabra. Barcelona: Seix Barral, 1968. 2d ed., Barral Ed., 1972. *3d ed., Barral Ed., 1977. [Complete works to date. Each edition adds new works.]
Breves acotaciones para una biografía. Las Palmas: Inventarios Provisionales, 1971.
Procedimientos narrativos. Santander: Isla de los Ratones, 1972.
Muestra, corregida y aumentada, de algunos procedimientos narrativos y de las actitudes sentimentales que habitualmente comportan. Madrid: Turner, 1976. 2d enlarged ed., 1977.
"Harsh World" and Other Poems. Trans. Donald D. Walsh. Princeton: Princeton Univ. Press, 1977. [Selected poems, in a bilingual edition.]
Poemas. Madrid: Ed. Cátedra, 1980. [Anthology, with a preface by the poet.]

B. SELECTED CRITICAL STUDIES

Alarcos Llorach, Emilio. *Angel González, poeta (variaciones críticas).* Oviedo: Univ. de Oviedo, 1969.
Benson, Douglas. "Angel González y 'Muestra (1977)': las perspectivas múltiples de una sensibilidad irónica." *Revista Hispánica Moderna:* in press.
————. "La ironía, la función del hablante y la experiencia del lector en la poesía de Angel González," *Hispania* 64 (1981): 570-81.
————. "Linguistic Parody and Reader Response in the Worlds of Angel González." *Anales de la Literatura Española Contemporánea* 7 (1982): in press.
Brower, Gary. "Breves acotaciones para una bio-bibliografía de la vidobra de Angel González." *Mester* 5, no. 1 (1974): 10-12.
Delgado, Bernardo. "Las tres voces de Angel González." *Jugar Con Fuego* [Avilés, Asturias], 3-4 (1977): 77-86.
González Muela, Joaquín. "La poesía de Angel González en su primer período." In R. Pincus Sigele and Gonzalo Sobejano, eds., *Homenaje a Casalduero: crítica y poesía,* pp. 189-99. [A slightly different version is included in *La nueva poesía española,* pp. 31-43.] Madrid: Ed. Gredos, 1972.
Jiménez, José Olivio. *Diez años de poesía española,* pp. 281-304.
Martino, Florentino. "La poesía de Angel González." *Papeles de Son Armadans* 57 (1970): 229-47.
Miller, Martha LaFollette. "Literary Tradition Versus Speaker Experience in the Poetry of Angel González." *Anales de la Literatura Española Contemporánea* 7 (1982): in press.
Rodríguez Padrón, Jorge. "Angel González: 'Tratado de urbanismo." *Cuadernos Hispanoamericanos,* no. 216 (1967): 674-80.

Singleterry, Gary. "The Poetic Cosmovision of Angel González." Ph.D. diss., Univ. of New Mexico, 1972.

MANUEL MANTERO

A. BOOKS OF POETRY

Mínimas del ciprés y los labios. Arcos (Cádiz): Col. Alcaraván, 1958.
Tiempo del hombre. Madrid: Col. Agora, 1960.
La lámpara común. Madrid: Col. Adonáis, 1962.
Misa solemne. Madrid: Ed. Nacional, 1966.
*Poesía (1958-1971). Barcelona: Plaza & Janés, 1972. [Includes a previously unpublished section, "Poemas exclusivos."]
Ya quiere amanecer. Madrid: Col. Dulcinea, 1975.
Crates de Tebas. El Ferrol: Col. Esquío, 1980.
Memorias de Deucalión. Barcelona: Plaza & Janés, in press.

B. SELECTED CRITICAL STUDIES

Cano, José Luis. *Poesía española contemporánea,* pp. 214–18.
Hernández, Antonio. *Una promoción desheredada,* pp. 193-96.
Molina Campos, Enrique. "Poesía de Manuel Mantero." *Cal* [Seville], no. 26 (1978): 22-26.
Roldán, Mariano. " 'Tiempo del hombre' o el sevillantismo esencial de Manuel Mantero," *Insula,* no. 172 (1961): 4.
Ruiz Copete, Juan de Dios. "Manuel Mantero o la poesía de la observación profunda." *Poetas de Sevilla,* pp. 297-308. Seville: Caja de Ahorros Prov. de San Fernando, 1971.
Uceda, Julia. "El sitio del hombre en la poesía de Manuel Mantero." *Insula,* no. 192 (1962): 13.
Villar, Arturo del. " 'Misa solemne,' de Manuel Mantero." *Alerta* [Santander], March 10, 1967.

CLAUDIO RODRÍGUEZ

A. BOOKS OF POETRY

Don de la ebriedad. Madrid: Ed. Rialp, 1953.
Conjuros. Santander: Ed. Cantalapiedra, 1958.
Alianza y condena. Madrid: Revista de Occidente, 1965.
*Poesía 1953-1966. Madrid: Plaza & Janés, 1971.
*El vuelo de la celebración. Madrid: Visor, 1976.
Antología poética, ed. Philip W. Silver. Madrid: Alianza Editorial, 1981. [Contains a useful introduction.]

B. SELECTED CRITICAL STUDIES

Bousoño, Carlos. "Prólogo: La poesía de Claudio Rodríguez." In Rodríguez, *Poesía 1953-1966,* pp. 7-35.

Bradford, Carole A. "Francisco Brines and Claudio Rodríguez: Two Recent Approaches to Poetic Creation." *Crítica Hispánica* 2 (1980): 29-40.

————. "Transcendent Reality in the Poetry of Claudio Rodríguez." *Journal of Spanish Studies—Twentieth Century* 7 (1979): 133-46.

Cano, José Luis. *Poesía española contemporánea*, pp. 153-64.

————. Review of *El vuelo de la celebración. Insula*, no. 359 (1976): 8.

Gonzalez Muela, Joaquín. *La nueva poesía española*, pp. 59-80.

Jiménez, José Olivio. "Claudio Rodríguez entre la luz y el canto: sobre 'El vuelo de la celebración.' " *Papeles de Son Armadans* 87 (1977): 103-24.

————. *Diez años de poesía espñola*, pp. 145-74.

Mandlove, Nancy. "Carnal Knowledge: Claudio Rodríguez and 'El vuelo de la celebración,' " *American Hispanist* 4, no. 32-33 (1979): 20-23.

Miller, Martha La Follette. "Elementos metapoéticos en un poema de Claudio Rodríguez." *Explicación de Textos Literarios* 8 (1979-80): 127-36.

————. "Linguistic Skepticism in 'El vuelo de la celebración.' " *Anales de la Literatura Española Contemporánea* 6 (1981): 105-21.

Mudrovic, William Michael. "Claudio Rodríguez's 'Alianza y condena': Technique, Development, and Unity." *Symposium* 33 (1979): 248-62.

————. "The Poetry of Claudio Rodríguez: Technique and Structure." Ph.D. diss., Univ. of Kansas, 1976.

————. "The Progression of Distance in Claudio Rodríguez's 'Conjuros.' " *Hispania* 63 (1980): 328-34.

Núñez, Antonio. "Encuentro con Claudio Rodríguez." *Insula*, no. 234 (1966): 4.

Sala, José M. "Algunas notas sobre la poesía de Claudio Rodríguez." *Cuadernos Hispanoamericanos*, no. 334 (1978): 125-41.

Sobejano, Gonzalo. " 'Espuma' de Claudio Rodríguez," *Consenso-Revista de Literatura* 2, no. 3 (1978): 37-50.

Villar, Arturo del. "El don de la claridad de Claudio Rodríguez." *Estafeta Literaria*, no. 592 (1976): 20-23.

CARLOS SAHAGÚN

A. BOOKS OF POETRY

Hombre naciente. [Onil, Alicante]:Silbo[1955].

Profecías del agua. Madrid: Ed. Rialp, 1958.

Como si hubiera muerto un niño. Barcelona: Instituto de Estudios Hispánicos, 1961.

Estar contigo. León: Colección Provincia, 1973.

* *Memorial de la noche (1957-1975).* Barcelona: "El Bardo," Ed. Lumen, 1976. [Collected poems.]

Primer y último oficio (1973-1977). León: Col. Provincia, 1979.

B. SELECTED CRITICAL STUDIES

Caballero Bonald, J. M. "Carlos Sahagún: 'Como si hubiera muerto un niño.' " *Insula*, no. 186 (1962): 6.

Cano, José Luis. *Poesía española contemporánea*, pp. 224-28.

Manrique de Lara, José Gerardo. "La poesía de Carlos Sahagún." In *Poetas sociales españoles* pp. 161-67. Madrid: EPESA, 1974.

Moreno Castillo, Enrique. "Memorial de la noche." In Sahagún, *Memorial de la noche,* pp. 5-6.

Rodríguez Puértolas, Julio. "La poesía de Carlos Sahagún: niños y ríos." *Norte* 3 (1969): 45-52.

JOSÉ ANGEL VALENTE

A. BOOKS OF POETRY

A modo de esperanza. Madrid: Adonais, 1955.

Poemas a Lázaro. Madrid: Indice, 1960.

Sobre el lugar del canto. Barcelona: Colliure, 1963.

La memoria y los signos. Madrid: Revista de Occidente, 1966.

Siete representaciones. Barcelona: El Bardo, 1967.

Breve son. Barcelona: El Bardo, 1968.

Presentación y memorial para un monumento. Madrid: Col. Poesía Para Todos, 1970.

El inocente. Mexico City: Joaquín Mortiz, 1970.

*Punto cero (Poesía 1953-1971). Barcelona: Barral Ed., 1972.

Interior con figuras. Barcelona: Barral Ed., 1976.

Material memoria. Barcelona: La Gaya Ciencia, 1979.

Punto cero (Poesía 1953-1979). Barcelona: Ed. Seix Barral, 1980.

B. SELECTED CRITICAL STUDIES

Bousoño, Carlos. "La poesía de José Angel Valente y el nuevo concepto de originalidad." *Insula,* no. 174 (1961): 1, 14.

Cano, José Luis. *Poesía española contemporánea,* pp. 141-52.

Daydí-Tolson, Santiago. "La poética de lo social: 'Sobre el lugar del canto' de José Angel Valente." *Journal of Spanish Studies-Twentieth Century* 6 (1978): 3-11.

―――. "Los efectos de la resonancia en la poesía de José Angel Valente." In *The Analysis of Literary Texts,* ed. Randolph D. Pope, pp. 107-18. Ypsilanti, Mich.: Bilingual Press, 1980.

―――. "Voces de la tribu: la poesía de José Angel Valente." Ph.D. diss., Univ. of Kansas, 1973.

Jiménez, José Olivio. *Diez años de poesía española,* pp. 223-42.

Lertora, Juan C. " 'Poemas a Lázaro': líneas de entrada a una poética." *Cuadernos Hispanoamericanos,* no. 341 (1978): 393-400.

Macrí, Oreste. "Memoria e segni nella poesia di José Angel Valente." *L' Approdo Letterario* 12 (1966): 78-92.

Marra-López, José R. "La poesía de José Angel Valente." *Insula,* no. 219 (1965): 5.

Marson, Ellen Engelson. *Poesía y poética de José Angel Valente.* New York: Eliseo Torres, 1978.

Martino, Florentino. "La poesía de José Angel Valente." *Papeles de Son Armadans* 51 (1968): 144-62.

Persin, Margaret H. "José Angel Valente y la ansiedad de la influencia." *Explicación de Textos Literarios* 8 (1979-1980): 191-200.

———. "José Angel Valente: Poem as Process." *Taller Literario* 1, no. 1 (1980): 24-41.

———. "Underlying Theories of Language in José Angel Valente's 'Poemas a Lázaro.'" [Unpublished.]

Risco, Antonio. "Lázaro en la poesía de José Angel Valente." *Hispania* 56 (1973): 379-85.

Rodríguez Padrón, Jorge. "La poesía de José Angel Valente." *Cuadernos Hispanoamericanos,* no. 222 (1968): 683-87.

Notes

1. THE GENERATION OF 1956–1971

1. Salient critical studies of these poets as a group include José Olivio Jiménez, "Poética y poesía de la joven generación española, *Hispania* 49 (1966): 195-205; and idem, *Diez años de poesía española (1960-1970)* (Madrid: Insula, 1972), pp. 15-32 (reissued, with some changes, as an appendix to the 2nd ed. of *Cinco poetas del tiempo* [Madrid: Insula, 1972]). Jiménez's *Diez años* and José Luis Cano's *Poesía española contemporánea: las generaciones de posguerra* (Madrid: Guadarrama, 1974) include valuable studies of the individual poets of the group. Carlos Bousoño has written significant studies on these poets, which also are useful in seeing the import of the group as a whole. See his introductions to Claudio Rodríguez's *Poesía 1953-1966* (Madrid: Plaza & Janés, 1971) and to Francisco Brines's *Poesía 1960-1971: ensayo de una despedida* (Barcelona: Plaza & Janés, 1974).

2. See for example Félix Grande's thorough *Apuntes sobre poesía española de posguerra* (Madrid: Taurus, 1970), pp. 12-16; and Victor G. de la Concha, *la poesía española de posguerra: teoría e historia de sus movimientos* (Madrid: Ed. Prensa Española, 1973), pp. 118-22, 187-243.

3. See Grande, *Apuntes,* pp. 21-33, and G. de la Concha, *Poesía española,* pp. 311, 340, 351-63. Biruté Ciplijauskaité offers a valuable study of the poetics of these and other post-War writers in *El poeta y la poesía* (Madrid: Insula, 1966), pp. 403-68. She makes the very pertinent observation (p. 406) that the initial impulse to social poetry did not immediately produce a new style. Ciplijauskaité does not make many distinctions between the poets of the 1940s and 1950s and the more recent ones that I am studying; such distinctions were not yet clear in the early 1960s, when her book was written. For examples of the "rehumanized" poetry of the 1940s and 1950s, see *Antología consultada de la joven poesía española* (Valencia: Distribuciones Mares, 1952); and Rafael Millán, ed., *Viente poetas españoles* (Madrid: Agora, 1955).

4. See Grande, *Apuntes,* pp. 33-38. Grande attributes less impact to *Sombra del paraíso* than seems merited. It is also important to note that Aleixandre's later book of poetry *Historia del corazón* (1955) fits into the current of social concerns in poetry that was becoming pervasive at the time.

I use the term Generation of 1927 because of its general acceptability, despite its limitations. On this issue, see my *Estudios sobre poesía española contemporánea—la generación de 1924-1925* (Madrid: Gredos, 1968, 1981), chapter 1.

5. Grande discusses the historical significance of these books (*Apuntes,* pp. 47-49).

6. See Bousoño, "Poesía contemporánea y poesía postcontemporánea," in *Teoría de la expresión poética,* 4th ed. (Madrid: Gredos, 1966), pp. 566-69. The whole essay, originally published in 1961, gives a valuable interpretation of post-Civil War poetry in contrast to "contemporary" poetry (that written in Europe between Baudelaire and World War II).

7. Aleixandre, *Algunos caracteres de la nueva poesía española* (Madrid: Instituto de España, 1955), p. 8.

8. Ibid., pp. 28-29.

9. Grande, *Apuntes,* pp. 39-44.

10. This vision is perhaps best exemplified by José Mariá Castellet's introduction to his anthology *Veinte años de poesía española, 1939-1959* (Barcelona: Seix Barral, 1960), which sees post-Civil War poetry as a movement toward realism and away from the "dehumanization" of earlier verse. From today's perspective it is obvious that poetry did not develop along those same lines in the 1960s, and that Castellet's dichotomy was

exaggerated; his interpretation, nevertheless, is an interesting example of the way the situation was seen by many writers in 1960. The inaccurate nature of Castellet's portrayal of post-War poetry as antisymbolist is pointed out by E. Inman Fox in "La poesía social y la tradición simbolista," *La Torre* 17, no. 64 (1969): 47-62.

11. See Carlos Edmundo de Ory, "Manifiesto del postismo," in his *Poesía 1945-1969*, ed. Félix Grande (Barcelona; EDHASA, 1970), pp. 279-87; and Pere Gimferrer, "Notas parciales sobre poesía española de posguerra," in Salvador Clotas and Gimferrer, *Treinta años de literatura* (Barcelona: Kairós 1971), pp. 103-05. The whole essay (pp. 91-108) offers an important "revisionist" look at post-Civil War poetry, stressing the fossilization of language that occurred in its first phase and the reactions which it evoked.

12. See Carnero, *El grupo 'Cántico' de Córdoba* (Madrid: Ed. Nacional, 1976).

13. Valente, "Tendencia y estilo," *Las palabras de la tribu* (Madrid: Siglo XXI de España Ed., 1971), p. 11; Rodríguez, in Francisco Ribes, ed., *Poesía última: selección* (Madrid: Taurus, 1963), p. 88; Sahagún in Ribes, *Poesía última,* p. 123.

14. Badosa, "Primero hablemos de Júpiter (La poesía como medio de conocimiento)," *Papeles de Son Armadans* 10 (1958), no. 28: 32-46, and no. 29: 135-59. The quote comes from no. 29, pp. 149-50. Badosa sets his essay against Carlos Bousoño's view of poetry as communication, expressed in the various editions of the latter's *Teoría de la expresión poética.* But it is more useful as an attack on cruder visions of poetry as vehicle for social messages than as a denial of Bousoño's fuller view of poetry as conveying complex expeirences.

See also a brief but perceptive earlier essay by Carlos Barral, "Poesía no es comunicación," *Laye,* no. 23 (1953): 23-26. Barral indicates the way in which facile social poetry limits the role of the reader; his essay, however, was not widely read.

15. Sahagún and Rodríguez in Ribes, *Poesía última,* pp. 120, 87; Valente, "Conocimiento y communicación," *Las palabras de la tribu,* p. 10. The original version of this essay appeared in Ribes, *Poesía última.*

16. Badosa, "Primero hablemos de Júpiter," no. 28, p. 39; no. 29, p. 149. Recently Angel González has written: "Porque las palabras del poema configuran con especial intensidad ideas o emociones, o a veces incluso llegan a crearlas." González, *Poemas* (Madrid: Cátedra, 1980), p. 23.

17. See their statements in Ribes, *Poesía última,* pp. 58-59, 87-92, 155-61. The quotation from Rodríguez appears on p. 88.

18. Gimferrer, *Treinta años,* pp. 95-97.

19. Brines, *Insistencias en Luzbel* (Madrid: Visor, 1977), p. 37; and Valente, *Punto cero* (Barcelona: Barral, 1972), pp. 122-23. See also Margaret Persin, "Underlying Theories of Language in José Angel Valente's *Poemas a Lázaro";* and Maria Nowakowska Stycos, "Poemas o silencío" (both unpublished).

20. González, in José Batlló, ed. *Antología de la nueva poesía española* (Madrid: El Bardo, 1968), p. 342.

21. See their statements in ibid., pp. 325 and 352, respectively.

22. José Olivio Jiménez gives a good general comment on their social poetry (*Diez años,* p. 21).

23. Ibid.

24. In an interview, Rodríguez has stated: "Lo importante es la aventura del lenguaje y el pensamiento a través de la palabra. . . . Se trata de cómo las palabras van creando no sólo el pensamiento sino la emodión y la contemplación sensorial." See Federico Campbell, *Infame turba* (Barcelona: Lumen, 1971), p. 119; see also Batlló, *Antología,* p.353. See Sahagún in Ribes, *Poesía última,* p.120.

25. In a brief but important study, Philip Silver has made clear significant ways in which these poets connect with the Generation of 1927, and has suggested a reorientation of the history of Spanish poetry. See his "New Spanish Poetry: The Rodríguez-Brines Generation," *Books Abroad* 42 (1968): 211-14.

26. Batlló, *Antologia,* p. 334.

27. References to diverse critics and critical theories that I have found helpful can be found in succeeding chapters, in context. On "reader criticism" in general, see Wolf-

gang Iser, *The Act of Reading* (Baltimore: Johns Hopkins Univ. Press, 1978); Stanley Fish, *Is There a Text in This Class?* (Cambridge: Harvard Univ. Press, 1980); Umberto Eco, *The Role of the Reader* (Bloomington: Indiana Univ. Press, 1979). For a different, more explicitly psychological approach, see Norman Holland, *The Dynamics of Literary Response* (New York: Oxford Univ. Press, 1968). My earlier work in reader criticism is contained in *Poetas hispanoamericanos contemporáneos* (Madrid: Ed. Gredos, 1976).

28. See Bousoño's introduction to Francisco Brines, *Poesía 1960-1971*, pp. 24-26, which gives one of the best overall descriptions of this generation. Also see Florencio Martínez Ruiz's introduction to his *La nueva poesía española: antología crítica* (Madrid: Biblioteca Nueva, 1971), pp. 12-19.

29. On the way in which the works of these older poets fit the trends of the "second post-War generation" see Jiménez, *Diez años*, pp. 33-99, 123-43.

30. Ibid., pp. 123-28.

31. Ibid., pp. 33-71, 123-43.

32. See Bousoño, "Poesía contemporánea," pp. 566–69.

33. Bousoño, in Brines, *Poesía 1960-1971*, pp. 11-33. This prologue makes clear Bousoño's sympathetic interest in the work of this generation, and the role that he played as a supporter and guide to its members. This role can be related to Bousoño's own poetry of the 1960s, which reveals many characteristics in common with those of the younger poets.

34. See his essay "Conocimiento y comunicación," *Las palabras de la tribu*, pp. 3-10.

35. Batlló, *Antología*, p. 12. For an interesting picture of the personal tensions experienced by this generation and of the repressions it faced, see Carlos Barral's *Años de penitencia* (Madrid: Alianza Editorial, 1975).

36. Petersen, *Filosofía de la ciencia literaria*, Spanish trans. (Mexico City: Fondo de Cultura Económica, 1946), pp. 164-168.

37. See Julián Marías, *El método histórico de las generaciones* (Madrid: Revista de Occidente, 1949), pp. 123-25; also my comments on generations in *Estudios sobre poesía española contemporánea*, 2nd ed., pp. 52-68.

38. José Emilio Portuando makes very common-sense statements to this effect in his *La historia y las generaciones* (Santiago de Cuba: Manigua, 1958), p. 38. One of the best practical applications of the generational scheme is José Arrom's *Esquema generacional de las letras hispanoamericanas* (Bogotá: Instituto Caro y Cuervo, 1963), which for the first time organizes Latin American literary history sensibly.

39. Marías, *El método histórico*, pp. 97-98, 169-78.

40. Arrom, *Esquema generacional*, pp. 15-20.

41. Badosa, "Primero hablemos de Júpiter."

42. Specific references to these and other books are given in the bibliography.

43. Also very important are Gimferrer's "Notas parciales," in *Treinta años*, in their revised assessment of post-War literature and their emphasis on the creativity of the latter period; Félix Grande's *Apuntes sobre poesía española de posguerra;* and José Luis Cano's *Poesía española contemporánea*, which collects previously published essays. Taken together, these works make clear that the generation has become established as a major factor in twentieth-century Spanish poetry.

44. (Barcelona: Barral, 1970.) See also Enrique Martín Pardo, ed., *Nueva poesía española* (Madrid: Scorpio, 1970).

45. For overviews of the work of these writers, see José Olivio Jiménez, *Diez años*, pp. 24-30; and Castellet's prologue to *Nueve novísimos*, pp. 33-47.

2. FRANCISCO BRINES

Francisco Brines was born in Oliva (Valencia) in 1932, and completed studies in law at Salamanca and in letters at Madrid. His books of poetry are as follows: *Las brasas* (1960, 1971), *El Santo Inocente* (1965), *Palabras a la oscuridad* (1966), *Aún no* (1971), and *Insistencias en Luzbel* (1977). All but the last are included in his *Poesía 1960-1971* (1974), from which quotations in this chapter are taken. Full publication facts are given in the bibliography.

1. See José Olivio Jiménez, *Cinco poetas*, 2nd ed., pp. 417-75; idem, *Diez años*, pp. 175-204; and Carlos Bousoño, "Prólogo," in Francisco Brines, *Poesía 1969-1971: ensayo de una despedida* (Barcelona: Plaza & Janés, 1974), pp. 11-94.

2. See Iser, *Act of Reading*, pp. 18-19, 20-27, 62-79. Iser describes the implied reader as "a textual structure anticipating the presence of a recipient without necessarily defining him: this concept prestructures the role to be assumed by each recipient.... Thus the concept of the implied reader designates a network of response inviting structures, which impel the reader to grasp the text" (p. 34). Concerning the progressive way in which a text creates an experience, see Stanley Fish, "Literature in the Reader: Affective Stylistics" (1970), in *Is There a Text in This Class?*, pp. 21-67 (see also pp. 1-17).

3. Iser, *Act of Reading*, pp. 87-92. Bousoño has indicated, in general terms, the presence of this effect in the poetry of Brines ("Prólogo," pp. 46-47).

4. See Jiménez, *Cinco poetas*, pp. 414-25.

5. See Bousoño, "Prólogo," pp. 33–38, 68, 72.

6. The concept of "defamiliarization" is explained by the Russian formalist critic Viktor Shklovsky; see his essay "Art as Technique," in *Russian Formalist Criticism*, trans. and ed. by Lee T. Lemon and Marion J. Reis (Lincoln: Univ. of Nebraska Press, 1965), pp. 13-22. The concept is most helpful in explaining ways in which the implied reader's expectations are altered. Using examples from Russian fiction, Shklovsky examines cases in which a change in the appearance of a common scene or event calls attention to it and leads us to the meaning created in the text.

In a very broad sense, we might also see this poem as an example of intertextuality: it sets its own rather unusual way of presenting man and nature against the normal way in which we have seen them presented in other writings. If we define "text" as not necessarily a particular literary work but rather any reality, read or recalled, that the reader has at his disposal and which affects the reading of the poem he is confronting, then we can say that this poem clearly sets itself up against a previous text. Attention to intertextual relationships of this sort has allowed critics to take a less static view of the works they study, and to show how such works expand their meanings as they are read. See Roland Barthes, "From Work to Text," in *Textual Strategies*, ed. J. V. Harari (Ithaca: Cornell Univ. Press, 1979), pp. 73–81, and Jonathan Culler, *The Pursuit of Signs* (Ithaca: Cornell Univ. Press, 1981), pp. 37-39, 100-107.

7. Concerning "disemia," see Bousoño, "Prólogo," pp. 60-63. Other explanations of this process can be found in Bousoño's prologue to Claudio Rodríguez, *Poesía 1953-1966*, pp. 15-17; and in his *Teoría de la expresión poética*, 4th ed., pp. 149-60.

8. Regarding dramatic monologue, see Robert Langbaum, *The Poetry of Experience* (New York: W. W. Norton, 1957), chapter 2. Similar defamiliarizations occur in other poems of *Las brasas*. In another work from "Poemas de la vida vieja" a man remains passive while nature seems alive and a chair is humanized (p. 110). In the last poem from "El barranco de los pájaros" a man loses individuality as several of his parts fit into natural processes (p. 129). The processes I have been studying seem fundamental to the book as a whole.

9. In 1965 Brines had published *El Santo Inocente*, included later in *Poesía* under the title "Materia narrativa inexacta."

10. Jiménez, *Diez años*, pp. 175-92.

11. In a work dealing with fiction but also applicable to dramatic monologues and to much of recent Spanish poetry, Gonzalo Díaz Migoyo indicates that any time we are faced with an individualized first-person speaker, we take for granted that behind him stands an author who is manipulating his perspective. See his *Estructura de la novela* (Madrid: Ed. Fundamentos, 1978), p. 67. On point of view in poetry, see also my *Poetas hispanoamericanos contemporáneos*.

12. This poem therefore reveals some of the qualities which Michael Riffaterre discusses in *Semiotics of Poetry* (Bloomington: Indiana Univ. Press, 1978), pp. 1-22. Riffaterre shows how certain displacements and distortions on the literal level lead the reader

to reexamine a text from a new vantage point and thus to discover its significance. His view will be very useful to our understanding of the work of Angel González (Chapter 4); it is helpful in understanding some of Brines's texts. I would argue, however, that in many of Brines's poems the defamiliarization already occurs on the literal level and at the first reading.

This poem depends even more clearly on an intertextual relationship for its effect, since it anticipates the reader's stock response to the *topos* of lovers in harmony with nature and then proceeds to modify that response. This intertextual relationship is the key to its dynamic nature, confirming Barthes's notion that intertextuality "asks the reader for an active collaboration" (*Textual Strategies,* p. 80). See also Iser, *Act of Reading,* pp. 69-95.

13. Bousoño, "Prólogo," pp. 39-40, 92-93.

14. Brines, *Insistencias en Luzbel* (Madrid: Visor, 1977). Quotations are taken from this edition. Regarding this book, see Alejandro Amusco, "Francisco Brines: estética de la nada y del sufrimiento," *Insula,* no. 376 (1978): 1, 12; also Carole Bradford, "The Dialectic of Nothingness in the Poetry of Francisco Brines," *Taller Literario* 1, no. 2 (1980): 1-12.

15. Brines, in an interview with Antinio Nuñez; see Nuñez, "Encuentro con Francisco Brines," *Insula,* no. 242 (1967): 4. On Brines's poetics, see Carole Bradford, "Francisco Brines and Claudio Rodríguez: Two Recent Approaches to Poetic Creation," *Crítica Hispánica* 2 (1980): 29–40.

3. CLAUDIO RODRÍGUEZ

Born in Zamora in 1934, Rodríguez obtained a degree in letters and has taught literature in Nottingham, Cambridge, and Madrid, where he now lives. His published poetry consists of the following books: *Don de la ebriedad* (1953), *Conjuros* (1958), *Alianza y condena* (1965), and *El vuelo de la celebración* (1976). The first three, together with an excellent study by Carlos Bousoño, are included in Rodríguez's *Poesía 1953-1966* (1971), from which the quotations in this chapter are taken. In 1981, Alianza Editorial in Madrid published an *Antología poética* of Rodríguez's work.

1. See Rodríguez, *Poesía 1953-1966,* pp. 11-12; William Michael Mudrovic, "The Poetry of Claudio Rodríguez: Technique and Structure" (Ph.d. diss., Univ. of Kansas, 1976); and José M. Sala, "Algunas notas sobre la poesía de Claudio Rodríguez," *Cuadernos Hispanoamericanos,* no. 334 (1978): 134.

2. Bousoño, "Prólogo: La poesía de Claudio Rodríguez," in Rodríguez, *Poesía,* p. 16. Hereafter cited as "Prólogo" (Rodríguez). My translation.

3. Regarding the "implied reader," see Iser, *Act of Reading,* pp. 18-19, 20-27, 62-79.

4. See Barthes, *S/Z, An Essay* (1970), trans. Richard Miller (New York: Hill & Wang, 1974), pp. 5-27.

5. In his prologue to *Poesía 1953-1966,* Bousoño discusses metaphor and allegory in the poetry of Rodríguez. He considers this poetry metaphoric rather than symbolic because he sees symbol as related to irrational and emotive meanings, not as logically explicable as the ones present in Rodríguez's poetry. For Bousoño (pp. 15-17), the exact correspondences in this poetry indicate the presence of metaphor and allegory, even if they are rather unusual. Since I consider the wider meanings of these poems enigmatic and subjective in nature, and cannot see them reduced to exact correspondences, I prefer to speak of a symbolic level.

6. It might seem contradictory to speak of a representational "code," since the representational level of the poem is presumably present before any coding takes place. Nevertheless, Rodríguez uses specific words which keep highlighting this representational level; in seeing these words as a specific code rather than merely as the underlying level of the poem, we are better able to appreciate the work's effect.

7. See Mudrovic, "Poetry of Claudio Rodríguez," p. 70.

8. Shklovsky, "Art as Technique," pp. 13-22.

9. One could argue that the humorous level is not produced by a separate code but rather by a mixture of the representational, symbolic, and cultural codes. This would not alter my view of the effects achieved, since there is clearly a humorous *level* operating. By speaking of a humorous code, one can isolate specific acts (the rooster's stepping on the clothes) which serve exclusively to produce contrast and humor, but the term is not indispensable.

10. This could lead a critic to keep unfolding the poem and "deconstructing" its meaning in a way exemplified by, among others, J. Hillis Miller in "Ariachne's Broken Woof," *Georgia Review* 31 (1977): 44-60. My own approach has been more logocentric in an effort to define basic characteristics and effects of Rodríguez's poetry.

11. For a good overall view of these books, see Jiménez, *Diez años,* pp. 145-46; Cano, *Poesía española contemporánea,* pp. 153-57; and Bousoño, "Prólogo" (Rodríguez), pp. 9-16.

12. In Batlló, *Antología,* p. 353.

13. Bousoño, "Prólogo" (Rodríguez), pp. 11-17.

14. Jiménez, *Diez años,* pp. 146-48. Rodríguez, quoted in Antonio Núñez, "Encuentro con Claudio Rodríguez," *Insula,* no. 234 (1966): 4.

15. See Jiménez, *Diez años,* pp. 173-74. Rodríguez himself has stated in an interview that "dentro de la alianza existe la condena, igual que dentro de la condena existe la alianza. Es un proceso (para decirlo con una palabra muy cursi) dialéctico." In Campbell, *Infame turba,* p. 230.

16. On this aspect of the poetry of Rodríguez and other poets of the period, see Cano, *Poesía española contemporánea,* pp. 153-54; and Jiménez, *Diez años,* pp. 146-48.

17. Bousoño, "Prólogo" (Rodríguez), pp. 17-22. Another good study of the book is William M. Mudrovic's "Claudio Rodríguez's 'Alianza y condena': Technique, Development, and Unity," *Symposium* 33 (1979): 248-62.

18. For a more archetypal reading of this poem see Carole A. Bradford, "Transcendent Reality in the Poetry of Claudio Rodríguez," *Journal of Spanish Studies-Twentieth Century* 7 (1979): pp. 137-138.

19. See ibid., pp. 139-44; and José Luis Cano's review of the book in *Insula,* no. 359 (Oct. 1976): 8.

20. The double view of reality we have seen in the last few poems studied, in which each text points to both creation and destruction, is related to the implicit tension in Rodríguez's poetry which has been perceptively studied by José Olivio Jiménez (*Diez años,* pp. 145-74).

4. ANGEL GONZÁLEZ

González was born in Oviedo in 1925; he obtained degrees in law and journalism, and has worked as a public official and a teacher. His volumes of poetry include: *Aspero mundo* (1956); *Sin esperanza con convencimiento* (1961); *Grado elemental* (1962); *Palabra sobre palabra* (1965) (individual book); *Tratado de urbanismo* (1967); *Breves acotaciones para una biografía* (1971); *Procedimientos narrativos* (1972); and *Muestra, corregida y aumentada, de algunos procedimientos narrativos y de las actitudes sentimentales que habitualmente comportan* (1976, 1977). (The last was later called *Breve muestra de algunos procedimientos narrativos* and included under the title "Procedimientos narrativos" in the 1977 edition of *Palabra sobre palabra.*) His complete works were published under the title *Palabra sobre palabra* by Seix Barral in 1968, and by Barral Editores in 1972 and 1977, respectively (with new works added each time). All quotations from González's poetry are taken from the 1977 edition of this collection (the third edition of González's collected works, although it is called "Segunda edición" in the volume, being the second by Barral Editores). In 1980, Ediciones Cátedra published a selection of González's work entitled *Poemas* and edited by the author.

1. For good thematic studies of González's poetry, see Emilio Alarcos Llorach, *Angel González, poeta (variaciones críticas)* (Oviedo: Universidad de Oviedo, 1969), pp. 9-52; Jiménez, *Diez años,* pp. 281-304 (on *Tratado de urbanismo*); and Gary Singleterry, "The

Poetic Cosmovision of Angel González" (Ph.D. diss., Univ. of New Mexico, 1972). The latter stresses the search for a cosmic love and the presence of a "tú" that represents it.

2. See Alarcos, *Angel González*, pp. 57-169.

3. On González's use of irony, see ibid, pp. 31-38; Joaquín González Muela, *La nueva poesía española* (Madrid: Ed. Alcalá, 1973), p. 31: and above all Douglas Benson, "La ironía, la función del hablante y la experiencia del lector en la poesía de Angel González," *Hispania* 64 (1981): 570-81.

4. In *Semiotics of Poetry* (Bloomington: Indiana Univ. Press, 1978), Michael Riffaterre posits and examines ways in which a text uses indirection to motivate a rereading of a text and to lead the reader from the literal to the second or semiotic level. (See especially pp. 1-22.) Riffaterre describes three kinds of indirection or transformation: by displacement (when one sign stands for another, exemplified by metaphor and metonymy); by distortion (where there is ambiguity or contradiction); and by the creation of a new principle of organization "out of linguistic items which may not be meaningful otherwise" (p. 2).

Many of the transformations that I examine could also be explained by the concept of "defamiliarization" as used by Viktor Shklovsky, who has examined the way in which a literary work makes a known reality "strange" to create its own meanings. (See Shklovsky, "Art as Technique," pp. 13-22.) But that approach would not take sufficient account of the ways in which González forges seemingly incomprehensible realities which require the reader's discovery of a governing principle, and a subsequent rereading on another level. Many of the poems I study here are also intertextual, since they juxtapose González's new text with a previous one. Others, however, set themselves not against any identifiable text or reality but against basic laws of nature or assumptions of human life. Riffaterre's more encompassing scheme seems to offer a better common denominator for the process I examine.

5. See for example Alarcos, *Angel González*, pp. 21-27.

6. See Benson's study of the poem that serves as prologue to *Aspero mundo*, in "La ironía," pp. 570-71. Florentino Martino has noted how González offers a skeptical vision and avoids metaphysical anguish. See his "La poesía de Angel González," *Papeles de Son Armadans* 57 (1970): 229-31.

7. Looking at this text as a speech act, we would say that its speaker violates the "cooperative principle" in his way of communicating with the person addressed. As H. B. Grice has pointed out, one of the maxims of the cooperative principle is to be truthful; yet attributing one's physical characteristics to someone else's beliefs violates a basic "truth" of human life. The violation is so obvious and so intense that it has to be an example of flouting a maxim—of deliberately breaking it for effect. On this issue see Grice, "Logic and Conversation," in Peter Cole and J. L. Morgan, eds., *Syntax and Semantics* 3 (New York: Academic Press, 1975): 41-58.

8. Many of the transformations to be studied here are based on metaphors, since they involve unusual comparisons created by the poet. What makes them significant, however, is not their metaphorical nature but their violation of accepted premises or realities, and the effects this produces. This allows González to render an emotive meaning with freshness and precision. (Martino, "Poesía de Angel González," p. 232, notes this quality of his work.)

9. As has been noted by Alarcos (*Angel González*, pp. 31-32), and Benson, "La ironía," p. 578.

10. See Benson, ibid., p. 578.

11. Grice considers irony a denial and flouting of the maxim of quality, the requirement that the speaker be truthful ("Logic and Conversation," pp. 52-58). I would say that in this poem the *speaker* denies this maxim and therefore becomes unreliable to us; the *implied author* who makes him deny it flouts his denial at us, and in this fashion turns us against the speaker's traditional vision of the dignity of man.

12. Alarcos (*Angel González*, pp. 38-40) gives an excellent overview of the book's theme.

13. Jiménez, *Diez años,* pp. 291–93. See also Alarcos, *Angel González,* pp. 40-44, 49; and Martino, "Poesía de Angel González," pp. 242-46.

14. Jiménez (*Diez años,* p. 295) has commented very well the reversal of Vallejo's "Masa" present in this text. On the cooperative principle, see note 7 above.

15. Alarcos's examination of various ways in which González combines and inter-mixes serious and ironic planes suggests, in my opinion, that such combinations are also a process of transformation which leads the reader to a reappraisal of the work. See Alarcos, *Angel González,* pp. 150-58.

16. Benson, in a fairly brief section devoted to the recent poetry ("La ironía," p. 579), notes the importance of juxtapositions between ironic perspectives and more idealized ones and the resultant complexity of the works. But his main focus is still on the irony, and he does not examine the ways in which distortions and displacements function.

17. We can see a violation of the speech act maxim of relevancy and the cooperative principle on the part of the woman who uses restaurant language and conventions in responding to a love declaration (see Grice, "Logic and Conversation," pp. 41-49). This violation sets up the violation of rules of behavior which the whole poem represents.

18. See Miller, "Ariachne's Broken Woof," pp. 44-60. Also see Miller's "Stevens' Rock and Criticism as Cure, II," *Georgia Review* 30 (1976): 330-48.

19. On all this see J. Hillis Miller, "Williams' 'Spring and All' and the Progress of Poetry," *Daedalus* 99 (1970): 405–34, in which the critic uses Williams's transformation of a Rimbaud poem to illustrate the process. Riffaterre has commented on the ways in which humor is used in poetry to point out intertexual relationships and replace referential meaning with evocations of other levels and texts, creating "the continuous experience of a verbal detour" (*Semiotics of Poetry,* p. 138).

5. GLORIA FUERTES

Gloria Fuertes was born in Madrid in 1918; she has been an office worker, a librarian, and an editor of children's magazines. She has also taught literature as a visiting professor in American universities. Although she indicates that she has been writing poetry since her early youth, her books appeared in the same period as those of the other writers I am studying here. Aside from several volumes that were directed at children, she has published the following books of poetry: *Isla ignorada* (1950); *Antología y poemas del suburbio* (1954); *Aconsejo beber hilo* (1954); *Todo asusta* (1958); ... *Que estás en la tierra* (1962; an anthology, including some previously unpublished poems); *Ni tiro, ni veneno, ni navaja* (1965); *Poeta de guardia* (1968); *Cómo atar los bigotes al tigre* (1969); *Sola en la sala* (1973); and *Cuando amas aprendes geografía* (1973). In 1970 Plaza and Janés published Fuertes's *Antología poética (1950-1969),* with an introduction by Francisco Ynduráin; in 1975 Cátedra published Fuertes's complete works to date (excluding children's verse) under the title *Obras incompletas.* All references to her poetry in this chapter are taken from the third edition of this book, published in 1977. In 1980, after this chapter was written, there appeared a new volume of Fuertes's poetry entitled *Historia de Gloria (amor, humor y desamor).*

1. On the way in which social issues are handled creatively in Fuertes's poetry, see J. P. González Martín, *Poesía hispánica 1939-1969* (Barcelona: El Bardo, 1970), p. 97; Cano, *Poesía española contemporánea,* pp. 174-76; and Francisco Ynduráin "Prólogo," in Fuertes, *Antología poética 1950-1969,* pp. 26-28, 30-31.

2. See Margaret H. Persin, "Humor as Semiosis in the Poetry of Gloria Fuertes," *Revista Hispánica Moderna,* in press; and Ynduráin, "Prólogo," p. 20.

3. I am using "text" in its broad sense: a text is not only or necessarily a specific literary work, but any reality, recalled or read, that the reader has at her disposal and which affects her attitude to other texts that she confronts. As Jonathan Culler indicates: "A work can only be read in connection with or against other texts, which provide a grid through which it is read and structured by establishing expectations which enable one to pick out salient features and give them a structure." (*Structuralist Poetics* [Ithaca: Cornell

Univ. Press, 1975] p. 139.) In the case of Fuertes's poetry, we will see how the deliberate infusion of other and conflicting texts produces intertextuality, a weaving together of texts that leads to the final meaning and experience of the work.

This broader view of intertextuality is very well defined by Culler in his more recent book, *The Pursuit of Signs*, pp. 37-39, 100-108; as well as by Roland Barthes in "From Work to Text," in *Textual Strategies*, ed. Josué V. Harari, pp. 73-81. It is especially useful in helping us to see a work as less static and more dynamic, in stressing ways in which the meanings derived by a reader emerge from a confrontation between the text at hand and previous texts. Fuertes's poems achieve their effects by denying or modifying the presuppositions of those previous texts. (On the notion of presupposition, see Culler, *Pursuit of Signs*, pp. 112-18).

4. Fuertes's poems often depend on the reader to have a certain attitude to their subject, and then undercut that attitude to produce their effect. Following Hans Robert Jauss's formulation, we might say that these poems assume the "horizon of expectations" of a typical modern city dweller and then twist or frustrate that set of expectations. This does raise questions on the reception of these poems by readers of other times and cultures. On this topic see Jauss, "Literary History as a Challenge to Literary Theory," *New Literary History* 2 (1970): 7–37.

5. Some of the cases of intertextuality we will see also fit the narrower definition espoused by Gustavo Pérez Firmat in "Apuntes para un modelo de la intertextualidad en la literatura," *Romanic Review* 69 (1978): 1-14. Pérez Firmat limits intertextual correspondences to those established with specific literary works, explicitly cited by the text at hand. He suggests that in these cases the reader in fact experiences a "new" text, a product of the interplay within her consciousness of the one being read with the previous ones being evoked.

6. On this issue see Jauss, "Literary History," pp. 7-37; and note 4 above.

7. See "Poema," p. 55, and "Hago versos, señores!" p. 137.

8. Ynduráin, "Prólogo," pp. 34-36.

9. Ibid., pp. 31-33; see also Cano, *Poesía española contemporánea*, pp. 176-77.

10. I nonetheless feel that the concept of intertexuality is the most helpful one in explaining this aspect of Fuertes's poetry. Not only does it allow us to discuss poems which suggest another text that might not have an easily definable code ("Me crucé con un entierro"); it also places appropriate stress on the way in which these poems counterpose different works and different traditions in order to produce new visions. The counterpositions we have seen in these last two poems are somewhat akin to what Carlos Bousoño has called "superposiciones" and "ruptura del sistema," since they point in two directions at once and set up two simultaneous frames of reference. (Other examples of intertexuality in Fuertes's work, however, do not fit these concepts.) See Bousoño, *Teoría de la expresión poética*, 4th ed. (Madrid: Gredos, 1966), pp. 231-34, 270-73.

11. Persin has commented perceptively on the effect of the last line of this poem, and on the humor and meaning produced by it ("Humor as Semiosis").

12. Ynduráin, "Prologo," pp. 36-37.

13. Ibid., pp. 38-42; see also Fuertes's statements on her poetry in Batlló, *Antología*, pp. 337-38.

14. Batlló, *Antología*, p. 338.

15. As Ynduráin has noted ("Prologo," p. 42), Gloria Fuertes frequently recites and records her poetry and is very conscious of her effect on the listener. The intertextual plays and denials of reader expectations which we have seen undoubtedly contribute to this effect.

6. JOSÉ ANGEL VALENTE

José Angel Valente was born in Oviedo in 1929, studied at the universities of Santiago and Madrid, and taught Spanish literature at Oxford. He has worked as an official of the United Nations in Geneva. His books of poetry include: *A modo de esperanza*

(1955); *Poemas a Lázaro* (1960); *Sobre el lugar del canto* (1963; an anthology composed of poems that had appeared in earlier books or would appear in the next one); *La memoria y los signos* (1966); *Siete representaciones* (1967); *Breve son* (1968); *Presentación y memorial para un monumento* (1970); *El inocente* (1970); *Punto cero (Poesía 1953-1971)* (1972; Valente's complete poetry through 1971); *Interior con figuras* (1976); *Material memoria* (1979); *Punto cero (Poesía 1953-1979)* (1980). Valente's prose works include *Las palabras de la tribu* (1971; critical essays); *El fin de la edad de plata* (1973; essays and prose poems); and *Número trece,* a 1973 book of essays confiscated by the censor. All quotations in this chapter are taken from *Punto cero,* 1972 edition. (The 1980 edition appeared after this book was completed.)

1. Valente, *Las palabras de la tribu* (Madrid: Siglo XXI de España, 1971), p. 7. (The essay originally appeared in Francisco Ribes, *Poesía última: selección.*)

2. Ibid., pp. 6, 26-27, 11, 14-15.

3. See Valente, *Punto cero* (Barcelona: Barral Editores, 1972), pp. 61-62; and Margaret H. Persin, "José Angel Valente: Poem as Process," *Taller Literario* 1, no. 1 (1980): 24-41. In a later (unpublished) article, "Underlying Theories of Language in José Angel Valente's *Poemas a Lázaro,*" Persin suggests that the poet's failed efforts to capture essential meanings become in themselves a positive creative process.

4. See Cano, *Poesía española contemporánea,* pp. 141-43.

5. On this subject see Riffaterre, *Semiotics of Poetry,* especially pp. 2-6, 19-22.

6. This feature of Valente's poetry has been perceptively studied by Persin in "Poem as Process," pp. 24–41.

7. See Cano, *Poesía española contemporánea,* p. 142; and Santiago Daydí-Tolson, "Voces de la tribu: la poesía de José Angel Valente" (Ph.D. diss., Univ. of Kansas, 1973), p. 64.

8. See Miller, "Ariachne's Broken Woof," pp. 44-60.

9. Santiago Daydí-Tolson has studied the use of allusions and "resonances" in Valente's poetry in "Los efectos de la resonancia en la poesía de José Angel Valente," in *The Analysis of Literary Texts,* ed. Randolph D. Pope (Ypsilanti, Mich.: Bilingual Press, 1980), pp. 107-18; and also, more fully, in his dissertation "Voces de la tribu."

10. Daydí, "Voces," pp. 27-32. This poem gives an example of the intertextualities already present in Valente's early work.

11. This use of a second level calls to mind Carlos Bousoño's study of bisemic symbols; see his *Teoría de la expresión poética,* 4th ed., pp. 145-50. Valente, however, creates not so much a single symbolic plane set behind the representational level of a poem, as various patterns which produce a variety of new dimensions of meaning when we reread the text. (In "El adiós," for example, we discover a new interpretation of the story rather than a symbolic level—and then move to a new reading.)

12. See Daydí, "Voces," pp. 96–107.

13. Carlos Buosoño has studied the symbolic nature of this poem in "La poesía de J. A. Valente y el nuevo concepto de originalidad," *Insula,* no. 174 (1961): 1. Margaret Persin discusses the reader's participation in the search for knowledge and hence in the process of the poem ("Poem as Process," pp. 31-34.)

14. Persin, "Poem as Process," pp. 32-34. In Barthes's terms, this would be a "hermeneutic code," defining an enigma to be solved.

15. Ibid., pp. 33-34.

16. Interestingly, Persin (ibid., p. 41, note 9) and Bousoño ("Poesía de J. A. Valente," p. 1) give different explanations of the symbolism, suggesting that the symbolic explanation too is subject to a reader's "re-creation."

17. Persin, "Poem as Process," p. 29.

18. Daydí, "Voces," p. 191.

19. José Olivio Jiménez sees the ending of this poem as signalling a preservation of the man's life in a "communal song." See his *Diez años,* p. 233.

20. Ibid., pp. 223-42; see especially pp. 241-42.

21. For a general characterization of this poetry, see Jiménez, ibid., pp. 225-26. A detailed study can be found in Daydí, "Voces," pp. 199 ff.

22. Margaret H. Persin has done a detailed study of the intertextuality present in another poem from this book, in "José Angel Valente y la ansiedad de la influencia," *Explicación de Textos Literarios* 8 (1979-1980): 191-200. Comparing Valente's "Estatua ecuestre" with an antecedent by Jorge Guillén, she has drawn significant conclusions on the characteristics of their works.

23. See Pérez Firmat, "Apuntes para un modelo de la intertextualidad en la literatura," *Romanic Review* 69 (1978): 1-13. Pérez Firmat uses a narrow definition of intertextuality, one that limits intertextual correspondences to those established with specific literary texts, explicitly cited by the work at hand. This view allows him to discuss precisely the ways in which two texts collaborate and produce a new text within the reader's experience. It can serve as a basis for studies which follow the approach of Harold Bloom in *The Anxiety of Influence* (Oxford: Oxford Univ. Press, 1973) and which examine bonds and tensions that result when one work influences another. Pérez Firmat's approach does raise some questions. It does not account for the long chain of echoes to various previous antecedents that often exists in an intertextual correspondence; neither does it provide for intertextualities such as we have seen in the poetry of Gloria Fuertes, in which a text sets itself against other realities, forms of expression, or conventions. A broader definition is more useful in such cases, keeps us from forcing a work's meaning into too narrow a mold, and helps to stress the ways in which meaning emerges dynamically from a confrontation between a text and many surrounding realities. On this topic see Roland Barthes, "From Work to Text," pp. 73-81; and especially Jonathan Culler, *In Pursuit of Signs*, pp. 37-39, 100-118.

7. JAIME GIL DE BIEDMA

Gil de Biedma was born in Barcelona in 1929 and has lived there most of his life; he obtained a law degree at Salamanca in 1951, and works in business. His poetry books include: *Según sentencia del tiempo* (1953), comprising twelve early poems, of which only a few are included in later collections; *Compañeros de viaje* (1959), composed of the sections "Por vivir aquí" and "La historia para todos"; *Moralidades, 1959-1964* (1966); and *Poemas póstumos* (1968, 1970). A good part of his poetry was collected in *Colección particular* (1969), a volume that never went on sale and of which only a few copies remain. Many of Gil de Biedma's love poems were included in *En favor de Venus* (1965). His complete poetry to date, with some poems added and a few deliberately left out, was published in 1975 by Barral Editores under the title *Las personas del verbo*. All quotations from his poetry in this chapter are taken from this volume. A later (1982) edition appeared while this chapter was in press. Gil de Biedma is also the author of an important critical study, *Cántico: el mundo y la poesía de Jorge Guillén* (Barcelona: Seix Barral, 1960), and a book of memoirs, *Diario de un artista seriamente enfermo* (Barcelona: Lumen, 1974).

1. See for example Martínez Ruiz, *La nueva poesía española*, pp. 83-84.

2. See Gimferrer, "La poesía de Jaime Gil de Biedma," *Cuadernos Hispanoamericanos*, no. 202 (Oct. 1966): pp. 240-45. Jiménez, *Diez años*, pp. 210-13.

3. Gil de Biedma's concern with time is apparent in the book's preface, in which he discusses the passage of time in relation to his slow writing pace: "Pero la lentitud también tiene sus ventajas. En la creación poética, como en todos los procesos de transformación natural, el tiempo es un factor que modifica a los demás. Bueno o malo, por el mero hecho de haber sido escrito despacio, un libro lleva dentro de sí tiempo de la vida de su autor" (p. 15). One should also note that the poem "Arte poética" (p. 37), with which the main part of the book begins, lays stress on the effects of time on human consciousness, and on poetry as a response to it; and that the book is headed by a quote from Antonio Machado which includes the following verses: "Con negra llave el aposento frío / de su tiempo abrirá" (p. 18).

4. Jiménez, *Diez Años*, p. 210.

5. "Retrato" is the first poem of Machado's *Campos de Castilla* and appears as No. 97 in his *Poesías completas*, 11th ed. (Madrid: "Austral," Espasa-Calpe, 1966), pp. 76-77.

6. See Jiménez, *Diez años*, p. 213.

7. As has been noted by Gimferrer, "La poesía de Jaime Gil de Biedma," pp. 241-42.

8. See Juan Rodríguez Padrón, "Jaime Gil de Biedma desde sus "Poemas póstumos," *Cuadernos Hispanoamericanos,* no. 237 (1969): p. 788-95.

9. In an interview with Federico Campbell, Gil de Biedma indicated that he wrote this poem as a way of facing and overcoming a temptation to suicide; he also noted that it reflects the death of a part of himself and of an epoch in his life, which would support a metaphoric reading of the text such as the one I am presenting. See Campbell, *Infame turba,* pp. 247-48.

10. In *Jaime Gil de Biedma* (Madrid: Júcar, 1980), published after this chapter was completed, Shirley Mangini González has studied very perceptively the use of speaker, tone, and point of view in Gil's poetry.

8. CARLOS SAHAGÚN

Born in Onil, Alicante, in 1938, Sahagún completed his studies in Madrid and has taught literature in Segovia and in Barcelona, where he now resides. He was a visiting lecturer in Exeter, England, in 1960-1961. He has written criticism and edited various works, including an excellent anthology of earlier twentieth-century Spanish poetry. His books of verse include: *Hombre naciente,* published in 1955 and never included in his complete works; *Profecías del agua,* published in 1958, after winning the Adonáis prize the previous year; *Como si hubiera muerto un niño* (1961), winner of the Boscán prize; and *Estar contigo* (1973). His complete poetry to 1975, including some previously unpublished works, has been collected under the title *Memorial de la noche (1957-1975)* (1976); all quotations in this chapter are taken from this volume. In 1979, Sahagún published a new book of poetry, *Primer y último oficio (1973-1977),* which reached me after the draft of this chapter was completed.

1. The clarity and the artistic quality of Sahagún's verse have been noted by José Luis Cano in *Poesía española contemporánea,* pp. 224-31; and by Enrique Moreno Castillo in his prologue to Sahagún's *Memorial de la noche,* pp. 5-6.

2. I accept here the traditional view of metaphor as an implied comparison between two distinct realities. By thus comparing two elements which we would normally deem dissimilar, a metaphor casts new light on them and generates a new way of seeing a subject. (See Philip Wheelwright, *Metaphor and Reality* [Bloomington: Indiana Univ. Press, 1962], chapter 4). Sahagún, as we shall see, uses metaphors and similes to take an unusual perspective on past happenings and situations.

3. See Ricoeur, "The Metaphorical Process as Cognition, Imagination, and Feeling," in Sheldon Sacks, ed., *On Metaphor* (Chicago: Univ. of Chicago Press, 1978), pp. 151-55. On p. 151, Ricoeur writes: "The sense of a novel metaphor ... is the emergence of a new semantic congruence or pertinence from the ruins of a literal sense shattered by semantic incompatibility." This "new congruence" would involve, in "Río," the vision of a time as a place.

4. In this sense, the river exemplifies a function Paul de Man ascribes to metaphor, which creates objective correspondences to inner and subjective realities, and "freezes hypothesis, or fiction, into fact." (*Allegories of Reading* [New Haven: Yale Univ. Press, 1979] p. 151.) On the same page, De Man observes: "Metaphor is error because it believes or feigns to believe in its own referential meaning. This belief is legitimate only within the limits of a given text." Within the limits of "Río," a past time does have the consistency and the characteristics of a place viewed in the present. This way of using the metaphor of the river distinguishes Sahagún's poem from Manrique's *Coplas,* in which the equivalance of river to human life does not create such a "fiction" and serves mainly to represent the pattern of life leading to death.

5. See Bousoño, *Teoría de la expresión poética,* 4th ed., pp. 123-33.

6. On the "co-operative principle" see H. B. Grice, "Logic and Conversation," pp. 41-58.

7. Levin, *Semantics of Metaphor* (Baltimore: Johns Hopkins Univ. Press, 1977), pp. 116-27.

8. The view of metaphor and metonymy as two basic ways of arranging linguistic signs (the former operates by similarity and comparison, the later by contiguity) goes back to Roman Jakobson's formulation in "The Metaphoric and Metonymic Poles," in Jakobson and M. Halle, *Fundamentals of Language* (The Hague: Mouton, 1956), pp. 76-82. In a recent article Floyd Merrell has studied very perceptively how metaphoric and metonymic patterns interrelate and complement each other in fiction. Merrell indicates that metaphor adds a concrete and synchronic level to the diachronic development produced by metonymy and fills out the narrative's metonymic message. (See his "Metaphor and Metonymy: A Key to Narrative Structure," *Language and Style* 11 [1978]: 146-63.) A similar process underlies Sahagún's poetry, though metonymic patterns grow more directly out of key metaphors.

9. Drawing on Levin's view of metaphor (*Semantics of Metaphor*, pp. 116-27), we might say that the speaker is operating here as a poet who has tried to sustain his fictional premise of time as place and has lost his ability to do so; he has to return to the premises of our world, to accept the impossiblity of reversing time. This links the process of examining his life even more closely to the process of poetizing it, and highlights the metapoetic dimension of the work.

10. The section contains two more poems; the first laments the loss of a beloved and imagines their resurrection and reunion, while the second again evokes a beloved as the speaker meditates on his own death. These works are therefore not directly tied to the preceding ones, although they deal with the same themes of disillusion, loss, and death.

11. This takes us back again to Ricoeur's view of metaphor as a way of making us suspend the referential function of the reality described, and hence read the reality in a new way. See "On Metaphorical Process," p. 155.

9. ELADIO CABAÑERO

Cabañero was born in Tomelloso, in the province of Ciudad Real, in 1930. His books of poetry include: *Desde el sol y la anchura* (1956), *Una señal de amor* (1958), *Recordatorio* (1961), and *Marisa Sabia y otros poemas* (1963). These books have been collected in Cabañero's *Poesía (1956-1970)* (1970), with a prologue by Florencio Martínez Ruiz. All quotations in this chapter come from this collection.

1. See Martínez Ruiz's prologue to Cabañero's *Poesía (1956-1970)*, p. 12.

2. Ibid., p. 20; and Batlló, *Antología*, pp. 30, 35.

3. One should keep in mind Cabañero's very careful selection of vocabulary, his tendency to use local and archaic expressions in significant ways, and his ability to coin neologisms for poetic purposes. In an interview Cabañero praised earlier poets who renewed language through the novel use of old words. See Cabañero as quoted in Batlló, *Antología*, p. 335.

4. In his prologue (pp. 9-11), Martínez Ruiz describes Cabañero's arrival in Madrid around 1958, and suggests that it marked a turning point in his work; although the poet would continue to use images from his youth in his poetry, their more selective use and their organization into more symbolic patterns may be related to this change in circumstances.

5. See Bousoño, *Teoría de la expresión poética*, 4th ed., pp. 106-19.

6. It is important to note that in the 1968 interview published by Batlló, Cabañero defends the continued existence of social poetry in Spain, and indicates that social poetry is an attitude ("un estado general de conciencia") rather than a movement or fad. This statement also separates Cabañero from those social poets who had seen their work in more limited terms and had used the concept of social poetry in opposition to more consciously artistic works. See Batlló, *Antología*, p. 336.

7. Prologue, p. 21. On poetry as "concrete universal," see William Wimsatt, *The Verbal Icon*, 2nd ed. (New York: Noonday Press, 1958), pp. 69-83.

8. As Dámaso Alonso has defined it, an "encabalgamiento suave" is a run-on line that continues without break until the end of the following line; an "encabalgamiento abrupto," on the other hand, is a run-on line that leads into a break or caesura in the middle of the next one. As Alonso has demonstrated, the former produces a flowing effect, while the latter causes a dramatic break. See Alonso, *Poesía española: ensayo de métodos y límites estilísticos,* 2nd ed. (Madrid: Ed. Gredos, 1952), pp. 67-75.

9. The repeated use of the image of filming reality, as well as other images taken from the contemporary scene, suggests that Cabañero is using his imagery to crystallize a particular time, to set his book in a period of the mid-twentieth century.

10. ANGEL CRESPO AND MANUEL MANTERO

Both Crespo and Mantero have published a number of volumes of poetry, which are listed in the bibliography. Mantero has also published two books of criticism and several anthologies and editions. Crespo has written many critical studies, including books on the Duque de Rivas, Juan Ramón Jiménez, and concretist poetry, and has translated and edited Dante's *Divine Comedy* as well as Portuguese and Brazilian poetry. Quotations from Crespo's poetry are from *En medio del camino (Poesía, 1949-1970)* (1971). Quotations from Mantero's poetry are taken from *Poesía (1958-1971)* (1972). The volume comprises four previously published books, one unpublished book, and an important essay in which the poet discusses his work.

1. De la Rica, "Vanguardia de los años cincuenta (desde el ismo a la generación," *Papeles de Son Armadans* 37 (1965), no. 109: i-xvi; no. 110: xxv-xlviii; and no. 112: iii-xv. De la Rica uses the term generation rather loosely, and classifies as generation a group of poets whose period of collaboration lasted only a few years. If one assumes that a new generation does not come along more often than every fifteen years, Crespo has to be grouped with the other poets I am studying.

2. On the ways in which Crespo highlights the unusual nature of the everyday, see Linda Metzler, "The Poetry of Angel Crespo" (Ph.D. diss., Univ. of Kansas, 1978), especially chapter 1.

3. Gómez Bedate, "La contestación de la realidad en la poesía de Angel Crespo," *Revista de Letras,* no. 4 (1969): 617. See also Metzler's comments on this poem ("Poetry of Angel Crespo," pp. 50-51).

4. See Metzler's excellent analysis of this poem ("Poetry of Angel Crespo," pp. 69-72.

5. Ibid., pp. 83-85, 94.

6. Metzler has also analyzed this text; her reading defines the poem's central conflict as an intrusion of common reality into a peaceful scene (ibid., pp. 158-62).

7. See Mantero's introduction to *Poesía (1958-1971),* pp. 15-17.

Index

Note: All poems and books of poetry written by the authors here studied are indexed, as well as the first lines of untitled poems. Titles of critical works mentioned are not indexed, but names of critics (and all other persons) are. The index also includes references to a few topics and critical concepts, and to magazines to which substantive reference is made. The notes are only indexed for critics' names and for the poets here studied.